# Industrial Location and Regional Development in Backward Areas

# Industrial Location and Regional Development in Backward Areas

**Vipin Mathur**

**CYBER TECH PUBLICATIONS**
4264/3, Ansari Road, Daryaganj, New Delhi-110002 (India)
Ph.: 011-23244078. Fax: 011-23280028
E-Mail: cyberpublicationsdelhi@yahoo.com

**INDUSTRIAL LOCATION AND REGIONAL DEVELOPMENT IN BACKWARD AREAS**

**Vipin Mathur**



First Edition 2009



*Published by :*

**G.S. Rawat** for **Cyber Tech Publications**
4264/3, Ansari Road, Daryaganj, New Delhi-110002 (India)
Ph.: 011-23244078. Fax: 011-23280028
E-Mail: cyberpublicationsdelhi@yahoo.com

***Printed at*** Asian Offset Printers

# Preface

As soon as a national government assumes responsibility for the geographical impact of its actions, it needs to decide which areas merit its favorable attention. The answer is inevitably determined in part by political pressures, but it is clearly in the national interest to formulate and apply some more objective social and economic rationale.

We note an interesting shift in the use of terms to describe areas to which national public development assistance programs are directed. In the 1920s and 1930s, the British used to refer to their "depressed areas." Later, these same objects of solicitude were rechristened under the curiously neutral term of "special areas." Still more recently, they have come to be referred to as "development areas." In the United States in the 1930s, we used to refer to "problem areas," or "stranded areas"; later, to "redevelopment areas"; and now to "development areas," and to "growth centers within them. As to our less fortunate brethren across the seas, we used to refer to them as simply "poor" or "backward," or "low-income" countries. Later they became "undeveloped" and then "underdeveloped." Nowadays, it is considered more tactful to speak of the "less developed" or, better still, the "developing" countries.

Does this curious trend reflect anything besides euphemism-that is, a growing squeamishness about offending the sensitivities of people in the areas in question? Not necessarily; but perhaps we can read into the new terms a growing emphasis on the positive, and a belief that any and every region can and should be made to develop faster. We may descry also a disquieting indication that the ideal of place prosperity is enlisting greater support.

*—Author*

# CONTENTS

# 1

# Introduction

Two Five Year Plans have helped strengthen the foundations of economic and social life and stimulated industrial and economic growth and scientific and technological advance.

The Third Five Year Plan seeks to give a more precise content to the social objectives of the Constitution and represents a large advance towards their realisation. It takes account of the successes and the failures in the first two Plans and sets the tasks to be fulfilled in the perspective of development over the next fifteen years and more.

Work on the preparation of the Third Plan commenced towards the end of 1958 and was carried out in three main stages. The first, leading to the publication of the Draft outline early in July,1960, comprised detailed studies by working groups set up at the Centre and in the States. Parliament gave its general approved to the Draft Outline in August, 1960

The Draft Outline was discussed throught the country and served as the basis for the preparation of the plans of States. These were considered with the Chief Ministers of States between September and November, 1960. In January, 1961, the National Development Council made its recommendations concerning the overall size and the structure of the Third Plan; the Council also set up Committee on Savings to suggest ways of securing the maximum mobilisation of resources for the Third Plan. Finally, on May 31 and June 1,1961, the National Development Council considered the Draft Report on the Third Plan and generally approved it.

The objectives and priorities of the Third Plan were considered carefully by five Parliamentary Committees in November, 1960 and every effort has been made in this Report to avail of the suggestions and comments offered by before the Committee of Members of Parliament from different political parties presided over by the Primie Minister. The Consultative Committee of Members of Parliament associated with the Planing commission also reviewed the Plan at various stages.

Throughout the preparation of the Plan, leading public men scholars, proffessional associations, organisations representing industry and labour, and independent experts generously gave of the time and experience. The Planing Commission had the benefit of advice and suggestions from its Panel of Economists, Panel of Scientists, and Panels on Land Reform, Agriculture, Education, Health and Housing. It was also helped by studies initiated by the Programmee Evaluation Organisation, the Research Programmes Committee, the Committee on Plan Projects, the Central Statistical Organisation, the Indian Statistical Institute and other leading organisations engaged in research. Efforts to prepare plans at the district, block and village level specially for the development of agriculture, cooperation, education and rural industries, were an integral part of the process of drawing up the plans of States as well as the National Plan. These local plans are a vital element in the success of Panchayati Raj, which places in the hands of the people of each area the initiative and responsibility for their own development and the means and resources for rapid advance.

The preparation of the Third Plan been, thus, a vast national undertaking in which valuable contributions have come from many sources, and at every stage there has been the closet collaboration with the State Governments and the Central Ministers.

The Third Plan represents the first phase in a scheme of long- term development extending over-the next fifteen Years or so, the preparation of which will now be taken in hand. In the course of this period, India's economy must not only expand rapidly but must, at the same time, become self-reliant and self-generating. This long-term approach is intended to provide a general design of development for the country's natural resources, agricultural and industrial advance, changes in the social structure and an integrated scheme of regional and national development.

The Plan sets large objectives and targets for the five-year period. They are large only in comparison with the past, not in relation to needs or to the nation's capacity to achieve. They constitute a minimum which must be assured, but their true purpose is to open the way to a still more intensive endeavour and a deeper sense of urgency.

The size of the task and the many-sided challenge should not be underestimated. The greatest stress in the Plan has to be on implementation, on speed and thoroughness in seeking practical results, and on creating conditions for the maximum production and employment and the development of human resources. Discipline and national unity are the very basis of social. and economic progress and the achievement of socialism. At each step, the Third Plan will demand dedicated leadership at all levels, the highest standards of devotion and efficiency from the public services, widespread understanding and participation by the people, and willingness on their part to take their full share of responsibility and to bear larger burdens for the future.

## OBJECTIVES OF PLANNED DEVELOPMENT

The basic objective of India's development must necessarily be to provide the masses of the Indian people the opportunity to lead a good life. That indeed is the objective of all countries for their peoples, even though the good life may be defined in many ways. In the larger context of the world, the realisation of this objective for India, as for other countries, is intimately tied up with, and dependent on the maintenance of world peace. War, with the weapons of modern warfare, would not only be an end to all hopes of progress but would endanger the survival of the human race. Peace, therefore, becomes of paramount importance and an essential prerequisite for national progress. The existence of underdeveloped and poverty- stricken nations or peoples is itself an abiding danger to the maintenance of peace. It has, thus, been increasingly recognised that the welfare and peace of the world require the, extermination of poverty and disease and ignorance from every country, so as to build up a liberated humanity.

Each major culture and civilisation has certain distinctive features, rooted in the past, which bear the impress of that culture, India, with thousands of years of history, bears even now the powerful impress of her own distinctive features. They are today covered up by widespread and appalling poverty, the result of a traditional society and a static economy in the past petrified to some extent by colonial rule. But these essential features, though apparently associated with the traditional structure of society are in no sense an integral part of it. They are in fact a set of moral and ethical values which have governed Indian life for ages past, even though people may not have lived upto them. These values are a part of India's thinking, even as, more and more, that thinking is directed to the impact of the scientific and technological civilisation of the modern world. To some extent, the problem of India is how to bring about a synthesis between these two. Probably, no other country in the modern world would have produced a Gandhi; even Tagore, who was typically modem in his approach to life's problems, was, at the same time, steeped in India's old culture and thinking. His message is thus one of synthesis between these two.

To provide the good life to the four hundred million people of India and more is a vast undertaking, and the achievement of this goal is far off. But no lesser goal can be kept in view, because each present step has to be conditioned by the final objective. Behind the plans that are drawn up is the vision of the future, even as the Indian people had a vision of freedom and independence during the long years of their national struggle, and there is faith and confidence in that future. Fully conscious of existing difficulties the people have also the conviction that these difficulties will be overcome. The experience of the last ten years of planning and the large social and economic changes that have already taken place have brought a conviction that India can look forward with assurance to sustained economic progress. Even in this ancient land, for so long governed by tradition, the winds of change are blowing and affecting not only the dweller in the city but also the peasant in his field. At each stage, new conflicts and new challenges arise. They have to be met with courage and confidence. There is an excitement in this changing face of India as the drama of India's development plans unfolds itself.

The more immediate problem is to combat the curse of poverty, with all the ills that it produces, and it is recognised that this can only be done by social and economic advance, so as to build up a technologically mature society and a social order which offers equal opportunities to all citizens. This involves basic social and economic changes and the replacing of the old traditional order by a dynamic society. It involves not only the acceptance of the temper and application of science and modern technology, but also farreaching changes in social customs and institutions. To some extent, recognition of this twofold aspect of change has been present in the Indian mind for generations past. Gradually it has taken more concrete shape and has become the basis for planning.

It was inevitable that during India's struggle for freedom, the political aspect of Independence overshadowed everything else. Yet from its earliest beginnings, Indian nationalism had a large element of economic thinking and social reform. This was, to some extent, an unusual feature for a national movement. Freedom was considered the indispensable means to overcome mass poverty, to protect the farmer and the artisan, to create modem industry, to remove privilege and injustice and to reconstruct the entire fabric of India's social and economic life.

Beginning with Dadabhai Naoroji, whose paper on 'The Poverty of India' was resented as far back as 1876, a long line of national leaders placed these aims in the forefront of the national struggle. As the national movement grew and spread among the people of India, its social content became, deeper. With the, coming of Mahatma Gandhi, the movement spread with remarkable rapidity to the, peasantry and the workers of India.

To Gandhiji freedom was not merely a political objective, but the raising of the masses of the people from the poverty and degradation.He aligned himself with the masses of the Indian Indian people and more especially with those who were in the lowest rungs of the social ladder, Under his leadership the national movement came to identify itself more and more with the service of the masses and, progressively, a very large proportion of its membership came from amongst the peasants. The agrarian problem thus came to occupy a prominent place in its thinking even as, under Gandhiji's guidance, it made the uplift of the depressed and the underprivileged one of its major planks.

In this way, as the political struggle for Independence developed and took shape in mighty movements, it was a flied in some measure to India's basic social and economic problems and more particularly the agrarian problem. The social and economic aims of the struggle for freedom became progressively more definite. A comprehensive economic programme was adopted in 1931, and an agrarian programme in 1936. Towards the end of 1938, a National Planning Committee was constituted and, thus, the idea of planning came into prominence in India. The National Planning Committee could not carry on its work effectively because of the beginning of the Second World War. In the course of which many of its members found themselves in prison. But it considered nearly all aspects of planning and ultimately produced a series of studies containing social and economic and economic policies and programmes, which formed the basis of a more organised attempt at planning after Independence.

The Second World War resulted, by the compulsion of events, in the growth of some industries in India. Even before Independence was established, the Interim Government gave thought to planning and constituted an Advisory Planning Board to collect all the available material for it. Owing to the disastrous consequences of Partition and the vast numbers of people who were uprooted and driven out from Pakistan to India and India to Pakistan, there was some delay in giving effect to the recommendations of the Board. Early in 1950, following the adoption of the new Constitution by the Constituent Assembly of India, the Government of in a established the Planning Commission to assess the country's material, capital and human resources and to formulate a Plan for their most effective and balanced utilisation.

In the Constitution the basic objectives were set forth as "The Directive Principles of State policy Among those 'Directive Principles' were that :

*"The, State shall strive to promote the welfare of the people by securing and protecting, as effectively as it may, a social order in which justice, social, economic and political, shall inform all the insti- tutions of national life".*

Further that-

"The State shall, in particular, direct its policy towards securing-

(a) that the citizens, men and women equally., have the right to an adequate means of livelihood;

(b) that the, ownership and control of the material resources of the community are so distributed as best to subserve the common good;

(c) that the operation of the economic system does not result in the concentration of wealth and means of production to the common detriment."

These general principles were given a more precise direction in December, 1954, when Parliament adopted the 'socialist pattern of society' as the objective of social and economic policy. This concept, which embodies the values of socialism and democracy and the approach of planned development, involved no sudden change, and had its roots deep in India's struggle for freedom.

Thus, ever since Independence, two main aims have guided India's planned development-to build up by democratic means a rapidly expanding and technologically progressive economy and a social order based on justice and offering equal opportunity to every citizen'. To change a traditional society into a dynamic one, in a country with a vast population rooted in the past, was a tremendous task. To do this through peaceful and democratic means and by the consent of the people, made this task even more difficult. It was inevitable that India should accept peaceful and democratic means as these had been the very methods it had adopted in its struggle for freedom.

With these objectives in view, the First Five Year Plan faced this task with limited means and inadequate data. The immediate objectives it laid down were achieved and this success gave confidence to the nation. The Second Five Year Plan, being based on somewhat greater experience and more knowledge, set forth larger goals and a long-term Strategy for economic and industrial advance based on the socialist pattern of society. In describing the approach to planned development, the Second Five Year Plan stated :

> *" ... The task before an underdeveloped country is not merely to get better results within the existing framework of economic and social institutions, but to mould and refashion these so that they contribute effectively to the realisation of wider and deeper social values,*
>
> *"These values or basic objectives have recently been summed up in the phrase, socialist pattern of society'. Essentially, this means that the basic criterion for determining lines of advance must not be private profit, but social gain, and that the pattern of development and the structure, of socio-economic relations should be so planned that they result not only in appreciable increases in national income and employment but also in greater equality in incomes and wealth. Major decisions regarding production, distribution, consumption and investment and in fact all significant socio-economic relationships-must be made by agencies informed by social purpose. The benefits of economic development must accrue more and more to the relatively less privileged classes of society, and there should be progressive reduction of the concentration of incomes, wealth and economic power. The problem is to create a milieu in which the small man who has so far had*

*little opportunity of perceiving and participating in the immense possibilities of growth through organised effort is enabled to put in his best interest of a higher standard of life for himself and increased prosperity for the country. In the process, he rises in economic and social status. Vertical mobility of labour is thus no less important than horizontal mobility, for nothing is more destructive of hope and more inhibitive of effort than a feeling that the accident of birth or of a poor start in life is likely to come in the way of a capable person rising in life in terms of economic and social status...*

*"The socialist pattern of society is not to be regarded as some fixed or rigid pattern. It is not rooted in any doctrine or dogma. Each country has to develop according to its own genius and traditions. Economic and social policy has to be shaped from time to time in the light of historical circumstances. It is neither necessary nor desirable that the economy should become a monolithic type of Organisation offering little play for experimentation either as to forms or as to modes of functioning. Nor should expansion of the Public sector mean centralisation of decision-making and of exercise of authority. In fact, the aim should be to secure an appropriate devolution of functions and to ensure to public enterprises the fullest freedom to operate within a framework of broad directives or rules of the game .........*

*"....The accent of the socialist pattern of society is on the attainment of positive goals, the raising of living standards, the enlargement of opportunities for all, the promotion of enterprise among the disadvantaged classes and the creation of a sense of partnership among all sections of the community. These positive goals provide the criteria for basic decisions. The directive principles of State policy in the Constitution have indicated the approach in broad terms; the socialist pattern of society is a more concretised expression of this approach. Economic policy and institutional changes have to be*

*planned in a manner that would secure economic advance along democratic and egalitarian lines. Democracy, it has been said, is a way of life rather than a particular set of institutional arrangements. The same could well be said of the socialist pattern."*

When Independence came, India had a slender industrial base. Millions of her rural people suffered under the weight of a traditional agrarian structure. A long period of economic stagnation, against the back-ground of increasing pressure of population, followed by the burdens of the Second World War, had weakened the Indian economy. There was widespread poverty and want.

The partition of the country had uprooted millions of people and dislocated economic life. Productivity' in agriculture and industry stood at a low level. In relation to needs the available domestic savings were altogether meagre. The promise of freedom could only be redeemed if the economic foundations were greatly strengthened. The Constitution established equal rights of citizenship, and these had now to be expressed through rising levels of living and greater opportunities for the bulk of the people. It was essential to rebuild the rural economy, to lay the foundation of industrial and scientific progress, and to expand education and other social services.

These called for planning on a national scale, encompassing all aspects of economic and social life, for efforts to mobilise resources, to determine priorities and goals and to create a widespread outlook of change and technological progress. Thus, planned development was the means for securing with the utmost speed possible, a high rate of growth. reconstructing the institutions of economic and social. life and harnessing the energies of the people to the tasks of national development.

The leading features of the pattern of development envisaged in the Five Year Plans may be briefly stated. The basic objective is to provide sound foundations for sustained economic growth, for increasing opportunities for gainful employment and improving living standards and working conditions for the masses.

**Third Five Year Plan**

In the scheme of development, the first priority necessarily belongs to agriculture; and agricultural production has to be increased to the highest levels feasible. The Five Year Plans provide for a comprehensive and many-sided effort to transform the peasant's outlook and environment. The growth of agriculture and the development of human resources alike hinge upon the advance made by industry. Not only does industry provide the new tools, but it begins to change the mental outlook of the peasant. There can be no doubt that vast numbers of the peasantry today in India are undergoing this change of outlook as they use new tools and experiment with new methods of agriculture. Even the coming of the bicycle in large numbers to the villages of India is not only a sign of higher standards, but is a symbol of new and changing attitudes.

Agriculture and industry must be regarded as integral parts of the same process of development. Through planned development, therefore the growth of industry has to be speeded and economic progress accelerated. in particular, heavy industries and machine-making industries have to be developed, the public sector expanded and a large and growing cooperative sector built up. The public sector is expected to provide specially for the further development of industries of basic and strategic importance or in the nature of public utility services, other industries being also taken up by Government to the extent necessary. State trading. has also to be undertaken on an increasing scale according to the needs of the economy. In brief, in the scheme of development, while making full use of all available agencies, the public sector is expected to grow both absolutely and in comparison and at a faster rate than the private sector.

With the rapid expansion of the economy, wider opportunities of growth arise for both the public and the private sectors and in many ways their activities are complementary. The private sector includes not only organised industry but agriculture, small industry, trade and a great deal of activity in housing and construction and other fields. Progressively, it has to take the form of cooperative effort. Among the main objects of programmes undertaken by the Government are the expansion of facilities for the development of agriculture, specially irrigation, the building up of economic overheads such as rail and road transport, ports and power stations, and the expansion of education, health and other social services. Activities which are promoted through these facilities are in considerable part in-the hands of private individuals and organisations, and increasing numbers among them are being assisted. Thus, the Five Year Plans enlarge the scope for individual initiative as well as for co-operative and corporate effort.

It is mainly within a limited area in the field of large scale industrial enterprise that the question arises whether, in the special circumstances of the country, in accordance with the Industrial Policy Resolution of April, 1956, and in view of the social goals aimed at, particular tasks should be assigned to the public sector or to the private sector. In the context of the country's planned development the private sector has a large area in which to develop and expand. It has to function, of course, within the framework of national planning and in harmony with its overall aims, and there must be continuous stress on undertakings in the private sector acting with an understanding of obligations towards the community as a whole. At the same time, it is essential to ensure that the opportunities available in the private sector do not lead to the concentration of economic power in the hands of small numbers of individuals and businesses and that disparities in income and wealth are progressively reduced.

In the pattern of development envisaged in the Five Year Plans, cooperation is expected to become progressively the principal basis of Organisation in several branches of economic life, notably, in agriculture, small industry, distribution, construction and provision of essential amenities for local communities. Village and small scale industries have a crucial role in the development of the national economy, for, besides providing consumer and other goods and largescale employment, they offer a method of ensuring a more equitable distribution of the national income and the means for the utilisation of available resources in skill and manpower. Disparities in levels of development in different regions have to be steadily reduced and the benefits of industrialisation spread evenly between different parts of the country.

These aims have to be achieved, as the Industrial Policy Resolution specified, through the balanced and coordinated development of the industrial and agricultural economy of each region, and through planned urbanisation and the development of economic and social services. Frequently, in the early phases of development, there is a dilemma to be faced : whether it is better to concentrate on developing Tore favourably situated areas and thus securing quicker and larger returns from the investment, or to aim at more even development of the country, through greater attention to the more backward areas. Economic considerations have necessarily to be given importance, but certain social and regional aspects cannot be ignored. Indeed, as the economy develops, it becomes possible to provide for more intensive development in the less developed areas.

The policies described above constitute the larger part of the programme for achieving rapid economic development and for realising the socialist pattern of society. In such a scheme the basic criterion in determining social policies and the lines of economic advance must necessarily be the interest of the community as a whole, and especially of its weaker sections. Through its very success and dynamism, a rapidly developing economy throws up new problems of Organisation and management as well as of social policy. The existing social and economic institu- tions have, therefore, to be appraised from time to time in relation to their role in the nation's development. To the extent they do not adequately fulfil the social purpose or fail to secure the economic aims of planned development, they have to be replaced or transformed.

Development plans reflect the changes which are taking place in the country's economic and social structure as well as the directions in which this structure has to be reorganised and strengthened. In a democracy the pace of change depends to a large extent on increase in public understanding and in public response and on the growth of a scientific outlook on the part of large numbers of people. Besides the economic and social objectives, the educational aspects of planning are, therefore, of great importance. These are emphasised through the wide sharing of responsibility for drawing up and carrying out Plans and 'through the participation in the process of planning by organisations representing all sections of opinion as well as universities and educational institutions and voluntary social service agencies. On behalf of the community as a whole the State has a large responsibility for assessing the wider long-term needs of the nation as against the claims of individual, sectional or regional interests, and in setting the goals to be achieved.

## Progress Towards Socialism

It is a basic premise in India's Five Year Plans that, through democracy and widespread public participation, development along socialist lines will secure rapid economic growth and expansion of employment, reduction of disparities in income and wealth, prevention of concentration of economic power, and equal society. values and attitudes of the free and equal society. these are vital objectives. Where the bulk of the people live so close to the margin of poverty, the claims of social justice, of the right to work. of equal opportunity and of the minimum level of the living have great urgency. Economic activity must therefore, be so organised that the tests of production and growth and those of equitable distribution are equally met. A high rate of economic growth sustained over a long period is the essential condition for all citizens, and especially for those in low income groups or lacking the opportunity to work. Increase in population and the need for investment in basic productive capacities and in economic and social overheads, which yield their benefits after a considerable period, place large burdens on developing economy. On the one hand, they limit the extent to which, over the short period, living standards can be raised' on the other, to be borne at all, their burdens must be shared widely, calling for sacrifice, according to capacity, by every section of the community.

Progress towards socialism lies along a number of directions, each enhancing the value of the others. Above all, a socialist economy must be efficient, progressive in its approach to science and technology, and capable of growing steadily to a level at which the well-being of the mass of the population can be secured. In an underdeveloped country, a high rate of economic progress and the development of a large public sector and a cooperative sector are among the principal means for affecting the transition towards socialism. In the second place, a socialist economy should ensure equality of opportunity to every citizen. As a first step. it should provide for the basic necessities. in particular, for food, work, opportunity for education, reasonable conditions of health and a minimum level of income which, in the given circumstances, will ensure tolerable living standards. In the third place, through the public policies it pursues, a socialist economy must not only reduce economic and social disparities which already exist, but must also ensure that rapid expansion of the economy is achieved without concentration of economic power and growth of monopoly.

Finally, a society developing on the basis of democracy and socialism is bound to place the greatest stress on social values and incentives and on developing a sense of common interest and obligations among all sections of the community. On account of the rigidities of the caste system as well as economic differences, India's social structure already presented numerous inherent conflicts and barriers to economic advance. While some of the old distinctions are passing a process which is being speeded up- urbanisation and the growth of modern industry tend to introduce new disparities in levels of income and opportunity. In turn, these are reflected in modes of living, social behaviour and a general increase in the spirit of acquisitiveness. It is the aim of public policy to check undesirable tendencies and to ensure that these do not come in the way of building up a society which is fundamentally integrated from within and derives its strength from common values and a sense of shared citizenship.

## Equal Opportunities

The first condition for securing equality of opportunity and achieving a national minimum is assurance of gainful employment for developed country, failure to provide full employment can be traced to certain fundamental deficiencies in the economic structure. Until the industrial base has been greatly strengthened and education and other social services developed, the economy is unable to achieve a rate of growth sufficient to provide work at an adequate level of remuneration to the entire labour force. These processes of development necessarily take time and call for a scale of effort and investment which may be well beyond the capacity of the economy in the early stages, Poverty is most acute in areas which have heavy pressure of population or in which, on account of the scanty development of local resources, low levels of productivity persist and there is lack of continuous work. There must, therefore, be additional opportunities for work to enable the lowest income groups to earn enough through productive employment to meet their minimum needs. In the Third Plan, it is envisaged that, along with programmes of development for large and small industries, for agriculture and for economic and social services, there will also be a largescale programme for rural works especially in densely populated regions and for periods of under-employment during the slack agricultural seasons.

In advanced countries the development of education and other social services has played a large part in ensuring greater equality of opportunity to different sections of the population and greater social mobility. Social services have also helped to bring about a measure of redistribution of income and provide the basic necessities. In India too, the expansion of social services will exert a similar influence, specially through the extension of free and universal education at the primary level, provision of larger opportunities for vocational and higher education, grants of scholarships and other forms of aid, and improvement in conditions of health, sanitation, water supply and housing, Thus, programmes for the welfare of scheduled tribes and castes and other backward classes, for the provision of minimum amenities in rural areas for local development at the village level and for the housing of industrial workers and slum clearance and improvement, are to be viewed not merely as extensions of social services but as vital ingredients in the scheme of economic development. These and other social benefits have to be provided to a greater extent in the Third and subsequent Five Year Plans than has been possible over the past decade. They will call for larger resources, not only from the State, but also within each community, and for the participation of a growing number of voluntary workers.

As economic development proceeds, social security and insurance will come to have high priority. Through the scheme of provident funds and health insurance for industrial workers the first important steps in this direction have already been taken. In the course of the Third Plan, it is proposed to introduce a scheme of employment assistance for industrial workers and to make a small start with relief and assistance for destitute persons, orphans and physi- cally handicapped persons without means of support or livelihood. In areas in which the rural works programme is taken in hand, facilities for registration are to be provided for persons seeking work. Thus, social services along with intensive economic development, the provision of scholarships and other facilities in the field of train- ing and education and the beginnings of social security should go some distance in providing more equal opportunities to different sections of the community.

Increase in agricultural production, the growth of modern industry and of transport and power, and the development of the public and the cooperative sectors in the economy will create conditions which will make it possible to advance towards socialism and to improve living standards. These will gain 'greater social significance in the measure in which socialism develops at the level of the community and enlists widespread local effort. As the values of socialism and democracy become more pervasive, influencing everyday attitudes and behaviour, wider opportunities will open up for all sections in the community, and especially for the under-privileged.

A large segment of India's development plans reaches the mass of the people through community development. In promoting the growth of socialism at the level of the community amongst the rural people, therefore, the role assigned in the Five Year Plans to the community development movement should be specially stressed. Community development must seek, above all, to bring about increase in agricultural production, higher standards of productivity, and fuller utilisation of the available manpower and other resources. With its stress on the development of local initiative and responsibility and on cooperative self-help, the movement is designed to serve as a spearhead of a wide range of programmes of development, which include agriculture, cooperation, irrigation, village and small industries, rural electrification and the reform of the agrarian system. One of its major aims is to create conditions for the growth of a progressive cooperative rural economy with a diversified occupational structure in which the weaker sections of the community are brought speedily to the level of the rest. The development of a cooperative agroindustrial economy in rural areas is essential for ensuring that the benefits of industrialisation spread out evenly among different sections of the population and to different areas and for securing a large measure of integration between rural and industrial development in each region.

A recent development of the community development movement in the rural areas has been, what is called, Panchayati Raj, or democratic decentralisation. At the village, block and district levels, responsibility for development is entrusted to Village Panchayats, Panchayat Samitis and Zila Parishads, and they are given considerable powers. This is a revolutionary change in the structure of administration within the district and in the pattern of rural development, and is already producing significant results and changing the rural climate.

In the villages the task of building up socialism at the bass is facilitated as the policies of land reform and cooperative development are implemented and as the approach of bhoodan and gramdan and of common obligations begins to permeate within each rural community. In the towns and cities also there is equal need for appropriate social policies. The influx of population into urban areas leads not only to a worsening of living conditions for large section of new disparities. These developments in the values of land and property, to the creation of new disparities. These developments demand a variety of measures, including careful planning of the use of land, large scale programmes for land acquisition, housing and land allotment policies designed to assist the lower income groups and the poorer sections of the population, adequate taxation of capital gains and urban properties, avoidance of conspicuous and wasteful forms of construction, and public vigilance over conditions of tenancy and rents.

## DISTRIBUTION OF ECONOMIC POWER

The growth of the corporate private sector over the past decade has brought to the fore the question of the means by which economic growth will be secured without concentration of economic power and the emergence of monopolistic tendencies. As a rule, the process of rapid economic development tends to enlarge opportunities for well-established firms to expand their size and enter new fields of enterprise. As compared to new undertakings or to smaller enter- prises, they enjoy advantages in organisation and expertise, in access to the capital market and ability to secure foreign collaboration and,generally, in the resources which they are in a position to deploy. The fact that a significant proportion of the resources available for investment in industry arises within the corporate sector itself is another factor which makes it easier for an existing unit to expand than for a new one to come into being and take firm root. In several industries technological considerations favour the setting up of large-scale units with resultant savings in capital cost and in the cost of production. Consequently, certain difficult problems arise. On the one hand, to the extent to which large existing enterprises undertake development in accordance with the priorities set in the Five Year Plans and avail of essential economies of scale, they assist the growth of the economy. On the other, excessive economic power in relatively few hands and the uses to which it may be put, disturb the balance of power in a democracy, expose the social structure to new strains and tensions, and come in the way of diffusion of economic opportunities.

The tendency towards concentration of economic power has to be countered in a variety of ways' firstly, through the extension of the public sector into fields requiring the establishment of large scale units and heavy investments; secondly, through widening opportunities for new entrants and for medium and small-sized units as well as for industries organised on cooperative lines; and, thirdly, through effective exercise of Government's powers of control and regulation and use of appropriate fiscal measures.

The object, briefly, must be not merely to prevent concentration of economic power and the growth of monopolistic tendencies, but also to promote a pattern of industrial organisation which will lead to high levels of productivity and give full scope, within the framework of national planning, to new entrepreneurs, to medium and small scale enterprises and to cooperative organisations.

As a decisive instrument which the State can employ in preventing concentration of economic power and growth of monopolistic tendencies, the rapid expansion of the public sector serves a twofold purpose. It helps to remove certain basic deficiencies in the economic structure and, at the same time, it reduces the scope for accumulation of wealth and large incomes in private hands. In the generation and distribution of electric power, the public sector has now the principal share and is being rapidly enlarged. Its share in transport has also steadily increased. In large industries and minerals the total investment in the public sector during the Third Plan will be distinctly higher than that in the private sector.

As compared to 1950-51, by the end of the Third Plan, the contribution of the public sector will increase from less than 2 per cent to nearly a fourth in organised manufacturing industries and from less than a tenth to over a third in mineral production. While these are significant developments, careful attention must be given to factors which will increase the capacity of the public sector to expand still more rapidly, such as efficiency of operation, availability of trained managerial and technical personnel in larger numbers and ability to earn large surpluses. It is also essential that to the greatest extent feasible construction and supply functions for State undertakings should be entrusted to public and cooperative agencies. As the relative share of the public sector increases, its role in economic growth will become even more strategic and the State will be in a still stronger position to determine the character and functioning of the economy as a whole.

Within the field of activity entrusted to the private sector, the major aim of policy is to ensure broad-based owenership in industry, diffusion of enterprise and liberal facilities for new entrants, and the growth of cooperative organisations. Means for achieving these objectives are already available to a large extent, but need to be employed by the Central and State Governments and the various agencies functioning under them more purposefully and with greater coordination than in recent years. In licensing new industrial units and sanctioning the expansion of existing units, there must be considerable vigilance in permitting the growth of large existing businesses and, in the greatest measure possible, the entry of new firms should be facilitated and small and medium enterprises and cooperative organisations encouraged. In recent years a number of financial and promotional institutions have been established, such as the Industrial Finance Corporation, the State Finance Corporations, the Industrial Credit and Investment Corporation of India and others.

In the light of the experience gained during the Second Plan, these and other financial institutions should review their existing administrative policies and practices so as to ensure that their support to new entrants into industry and to medium and small enterprises as well as to cooperative undertakings is both speedy and adequate. They' should also devise suitable criteria for assessing progress in these directions. The State Bank of India as well as other commercial banks may be expected to play an increas- ing part in financing medium-sized, small and cooperative industries. The resources of the Life Insurance Corporation could also be of material assistance in the furtherance of these objectives. The Investment Centre recently established can assist in securing foreign exchange facilities for new enterprises. Finally, a brief reference may be made to the role of industrial estates and programmes for the development of village and small industries, rural electrification, regional planning and location of new townships which are described in later Chapters. These development programmes are among the most important positive steps under the Five Year Plans for taking the benefits of industrialisation to the smaller towns and villages.

In a developing economy taxation is one of the main instruments of social policy and, in accordance with the needs of the Plan, devices such as rebates, concessions and incentives have to be employed so as to prevent concentration of economic interests and to encourage new units as well as medium and small-scale businesses and cooperative undertakings. The provisions needed are already available within the existing framework of personal and corporate taxation, wealth tax, gift tax, capital gains tax and estate duty, and should be employed in an integrated manner.

Problems relating to tax evasion and tax avoidance and suitable measures for dealing with them are being given careful consideration. With the passing of the Companies Act, 1956, and the amendments recently undertaken, developments in company management such as inter-corporate investment, interlocking directorships, use of internal resources and the remuneration of directors and other top management personnel can be watched more closely and steps taken to ensure that the legislative provisions concerning them are administered effectively.

Powers under the Industries Development and Regulation Act can also be used to exercise control over production, distribution and prices to the extent neces- sary. To sum up, in dealing with the problems of concentration of economic power, there is already general agreement on the broad objec- tives, and the necessary legislative and other sanctions needed are in fact available for the greater part. It is, therefore, specially important in the present context that the content of measures and of the administrative methods and practices adopted in pursuance of them should in practice subserve the wider social purpose, and the existing arrangements should be re-examined in relation to the tasks and priorities of the Third Five Year Plan.

## DISPARITIES IN INCOME

Before the process of economic development gathers momentum, for the larger part inequalities arise from long-established features of a traditional society, such as feudal rights and tenures, or privileges and handicaps associated with the social structure. These vestiges of the past are the first to fall. Planned development has to hasten this process so as to enable the economy to move forward with less hindrance from within. Thus, the programme of land reform, with its stress on the abolition of intermediary rights, security and rent reduction for tenants and enforcement of ceilings on agricultural holdings, was calculated to release the productive forces of the rural economy. There has been progress in this direction but, owing to inadequate implementation of tenancy reforms and delays in carrying out the programme for ceilings on agricultural holdings, this has been less than was hoped for. Greater efforts are, however, now being made to give effect to legislation enacted in the States.

Disparities in income and wealth which arise from industrial and economic growth raise a series of complex problems. The first of these concerns differences in levels of earned income. In advanced countries these have now been greatly reduced. On the other hand, in underdeveloped countries, unless special measures are taken in the first phases of economic development, there is a tendency for them to become even larger than before. This is due to a variety of circumstances, more especially the relative scarcity of trained personnel, lack of social mobility, and the presence of inflationary influences. The essential problem here is to reduce the spread between the higher and the lower incomes and to raise the level of the minimum. This calls, among others, for large scale programmes of training and for steps to ensure that in all branches of the economy, both in the public and in the private sector, there is rapid growth of opportunities for merit.

Tax policies have an important role and should be used to bring the net earnings of those in high income brackets to reasonable levels. This is a question at present, not so much of attempting to set rigid ceilings, as of giving a general direction to public policy and to public thinking. In this connection it will be recalled that the Taxation Enquiry Commission considered a reasonable range of incomes after tax to be about thirty times the average family income, This broad objective should be progressively realised over the next two or three Plan periods. Although, in view of the low incomes of the bulk of the population, this range represents a considerable disparity, it could be further reduced as lower incomes rise.

An important aspect of the problem of income disparities concerns the gap between rural and non-rural incomes which tends to widen under the impact of industrial and economic development. Increase in agricultural productivity, reduction in the dependence on land and diversification of the economic structure of rural areas through the extension of industry and the development of social services on an adequate scale, and an agricultural price policy which is both fair to the urban consumer and fully safeguards the farmer's interest, are the principal means by which the gap between rural and urban incomes can be kept within narrow Emits. In a country with a large rural population, these policies have great significance.

In a growing economy, frequently high incomes are due in the main to the accrual of capital gains, to trading and speculative profits, and to perquisites of one kind or another which are permitted by law. A twofold approach is therefore called for. Firstly, through social policy, incomes arising from capital gains, speculation, etc. must be limited and the State should take its due share. Secondly, through extension and improvement of the tax system, steps must be taken to ensure that such incomes as do accrue are fully taxed, evasion of taxation is severely dealt with and opportunities for tax avoidance are reduced to the minimum.

With rapid development and expansion of employment, the incomes of the vast majority of workers in industry and services and of selfemployed workers like farmers and skilled artisans may be expected to increase steadily and, on the whole, in fair relationship to productivity. Those receiving fixed incomes, falling broadly in the lower middle-class groups, inevitably face special problems on account of the long-term tendency towards rise in prices. On the other hand, in these groups, through women entering employment in larger numbers and the growth of employment, there are also wider openings for augmenting the family income. For this group, equally with those in the lowest income groups, it is important that the prices of essential commodities should be kept down and social services, especially education, health and housing, should be brought within easy reach. At the other end of the scale, the greatest attention must be given to those who are totally unemployed or suffer from serious under-employment. The provision of employment opportunities has the foremost priority for them. Along with employment, education and social service benefits should also be extended as fully as possible.

## ECONOMIC AND SOCIAL INTEGRATION

The socialist pattern of society provides a major line of advance in a developing economy, which is becoming increasingly complex, and in which there is constant interplay of a variety of social, economic and other elements. Its realisation is necessarily a cumulative process resulting from progress along many different paths. For several reasons, in reaching this goal there is need now for a sense of urgency and a quickening of pace. It is true that the economic foundations must be well laid if the social objectives are to be attained. At the same time, any marked lag between economic and social development creates new stresses. Precise data are at present lacking, and without these it is difficult to devise definite measures. Accordingly, an expert committee set up by the Planning Commission in October, 1960, is at present engaged in reviewing changes in the levels of living which have occured in the course of the First and the Second Plans, in studying recent trends in the distribution of income and wealth and, in particular, in ascertaining the extent to which the operation of the economic system may have resulted in concentration of wealth and means of production.

Progress along each separate course has its own limitations. Sometimes, there may be conflict between different objectives and the means available for achieving them, and these have to be reconciled. Although many gaps remain, step by step within the scheme of planned development, the framework of socialism is being built up, but it has to be strengthened and made more purposeful in its actual working.

There must be fuller and more determined implementation of accepted policies and programmes in all spheres of public administration and of economic life and more critical tests of evaluation should be adopted. Moreover, at all times there should be due stress on the moral, human and spiritual values which give meaning to economic progress. Given the necessary unity and discipline in the nation, willingness to bear the burdens of development and a greater understanding by different sections of the community of what is due from them at the present juncture, both economic and social advance can be far more rapid than is generally realised.

Policies already initiated will go a long way to stimulate social mobility, strengthen such forces as the trade unions, the cooperative movement, voluntary organisations and the universities, and to create a broad-based constructive leadership in rural and urban communities. They will help to check concentration of economic power and the growth of monopoly, strengthen the bonds of cultural and economic integration, and assure to every citizen of India the right to work, to equal opportunity, and to a minimum level of living. In the last analysis, economic development is but a means to an end-the building up, through effort and sacrifice widely shared, of a society, without caste, class or privilege, which offers to every section of the community and to all parts of the country the fullest opportunity to grow and to contribute to the national wellbeing.

Planning is a continuous process and cannot be isolated for short periods. Thus, the Third Five Year Plan is a projection and a continuation of the First and Second Plans, and it will lead to the Fourth and subsequent Plans. Planning is a continuous movement towards desired goals and, because of this, all major decisions have to be made by agencies informed of these goals and the social purpose behind them. Even in considering a five-year period, forward and long-term planning has always to be kept in view. Indeed, perspective planning is of the essence of the planning process. As this process develops, there is a certain rhythm of expansion in the development of the people, and a sense of enterprise and achievement comes to them.

They are conscious of a purpose in life and have a feeling of being participants in the making of history. Ultimately, it is the development of the human being and the human personality that counts. Although planning involves material investment, even more important is the investment in man. The people of India today, with all their burdens and problems, live on the frontier of a new world which they are helping to build. In order to cross this frontier they have to possess courage and enterprise, the spirit of endurance and capacity for hard work, and the vision of the future.

# 2

# Balanced Regional Development

## GENERAL APPROACH

Balanced development of different parts of the country, extension of the benefits of economic progress to the less developed regions and widespread diffusion of industry are among the major aims of planned development. Successive Five Year Plans seek to realise these aims in larger measure. Expansion of the economy and more rapid growth increase progressively the capacity to achieve a better balance between national and regional development. In striving for such a balance, certain inherent difficulties have to be met, especially in the early phases of economic development. As resources are limited, frequently advantage lies in concentrating them at those points within the economy at which the returns are likely to be favourable. As development proceeds investments are undertaken over a wider area and resources can be applied at a large number of points, thereby resulting in greater spread of benefits. In the interest of development itself, the maximum increase in national income should be achieved and resources obtained for further investment.

The process is a cumulative one, each stage determining the shape of the next. In some fields, as in industry, intensive and localised development may be inevitable. Along with this, in other areas, the aim should be to provide for more dispersed advance in sectors like agriculture, small industries, power, communications and social services. Equally with industry, investment in economic and social overheads helps to create numerous promising centres for growth. Once a minimum in terms of national income and growth in different sectors is reached, without affecting the progress of the economy as a whole, it becomes possible to provide in many directions for a larger scale of development in the less developed regions. A large country with extensive natural resources, viewing each phase of its development in the perspective of a long-term plan, has the means riot only to realise a high and sustained rate of growth but also to enable its less developed regions to come up to the level of the rest.

The two aims-increase in national income and more balanced development of different parts of, the country-are thus related to one another and, step by step, it becomes possible to create conditions in which resources in terms of natural endowment, skill and capital in each region are fully utilised. Sometimes the sense of lagging behind in development may be due not so much to a slower rate of overall growth in the region as to inadequate or tardy development in specific fields, such as, agriculture, irrigation, power or industry or employment. In each region the nature of the problem and the impediments to rapid development in particular fields should be carefully studied, and appropriate measures devised for accelerated development. The essential object should be to secure the fullest possible utilisation of the resources of each region, so that it can contribute its best to the national pool and take its due share from the benefits accruing from national development.

The growth potential of each region should be fully developed, but the precise manner in which this goal is achieved and the stages of growth will not be identical. Some regional factors, such as those connected with physical features and geographical location, cannot be easily altered, but there are others which can be influenced by raising levels of education and skill, developing power and, generally, by applying science and technology on a larger scale. Large scale industries, specially basic and heavy industries, frequently serve as a spearhead of intensive and broad-based development. However, not all regions can offer equally favourable conditions for the development of industry. It is also possible to over-estimate the significance of the location of large industrial units in relation to the living standards of the bulk of the population. There are many examples, both of countries and of regions within a country, in which, with limited development in industry, an appreciable rise in living standards has been achieved through the fuller utilisation of local natural and human resources. There are also instances of areas around massive proJects where no great impact on the levels of living of the people is to be observed. Apart from the basic and capital goods industries and other large industries, there are other industries whose possibilities need to be fully explored, such as labour intensive industries of the traditional type, small scale industries of the modern type, agricultural processing industries, forest industries, assembly operations and recreational industries. Each region should endeavour to identify, plan for and promote industries which are specially suited to its conditions and for which it can provide relatively greater facilities.

## POLICIES FOR REGIONAL GROWTH

The general approach set out above was expressed through a variety of policies and programmes which were embodied in the Second Five Year Plan. Among the most important of these were:

(1) the priority given to programmes like agriculture, community development, irrigation, specially minor irrigation, local development works, etc. which spread over the entire area within the shortest possible time;

(2) provision of facilities such as power, water supply, transport and communications, training institutions, etc. in areas which were lagging behind industrially or where there was greater need for pro- viding opportunities for employment;

(3) programmes for the expansion of village and small industries; and

(4) in the location of new enterprises, whether public or private, consideration given to the need for developing a balanced economy in different parts of the country. in particular, this aspect was to be kept in view where the location of an industry was not determined almost

entirely by the availability of raw materials or other natural resources.

In addition to these measures, the Second Plan envisaged an effort to promote greater mobility of labour between different parts of the country and to organise schemes of migration and settlement from more to less densely populated areas. The Plan also suggested that there should be continuous study of the problem of regional disparities and suitable indicators of regional development should be evolved.

In drawing up and implementing the Second Plan, the regional aspects of development were dealt with in three different ways. Firstly, through the plans of States emphasis was given to programmes which had a direct bearing on the welfare of the people in different parts of the country. Secondly, special programmes were undertaken in particular areas where development had either received a temporary setback, or was being held back by certain basic deficiencies. In the third place, steps were taken to secure more dispersed development of industry which, in turn, creates conditions for development in several related fields.

Programmes of agriculture, community development, village and small industries, irrigation and power, communications and social services have the widest coverage, and aim at providing basic facilities and services to people in all regions. Since these programmes are included in the plans of States, it is largely through the shape given to State plans and the changes through which they pass in the course of the Plan period that the benefits of development are carried to every part of the country. River valley projects formed a most important segment in the plans of several States and large investments have been made in multi-purpose projects like the Hirakud, Kosi, Chambal, Rihand, D.V.C., Bhakra Nangal, Koyna and Nagar- junasagar. These and other projects. were essential for the development of vast regions in the country, some of which suffered from scarcity or unemployment or were otherwise poorly developed. Implementation of agricultural production and community development programmes, and of education and health schemes also, carried the benefits of development to the remotest areas. In addition to these general or overall programmes of development, both in the First and the Second Plan, special schemes were formulated for particular areas which had difficult problems to face. Thus, in 1953-54 a programme of permanent improvements in scar- city areas was taken in hand in several States at a, total cost of about Rs. 40 crores. The programme included medium as well as minor irrigation schemes, construction of embankments for flood protection and land reclamation and contour bunding schemes. Again, in 1957, when scarcity conditions developed in some States, the problem was studied and additional development programmes were taken up. For less developed areas situated in different States, such as, Vidharba and Marathwada, the eastern districts and other backward areas in Uttar Pradesh and hill areas in Punjab and Uttar Pradesh, the States concerned have frequently provided for special outlays within their plans, and have made special arrangements for the representatives of such areas to participate in making their own plans. In States like Madhya Pradesh, Orissa and Assam, additional programmes have been undertaken in areas inhabited by backward classes. These include roads and communications, multi-purpose development blocks, forest cooperative societies, and measures to improve upon the existing systems of shifting cultivation. A study of the problems of inaccessible areas in different States has also been undertaken by the Ministry of Food and Agriculture.

As regards the diffusion of industrial activity, so far as the larger industries are concerned, economic and technical considerations are always important and in practice only marginal deviations are feasible. The disadvantages which particular areas may have for the location of the larger projects are not always basic or irremediable for at times they may reflect only the lack of basic facilities and services. In the location of public sector projects, the claims of relatively backward areas have been kept in view wherever this could be done without giving up essential technical and economic criteria. The location of several important projects like the steel plants has been determined on the basis of expert study and on.

economic considerations. But as they are situated in areas which were hitherto industrially backward, the latter will benefit. Similarly, schemes for the development of certain natural resources such as lignite deposits in Arcot, iron ore in Orissa, bauxite deposits in Salem and lead and zinc deposits in Rajasthan will benefit areas which have been relatively less developed.

While, in the selection of sites for basic capital and producer goods industries, proximity to raw materials and other economic considerations have naturally been important, it was felt that in a wide range of consumer goods and processing industries it was possible to foster regional patterns of development. These in- clude cotton textiles, sugar, light engineering industries such as bicycles, sewing machines, electric motors, radio receivers, re- rolling of steel and non-ferrous metals from billets and semis, moulded plastics and manufacture and further processing of bulk drugs from penultimate products. Typical examples are the establishment of textile units in Rajasthan, Orissa, Assam and Punjab; sugar factories and distilleries in Andhra Pradesh, Madras, Mysore and Maharashtra; steel re-rolling mills in Assam, Madhya Pradesh, Kerala and North Bihar and tyre and tubes factory and electric lamps factory in Kerala. In the case of light engineering industries, the decision to sell steel at a uniform price at all rail-heads is an important step taken during the Second Plan for securing their wider dispersal. The policy followed regarding the licensing of new units in the sugar industry has assisted development in the peninsula. Similarly, new cotton textile mills have been encouraged to come up in areas in which the industry had not so far developed.

To some extent the development of new processes and new uses of raw materials has assisted in the spread of industry. Thus, a beginning was made with the use of bagasse as raw material for paper, and a number of paper factories based on the use of bagasse have been approved for being set up in sugarcane growing areas. In Uttar Pradesh a synthetic rubber plant is being established on the basis of alcohol, which was formerly being used mainly for admixture with petrol. A decision has been taken to license pig iron plants, each up to a capacity of about 100,000 tons, in areas where non-metallurgical coals locally available could be used, if necessary, along with coke produced from metallurgical coal. Besides increasing the production of pig iron this will ensure dispersal of the industry. In encouraging such developments care has of course to be taken to ensure that a balance is maintained between regional distribution and considerations of economy in production.

Village and small industries are spread all over the country and various forms of assistance provided by the Central and State Governments are made available in the areas according to the programmes which are undertaken. Industrial estates have been set up in all States, and increasingly they are to be located in the smaller towns and rural areas.

## REGIONAL POSSIBILITIES IN THE THIRD PLAN

With development on a scale larger and more comprehensive than in the recent past, the Third Plan provides extensive opportunity for the development of different parts of the country. Some of the most important programmes in the Plan fall necessarily within the plans of States. In drawing up these plans, the broad objectives have been to enable each State to contribute its best towards increasing agricultural production, to secure the largest measure of increase in income and employment feasible, to develop social services, in particular, elementary education, water supply and sanitation and health services in the rural areas, and to raise the levels of living for the less developed areas. Thus, State plans are intended to be oriented towards greater production and employment and the welfare of weaker sections of the population. Every effort has been made to propose outlays for different States after considering their needs and problems, past progress and lags in development, specially in social services, communications and power, likely contribution to the achievement of major national targets, and potential for growth, as well as the contribution in resources which they could themselves make towards the financing of their plans. In assessing the needs and problems of different States, such factors as population, area, pressure on cultivated land, commitments carried over from the Second Plan and those arising from large projects, and the state of technical and administrative services available have been taken into account. Thus, as far as possible, an attempt has been made to consider both national and State priorities. Taken as a whole, the size and pattern of outlays in the States under the Third Plan are calculated to reduce disparities of development between different States, although, in the nature of things, this is a process which must take time.

In addition to the role assigned to the plans of States, there are several important features in the Third Plan which will enlarge the possibilities of development in areas which have in the past been relatively backward. Thus, for instance, the intensive development of agriculture, extension of irrigation, village and small industries, large-scale expansion of power, development of roads and road transport, provision for universal education for the age-group 6- 11 years and larger opportunities for secondary, technical and vocational education, improvements in conditions of living and water supply, and programmes for the welfare of scheduled tribes and castes and other backward classes will go a long way to provide throughout the country the foundations for rapid economic development. Poverty and under-employment are specially acute in areas with heavy pressure of population and in those with scanty development of natural resources. The large programme of rural works, which it is proposed to undertake during the Third Plan, will help expand opportunities for work in these as well as other areas. In some parts of the country there will be considerable development in plantation industries, specially tea, coffee and rubber. Large industrial projects, river valley projects and others described later will also serve as vital centres for future growth.

Industrial location and development areas.-As explained earlier, for basic industries location has generally to be based on technical and economic considerations. Moreover, in the case of industries which may be able to export a significant proportion of their output, in the national interest the location of new or additional capacity has to be guided by the need to secure economies of scale and to enhance the ability to compete in foreign markets. But, subject to these broad considerations, the needs of areas which have the necessary potential for industrial development should be kept in view in the selection of sites for industrial projects both in the public and the private sector. The general approach has to be to avoid further concentration of industrial activity in areas where considerable development has already taken place or has been planned, but expansion in existing industries in such areas cannot, of course, be ruled out if it leads to greater economies in production. Similarly, as far as possible, care must be taken to set up new industries away from large and congested cities.

From decisions regarding location of projects in the public sector which have been reached so far, it is apparent that there will be a fair measure of dispersal and various regions will have a significant share in industrial development. As examples the following may be cited : expansion of the Rourkela steel plant and fertiliser factory in Orissa ; Nunmati oil refinery, fertiliser plant and use and distribution of natural gas in Assam; phyto-chemical plant, expansion in fertiliser capacity and construction of a shipyard in Kerala ; the synthetic drugs factory, refractories plant and expansion expansion of Hindustan Shipyard, Praga Tools and the Andhra Paper Mills in Andhra Pradesh; the security paper mill, basic refractories project and expansion of Nepa mills, the Bhilai steel plant and the Heavy Electrical Project in Madhya Pradesh ; the antibiotics factory, fertiliser factory, refractories plant and expansion of precision instruments factories in Uttar Pradesh develop- ment of copper deposits in Rajasthan a machine tool factory in Punjab ; surgical instruments' plant. raw film project, pilot iron and steel plant, Neiveli lignite high temperature carbonisation plant, teleprinter factory and a steel rolling mill in Madras ; oil refinery in Gujarat : and a cement factory in Jammu and Kashmir.

In the licensing of industrial projects in the private sector also, the claims of underdeveloped regions are kept in view and locations in such areas are suggested to prospective industrialists. The progress, programmes and Production targets of a number of industries in the private sector are examined from time to time with a view to securing the location of new capacity on a zonal basis. It is recognised that in future there should be even greater stress hi these directions. For example, it is proposed that the new textile mills to be established in the Third Plan period should, by and large, be distributed in regions where at present there is little capacity. Similar studies have been conducted in respect of some of the light engineering industries. Among illustrations of important projects in the private sector which are expected to be set up during the Third Plan in the less developed regions may be mentioned an aluminium plant and cellulose acetate factory in Uttar Pradesh ; a fertiliser factory, a nylon factory, caustic soda-P.V.C factory and a zinc smelter in Rajasthan ; synthetic rubber, polythylene and carbon black projects and paper pulp factory in Assam ; and an automobile rubber tyre factory and expansion of several existing plants in Kerala.

The Industrial Policy Resolution visualised that facilities such as power, water supply and transport should be made available in areas which are at present lagging behind industrially or where there is greater need for providing opportunities for employment, so that suitable industries could be established there. To give effect to this suggestion, the Third Plan includes a proposal for setting up 'industrial development areas' in backward regions. In such regions in selected areas basic facilities like power, water and communications are to be provided, and factory sites developed and offered for sale or on long lease to prospective entrepreneurs. The scheme has been drawn up primarily to promote medium-sized industries, but it is anticipated that, along with these. there will he wider scope for establishing small-scale industries, specially those of an ancillary character. It should also be possible to establish industrial estates within or in proximity to the proposed industrial development areas. The scheme has been broadly accepted by States and specific proposals are being worked out.

Large projects as nuclei of regional growth.-The benefits of a large project accrue in greater measure to the population of the region in which it is located if certain related or complementary programmes and schemes are undertaken. Therefore, as an essential feature of planning, every major project should be regarded as nucleus for integrated development of the region as a whole. Around the new irrigation projects for instance, a whole group of schemes aiming at the development of improved agriculture. horticulture, market centres and processing and other industries should be taken up . Similarly steel plants and other large industrial projects provide the basis for the development of small and medium industries and programmes of education and training and other activities. Such possibilities of development exist in all large regions in which new resources will be developed during the Third Plan, such as, Dandakaranya, the Rajasthan canal area, and the regions served by the Tungabhadra, Nagarjunasagar, Koyna, Chambal and several other projects. Problems of a somewhat different kind are posed by the growth of metropolitan cities and of large and growing cities. In metropolitan regions like Calcutta, Delhi, Bombay or others, it is necessary to pursue a series of programmes aiming at balanced regional development, including appropriate land and housing policies, establishment of new towns and decisions regarding the location of industries. Thus, in different types of regions the preparation of regional or area development plans should be undertaken at an early stage in the Third Plan. In this way, the benefits flowing from the location of new and vital centres of activity or the creation of new sources of wealth can be greatly increased and far more widely distributed.

## ROLE OF TECHNOLOGICAL DEVELOPMENTS

Development potentials of different regions need to be studied in relation to the possibilities which arise from advances in technology and science. For example, the handicaps of certain regions Such as Assam, Gujarat and Rajasthan arising from lack of deposits of coal may be materially reduced as hydel power, oil and atomic energy become available. From a long term point of view, this factor is of great importance in regional development. Similarly, improvements in transport and communications are already bringing distant regions nearer, as for instance in the case of Assam, Jammu and Kashmir and parts of Orissa, Madhya Pradesh and Rajasthan, and making it possible for them to share more fully in the general economic advance. Increase in the supply of electric power and the extension of rural electrification are important factors in opening up new possibilities of regional development. Several of the less developed areas in the country will register considerable progress in these directions during the Third Plan.

- Education and training - In areas which are less developed, lags in education are among the greatest handicaps in achieving rapid economic progress. Expansion of the general educational base through the programmes of free and compulsory primary education and provision of facilities for technical training is likely to make a steadily increasing contribution to the development of the less advanced regions. Financial provisions for these programmes have been made in the plans of States, but it is necessary to ensure that the resources earmarked for the development of primary education in the less developed areas and for the education of girls are effectively utilised. Facilities for the training of engineers, doctors, agricul- tural specialists, craftsmen and others are already being distributed throughout the country. The requirements of the population of relatively less developed areas in which new industrial projects may be located should be particularly borne in mind when programmes for technical, vocational and secondary education are implemented.
- Labour mobility.-In some parts of the country, there has been for long considerable mobility of labour. For instance, labour from Bihar works in the tea plantations in Assam and labour from Rajasthan works on roads and irrigation projects in Punjab and elsewhere. The redeployment machinery set up at the Centre and in the States for different areas assists movement of skilled personnel to new projects. The question of migration and mobility of labour is of course a wider one. The scope for transferring large numbers of unskilled workers from the more densely to the less densely populated parts of the country may at present be relatively limited.

However, it is apparent that skilled and semi-skilled workers can move from one area to another with much less difficulty and are absorbed more readily wherever the local economy is developing rapidly. It is, therefore, necessary that in areas of high density, besides assuring their own intensive development to as great an extent as possible, technical training programmes should be expanded considerably, so that a body of trained workers also become available for work elsewhere.

- Personnel for development.-The level of development depends to a considerable extent on the availability of competent adminis- trative and technical personnel and on the growth of a class of small and medium sized entrepreneurs who are prepared to venture into new fields and take risks and more generally, on the development of local initiative and leadership. Attention should be given to these aspects of development, for they point to handicaps which cannot be removed merely by providing resources to an under-developed region.

## STUDIES IN REGIONAL DEVELOPMENT

Continuous study of economic trends and rates of growth in different areas and of the programmes bearing on the less developed regions is useful in formulating programmes for more balanced regional development. Under developed areas which need special attention have to be more closely identified, their resources surveyed and the factors influencing their development examined. The concept of a 'region' also needs to be defined more clearly. There are regions within States as well as those which extend beyond them and depending upon the purpose in view, different concepts may be employed. Within every State, there are areas which are more under-developed than others. As explained earlier, problems of regional development also arise in a variety of other contexts as for,instance, in areas around major projects, areas where new resources are being developed, and metropolitan regions. For assessing levels of development in different regions, indicators of development based on agricultural production, industrial production, investment, unemployment, electricity consumption, irrigated area, value of output by commodity producing sectors, level of consumption expenditure, road mileage, primary and secondary education and occupational distribution of population, are useful, but they must be compiled on the basis of accurate statistical data and should be strictly comparable for different States or regions. Some work on these problems was done during the Second Plan, and it is proposed to continue it with the help of a special study group with which the Central Statistical Organisation, State Statistical Bureaus and the Indian Statistical Institute will be associated.

As a comprehensive indicator of economic progress estimates of 'State income' are of considerable interest in studies of development in different States and regions. There are complex questions connected with concepts, definitions and techniques of estimation of 'State' and 'regional' income, and these have a bearing on the practical value of various estimates. 'State income' may be considered either as the income originating within the boundaries of a State or as income accruing to its residents. The first concept corresponds to the 'domestic product' for the country as a whole, and the second to 'national income'. For a comparative study of the level of industrial and economic development among the States or regions, it is sufficient to have an estimate of income originating within the 'State' or 'region'. The estimates of income accruing to a State, on the other hand, may serve as a broad measure of the economic welfare of the residents of the State as a whole. In view of the importance of estimates of State income in future Plans, it has been agreed that the Central Statistical Organisation should undertake, in cooperation with State Statistical Bureaus, the task of preparing estimates of State income on a comparable annual basis. These estimates will have to be prepared on the basis of commodity production and income originating. Estimates of income in certain commodity sectors such as agriculture, industry, etc. on a comparable basis may be taken up in the first instance.

While estimates of State and regional income and compilation of data in respect of selected indicators would be useful, it is even more important to carry out systematic surveys for identifying the problems of different regions and assessing their needs and potentialities. Scientific and technical surveys in various fields are undertaken by agencies such as the Geological Survey of India, the Bureau of Mines, the Oil and Natural Gas Commission, the Central Water and Power Commission, the Indian Council of Agricultural Research. the Council of Scientific and Industrial Research and others. Techno-economic surveys of several States and Union Territories have been undertaken by the National Council of Applied Economic Research. The survey of the Damodar Valley region by the Institute of Technology, Kharagpur, and the universities of Calcutta and Patna, has reached an advanced stage. The Indian Statistical Institute has undertaken regional surveys in Mysore and Kerala as part of its scheme of study of the problems of regional planning. The bench-mark surveys and other studies of the Programme Evaluation Organisation and the Agro-Economic Research Centres provide information regarding the problems of rural areas at various stages of development. The city surveys and other studies organised under the auspices of the Research Programmes Committee offer valuable data bearing on urban and regional development problems. Surveys of metropolitan regions like Delhi and Bombay and those proposed for Calcutta have also considerable importance for planning. Thus, as a result of several steps which have been taken in recent years, a wide range of technical, economic and social data regarding the problems and possibilities of regional development have become available, and will assist planning for the future.

Development of regions and of the national economy as a whole have to be viewed as parts of a single process. The progress of the national economy will be reflected in the rate of growth realised by different regions and, in turn, greater development of resources in the regions must contribute towards acceleration the rate of progress for the country as a whole. Excessive emphasis on the problems of particular regions and attempts to plan for their development without relating their needs to the requirements of the national economy have to be guarded against, for, in the final analysis, it is as integral parts of the country that different regions can best hope to realise their full potential for growth. Balanced regional growth emerges eventually from a whole series of connected developments, many of which are of a long-term character. Over the short period, advance towards the goal will frequently seem small and incomplete.

This is true for individual regions and, equally, for the national economy as a whole. Whatever the present shortcomings, the aim must be that over a reasonable period all regions in the country should realise their potential for economic development and should attain levels of living not far removed from those of the nation as a whole. Progress in different regions must, therefore, be watched carefully, and additional steps taken to speed up development in particular areas which are found to be seriously lagging behind. In the perspective of long-term development, with the economy advancing rapidly towards the stage of self-sustained growth and with steady rise in the living standards of the people, regional and national development are essentially two different facets of a common objective.

# 3

# Employment and Manpower

## ANALYSIS OF THE PROBLEM

Employment has been a major objective of planning in India; it was so in the first two Plans and has assumed a special urgency in the Third. Full utilisation of the available manpower resources can be achieved after a considerable period of development. However, expansion of employment opportunities commensurate with the increase in the labour force over the Plan period is conceived as one of the principal aims of the Third Plan. In view of the numbers involved, provision of adequate employment opportunities is among the most difficult tasks to be accomplished during the next five years.

In the rural areas, both unemployment and underemployment exist side by side; the distinction between them is by no means sharp. In the villages, unemployment ordinarily takes the form of under- employment. In many parts of the country, during the busy agricultural seasons, shortages of labour are frequently reported, but over the greater part of the year, a large proportion of agricultural labour and others engaged in allied activities are without continuous employment.

The consequent drift of workers from villages to towns only serves to shift the focus of attention from rural areas to the urban. Though recent surveys show a somewhat higher rate of unemployment in the towns, this itself is a reflection of the lack of adequate work opportunities in rural areas. Urban and rural unemployment in fact constitute an indivisible problem.

In the urban areas, employment is linked with fluctuations in the state of business, transport and industry. Any change in conditions is reflected in an increase or decrease in employment figures. While this is generally true, towns-large and small-share with villages a measure of distress caused by under-employment.

The existing data are inadequate for building up a sufficiently detailed picture of the state of employment for the country as a whole and in its regional, urban and rural aspects. But statistics apart, there is a general belief, which is strengthened by the limited number of employment opportunities reported to the em- ployment exchanges and the pressure of employment seekers on them, that in terms of unemployment the economy suffered significant deterioration in the last five years. The high rate of growth of population, as reflected by the limited 1961 Census data, now available, would indicate that the problem is one of increasing complexity. This has been broadly confirmed by the findings of the Second Agricultural Labour Enquiry, the National Sample Survey and the studies undertaken by the Programme Evaluation Organisation. This, however, is not a complete statement. Development programmes have provided additional employment opportunities to a significant extent; but these are not being created fast enough to absorb the numbers who enter the labour force each year. If any further deterioration in the employment situation is to be avoided, the goal of planning must be to absorb in gainful employment in each five-year period at least the equivalent of new entrants to the labour force.

It is not easy to measure unemployment in an under-developed country. There is a tendency, specially among the self-employed, to share work between members of the family or the group. Where the available work opportunities are spread too thinly even to provide tolerable means of livelihood, a part of the population migrates in search of paid employment. It is in relation to this section of the population that the term "unemployed" can be used with some exactness. For the rest, one can only speak of under-employment for varying periods.

An important factor in planning for larger employment within the present occupational structure is that, for lack of employment opportunities, a considerable proportion of self-employed persons have to function below capacity and do much less work than in fact they are willing to. Statistics about under-employment depend very much on how the term is defined. At the present stage of development, it is difficult to determine the volume of Underemployment with reference to 'norms' of hours per day to be worked by individuals or other similar criteria. It is more meaningful to judge the amount of under- employment by the extent of additional work an individual may be willing to take up. This is the concept which has been adopted in the more recent rounds of the National Sample Survey.

The limited data at present available may be considered in relation to the following aspects of the employment problem; (a) numbers unemployed at the end of the Second Plan, (b) addition to the labour force during the Third Plan, and (c) assessment of additional employment likely to be secured through the implementation of the Plan as formulated. It is also necessary to take into account such mea- sures as would help to step up the employment effect of development schemes with a significant labour component, such as construction and small industries. Even if the full employment potential of the Plan is achieved, it will be necessary to think of special employment pro- grammes to cover the residual employment gap.

In the course of the Second Plan the additional employment opportunities created amounted to about 8 million, of which about 6.5 million were outside agriculture. The backlog of unemployment at the end of the Second Plan is reckoned at 9 million. This estimate is admittedly rough. It takes account of the estimate of unemployment as at the beginning of the Second Plan (5.3 million), the larger increase in labour force during the Second Plan period than had been visualised earlier (1.7 million), and the estimated shortfall in the employment target originally proposed for the Second Plan (about 2 million). In addition, under-employment in the sense of those who have some work but are willing to take up additional work cannot be precisely estimated, but is believed to be of the order of 15-18 million.

Increase in the labour force during a given period is calculated with reference to the proportion of men and women in the age group 15-59 years who are estimated as being gainfully employed or seeking employment. In the Draft Outline of the Third Plan, the increase in labour force had been worked out at 15 million, and it was pointed out that, if deterioration in the employment situation was to be avoided, additional employment opportunities of this order would have to be found during the Third Plan. Information for the 1961 Census regarding the age composition of the population and changes in the extent of participation in the labour force by men and women is not yet available and, at this stage, certain general assumptions on these aspects have to be made on the basis of the latest reports of the National Sample Survey. On such estimates as are at present possible, it appears that during the Third Plan the addition to the labour force may be of the order of 17 million, about a third of the increase being in the urban areas. When fuller data become available, it will be necessary to work out the increase in the labour force in relation to different States, so that each State may endeavour to realise the employment potential of programmes and projects under the Plan and consider the extent to which these could be supplemented by other measures. In a growing economy, mobility of labour, specially among skilled workers, is of great importance and should be encouraged and facilitated. However, in relation to the numbers involved, the effects of such mobility as Can be achieved in the next few years will be necessarily limited and will not affect the total size of the task to be undertaken in each State or region.

The employment objectives of the Third Plan need to be viewed in the perspective of a longer period. Increase in the labour force over the next 15 years may be of the order of 70 million. This consists roughly of about 17 million in the Third Plan, about 23 million in the Fourth and about 30 million in the Fifth Plan. The experience of the first two Plans has shown that a larger proportion of the employment opportunities generated during the period have gone to the non-agricultural sector. On the assumption that this trend will continue in future and also that about two-thirds of the increase in the labour force over the next 15 years is absorbed outside agriculture, it should be possible to reduce the proportion of the working force dependent on agriculture to around 60 per cent by 1976.

## ADDITIONAL EMPLOYMENT IN THE THIRD PLAN

There are inherent difficulties, in estimating the employment potential of the vast range of projects and programmes which form part of a plan of development stretching over a period of five years. In each sector of the Plan two major assumptions have to be made. The first is that through appropriate economic and other policies, production and employment will not be allowed to fall below the existing levels. Secondly, the various development programmes for which the Plan provides will be undertaken with the necessary efficiency and economy and continuity of output would be assured. In some fields, as in agriculture and trade, it is specially difficult to estimate the likely additional employment. Increase in agricultural production, to which the Plan devotes a fair share of resources, will lead primarily to reduction in under-employment, although there will also be a measure of net increase in employment opportunities. In less developed countries, the numbers engaged in trade are large, in relation to the work they are required to handle, so that the effect of expansion in the trading sector is more to reduce under-employment than to provide additional work opportunities to new entrants.

In industry, increase in investment and capacity does not lead to a proportionate growth of employment because new processes, specially in large-scale manufacture, have generally to be based on high productivity techniques. The choice of techniques becomes, thus, a matter of crucial importance for employment policy. In certain branches of industry, it is essential to adopt the scale and methods of production which will yield the largest economies. This has to be balanced by a deliberate effort in other fields to employ techniques which will be more labour-intensive and will save on capital resources, specially foreign exchange. Labour intensive methods have even wider application. in the field of construction in which, given the necessary organisation and advance planning, it is possible to use manpower to a greater extent than has been common in recent years. What techniques, should be adopted have to be determined not only according to the types of activities to be carried out, but also by the economic and social characteristics of the regions in which they are undertaken. In areas in which there is considerable pressure of population, special care must be taken to follow methods which, consistent with the overall objectives, make the maximum use of the available manpower resources.

In estimating the employment effects of the Plan, it is usual to distinguish two phases of employment-the construction phase and the continuing phase. Employment on construction, though temporary, postulates a certain order of investment even for maintaining it at a given level. Increase in construction employment can, therefore, be estimated with reference to the increase in investment over the previous Plan period. Since investment in construction is divided broadly between the labour component on the one hand, and machines, materials and services on the other, for working out the additional employment, the former has to be calculated with some precision.

In estimating continuing employment in fields such as agriculture, irrigation, industry, transport, social services, trade, etc., a variety of criteria have to be followed. For instance, development of agriculture, afforestation and irrigation facilities may in part reduce underemployment and in part provide full-time em- ployment to new entrants. It is by no means easy to ascertain the relative share, of the benefits to the under-employed and to new en- trants. Programmes of development like soil conservation, afforestation, land reclamation, flood control, settlement on land and the utilisation of irrigation facilities will provide means for employing new entrants to the labour force in addition to giving greater employment to those who are already at work. For this purpose certain norms have been adopted on the basis of experience accumulated over the last ten years.

In estimating additional employment in industries, depending upon their character, employment may have to be related either to the investment or to increase in levels of production after allowing for rise in productivity in some cases ; in others, reliance has to be placed on project reports and on information supplied to the Licensing Committee. In road transport, the criterion may be furnished by different indicators of increase in the volume of passenger and goods traffic. In the field of social services a variety of tests have to be adopted, depending upon the level at which the Plan intends to pro- vide these services to the community. For instance, in health services, the requirements of different types of personnel were assessed in relation to the population served. In education, the pupil-teacher ratio was used as the criterion.

Apart from the direct employment flowing from different development programmes, account has also to be taken of indirect em- ployment in such fields as trade, commerce and transport. In the Second Plan, indirect employment was reckoned at 52 per cent of the additional employment which could be attributed to development programmes under the Plan, both in the public and the private sectors. On the basis of recent studies it would be reasonable to assume for the Third Plan, indirect employment benefits at 56 per cent of the additional employment attributable to development programmes in the Plan. Finally, certain checks have to be applied to estimates of additional employment worked out for different sectors. Gradually, fuller data for such overall appraisal are becoming available.

These include the results of special surveys and investigations, project studies, employment market information gathered by the National Employment Service, and analysis of information provided in appli- cations submitted for industrial licences. Estimation of employment in relation to a plan of development involves a number of assumptions, which have to be continuously tested. In the nature of things, therefore, there can be no finality in estimates of employment which might be worked out in relation to a plan of development. Experience of the last ten years shows that there is need for continuous examination and improvement of methods and for assessment of the actual performance in relation to initial estimates of employment and investment. To facilitate this, a detailed statement of the as- sumptions made in calculating the additional employment potential of the Third Plan is given in Appendix C.

Following the methods of estimation explained above, it is reckoned that the Third Plan may provide additional non-agricultural employment of the order of 10.5 million and additional employment in agriculture of about 3.5 million. The additional non-agricultural employment is distributed broadly as follows :

***Additional non-agricultural employment***

***(in lakhs)***

| | sector | additional employment in the Third Plan |
|---|---|---|
| 1 | construction* | 23.00 |
| 2 | irrigation and power | 1.00 |
| 3 | railways | 1.40 |
| 4 | other transport and communications | 8.80 |
| 5 | industries and minerals | 7.50 |
| 6 | small industries | 9.00 |
| 7 | forestry, fisheries and allied services | 7.20 |
| 8 | education | 5.90 |
| 9 | health | 1.40 |
| 10 | other social services | 0.80 |
| 11 | government service | 1.50 |
| | total (1 to 11) | 67.50 |
| 12 | others' including trade and commerce at 56 per cent of total (1 to 11) | 37.80 |
| | grand tot l | 105.30 |

Besides additional employment outside agriculture and in agriculture described above, there will also be significant relief to underemployment, but it is difficult to indicate its extent in quantitative terms. In agriculture, only about a fourth of new employment potentialities have been taken acçount of for estimating additional employment and the remaining are expected to provide relief to under-employed persons. In village and small-scale industries, only full-time jobs have been accounted for in the table above. While the economy seeks to absorb as many workers, as possible into non- agricultural occupations, during the Third Plan it is expected that there will be a net addition to the total number of workers engaged in agriculture.

A large part of the increase in the labour force will take place in families who are at present dependent on agriculture. If employment opportunities do not develop sufficiently in the non- agricultural sectors, under-employment in agriculture will be further intensified, leading to lowering of living standards in a section of the community upon whom the growth in population has already borne harshly. It should also be stated that in the nature of things, estimates of additional employment arising from the Plan are subject to a considerable degree of uncertainty. If some of the assumptions made are not borne out by later experience, or if the various programmes and projects are not implemented in a sufficiently effective and continuous manner, the additional employment estimated above may not be fully realised.

If, in consequence of Plan programmes, employment opportunities are available for about 14 million persons, leaving aside the backlog of unemployment, even for providing work for the new entrants to the labour force, there is need to find additional employment opportunities for 3 million persons. This is considered to be an essential objective in the Third Plan.

At this stage it must be emphasised that although the validity of quantitative estimates is affected by the inadequacy and complexity of employment data, experience in the First and Second Plans show that employment targets could not be achieved in full because of shortfalls in performance in various sectors of the Plan. Every attempt has, therefore, to be made to avoid the recurrence of such a situation.

It is proposed that the problem should be approached along three main directions. Firstly, within the framework of the Plan, efforts should be made to ensure that the employment effects are spread out more widely and evenly than in the past. Secondly, a fairly large programme of rural industrialisation should be undertaken with special emphasis on programmes of rural electrification, development of rural industrial estates, promotion of village industries, and effective re- deployment of manpower. Even though, in the first instance, the introduction of new production techniques may result in a decrease in employment, it is expected that there will be significant Iong-term benefits in revitalising the rural economy. Thirdly, in addition to other measures for increasing employment through small industries, it is proposed to organise a rural works programme, which will provide work for an average of say, 100 days in the year for about 2.5 million persons and, if possible, more. Those programmes, and specially the proposal for rural works, will assist the general mass of the population and will also provide increased opportunities for the educated unemployed. The latter have, however, certain special problems of their own, which are briefly discussed in a later section of this chapter.

# 4

# Personnel Requirements and Training Programmes

## MANPOWER PLANNING

Of all the resources for development, perhaps the most fundamental at the present time is trained manpower. Owing to the rapid advance in science and technology and the growing complexity of industrial and economic Organisation, there is increasing demand for larger numbers of highly skilled and trained personnel drawn from different disciplines and functioning generally in composite teams rather than as individuals. As the economy develops, the requirements of individuals with more advanced and specialised training and of scientifically trained workers increase, while the need for persons at lower levels of skill and for the semi-skilled and unskilled steadily diminishes. It takes five years or more to give the, basic training needed by an engineer or a doctor, and a much longer period to provide research and practical experience essential for filling positions of greater responsibility. To secure the required outturn of scientific and technical personnel and build up an adequate foundation of scientific research may take a nation, a whole generation.

In relation to the long-term economic development of a country, the extent of trained manpower available and the training facilities established constitute a major determinant of the measure of advance which can be achieved in different directions. As the economy grows, there has to be emphasis not only on numbers but also on quality and experience. Problems of producing the requisite trained manpower have to be seen in their broader context. On the one hand, they bear upon the character of education at each stage in school And college and on life in the home ; on the other, they en- compass the entire system of management and organisation in industrial and other undertakings, and the lines along which research is undertaken and its results applied.

In the context of programmes for the training of manpower, the demands of rapid economic development are like those of a national emergency. It calls for the reorganisation and expansion of existing institutions, development of large numbers of new institutions, special measures for obtaining and training teachers and instructors, introduction of new techniques for intensifying training and shorten- ing the periods needed, expanding facilities for imparting practical training, and developing new ways of making use of trained personnel as a scarce key resource. In the light of experience and assessment of the developing needs of the economy there must be constant re- examination of ideas and practices in vogue in the field of training. In manpower planning the economy has to be viewed as a whole, the entire range of facilities and possibilities available in all undertakings, whether public or private, being deemed to be at the service of the community. There is need to encourage experiment and innovation on the part of every organisation and training institution and to provide ever-increasing opportunities for original and creative activity.

Over the first two Plans valuable experience in manpower planning has been gained in several fields. There has been considerable expansion in facilities for the training of scientists, engineers and technologists, of agricultural, veterinary and health and medical personnel and of skilled craftsmen. Steel plants and other major industrial projects have made it necessary to take up large-scale training, both within the country and abroad, and in this other nations have also generously shared their experience and facilities. Trained personnel are required in large numbers, not only for the development of industry and transport and power but also in many other fields. Rural development programmes undertaken in com- munity development and other areas have already involved large training programmes. As the role of democratic institutions at the district, block and village levels, of the cooperative movement, of municipal bodies and of voluntary organisations becomes more decisive in fields close to the welfare of the community as a whole, their need for trained personnel will become even more marked and much larger numbers of trained workers will be needed. Progress in education, health services, family planning and welfare programmes, as envisaged in the Third and later Plans, will also depend to no small. extent on the adequate supply of teachers and other trained personnel.

In each field personnel requirements have to be estimated carefully and over a long period. This calls for improved statistical information, and development of techniques of manpower assessment so that the necessary estimates call be made with reasonable accuracy and a comprehensive picture built up for the economy as a whole. Estimates of personnel requirements have necessarily to be reviewed from time to time in the light of changing needs and experience. Manpower planning is, thus, an integral part of the economic, plans formulated by the Central and State Governments and their agencies, and, within their own specific fields by industrial associations and other organisations representing different activities or interests as welt as by individual undertakings and institutions, both public and private. They call for constant interchange of knowledge and experience and for special investigations.

In view of the wide range of issues to be considered, and the great importance of manpower planning for the country's future development, it is proposed shortly to set up an Institute of Applied Manpower Research, which will work in close collaboration with the Central and State Governments and with industrial and other organisa- tions. Among the main aims of the Institute will be to provide a broad perspective of requirements of trained manpower for economic development in different fields, arrange for facilities for advanced training in manpower planning, develop methods for training and building, up the existing work-force, evolve methods for up the existing work-force, evolve methods for and, generally, secure the most effective utilisation of the country's human resources.

As compared to the First Plan, the Second Plan presented problems of manpower planning on a much large scale. To a consi- derable extent, profiting from the lessons of the Second Plan, steps were taken sufficiently in advance to secure trained personnel for the Third Plan. In many fields, though by no means in all, training programmes, which form part of the 'third Plan, are designed to produce trained workers for the still more intensive development envisaged in the Fourth and later plans. There are still large areas in which personnel with adequate experience will not be available in sufficient number, and small numbers of trained and experienced persons will have to carry a disproportionate load. In these fields, while making the maximum use of the available indigenous personnel, there should be no hesitation in taking advantage of technical assistance programmes and other sources for obtaining Such highly trained personnel as may be needed. Since the requirements of person- nel are commonly reckoned chiefly in terms of assumptions and possibilities, based on past or current experience and unforeseen demands will continue to be thrown up on account of the rapid technological changes within the country and abroad and the growing needs of the economy, the present estimates are likely to need upward revision. It will be of particular importance during the Third Plan to reassess requirements in different fields from time to time and to take a view of these requirements not merely for the Fourth Plan, but also for the Fifth Plan. In this Chapter it is proposed to set out briefly the present estimates of requirements of personnel and the training programmes for which the Third Plan provides in such fields as engineering, technology and science, agriculture and rural development, education, health and social welfare, and statistics and administration.

## ENGINEERING, TECHNOLOGY AND SCIENCE

Requirements of engineers and technicians may be considered at three principal levels-graduates, diploma holders and skilled craftsmen. In each group there has been rapid increase in the additions needed during each Plan period. On present estimates 5 1,000 additional engineering graduates are likely to be required for the Third Plan as compared to about 29,000 in the Second Plan. the demand in the Fourth Plan is estimated at about 80,000. Estimates for different branches of engineering are given in the Table below

***Table 1 : Estimated additional requirements for graduates in engineering and technology***

| | Second Plan | Third Plan | Fourth Plan |
|---|---|---|---|
| civil engineering | 12400 | 13000 | 20000 |
| mechanical engineering | 5300 | 15300 | 24000 |
| electrical engineering | 5600 | 10500 | 17000 |
| telecommunication engineering | 1600 | 2500 | 4000 |
| chemical engineering | 2300 | 3500 | 7000 |
| metallurgy | 700 | 1100 | 1600 |
| mining | 500 | 1600 | 2400 |
| others* | 1000 | 3500 | 4000 |
| total | 29400 | 51000 | 80000 |

The additional requirements of diploma holders in engineering and technology in the Third Plan are estimated at about 100,000 compared to about 56,000 in the Second Plan; estimates for the Fourth Plan are at present placed at about 125,000. The break-up of the additions needed by different branches of engineering is shown in the below Table.

With the stepping up of industrial development in the Third Plan and developments visualised for the Fourth Plan, the requirements of mechanical, electrical and chemical engineers Will increase relatively faster than those of civil engineers.

There will also be greater need for training specialists in branches like mining metallurgy and other technologies. These changing trends will be taken into account while determining the distribution of the addi- tional facilities for engineering education which are now being provided. In the course of the

Third Plan the admission capacity of engineering colleges will increase from 13,860 at the end of the Second Plan to 19,140, the corresponding increase in polytechnics being from 25,570 to 37,390. Provision is also being made for part time and correspondence courses in engineering and technology. Estimates of requirements and out-term of engineering personnel for the Third and Fourth Plans are indicated in the Table below

***Table 2 : Estimated additional requirements of diploma holders in engineering and technology***

| | Second Plan | Third Plan | Fourth Plan |
|---|---|---|---|
| civil engineering | 29000 | 39000 | 48000 |
| mechanical engineering | 12200 | 26000 | 33500 |
| electrical engineering | 10400 | 18000 | 22500 |
| telecommunication engineering | 600 | 600 | 800 |
| chemical engineering+ | 800 | 3500 | 5000 |
| metallurgy | 200 | 1100 | 1300 |
| mining | 600 | 4000 | 5000 |
| others* | 2000 | 7800 | 8900 |
| total | 55800 | 100000 | 125000 |

* Includes sugar technologists, jute technologists, leather technologists, architects and town planners, automobile, aeronautical, marine, public health and sanitary, and agricultural engineering personnel

\+ Training at the diploma level is provided by sandwich courses at training centres for chemical operators

The shortage of diploma holders, which has been considerable during the Second Plan, will not be altogether made up in the Third Plan. The present plans need to be reviewed further from this aspect and in the, light of more detailed information regarding the requirements of engineering personnel for major industrial programmes which is likely to become available as programmes are worked out. Estimates for the Fourth Plan are provisional and will be studied in greater detail with reference to the possibilities of long-term economic development indi- cated in Chapter II.

**Craftmen.** The requirements for craftmen during the Third Plan are estimated at nearly 1.3 million, about 810,000 being in en- gineering trades and the rest in non-engineering trades. Several industries as well as establishments under the Railways, Posts and Telegraphs, Defence, etc., have their own training programmes. A proportion of skilled and semi-skilled workers are also trained through traditional methods, the skills being imparted from father to son.

Facilities for institutional training at centres maintained by State Governments in collaboration with the Ministry of Labour & Employment, are, thus, required for a much smaller number. The number of industrial training institutes and centres has increased from 59 in 1955-56 to 167 in 1960-61, and the Third Plan provides for a further addition of 151.

The intake capacity increased correspondingly from 10,500 in 1955-56 to 42,000 at the end of the Second Plan, and will increase further during the Third Plan to 100,000. The apprenticeship training scheme, which was to be implemented by industry on a voluntary basis with a measure of support from Government, did not make much progress during the Second Plan. Legislation will be shortly introduced for placing apprenticeship on a compulsory basis. The programme for evening classes for industrial workers will also be extended.

Inservice training programmes.-Over the Second Plan inservice training programmes have been introduced by a large number of organisations, both public and private. These will be further enlarged.

Thus, the major industrial enterprises have, set up their own training schools, and some of them have also provided facilities for apprenticeship training. For the training of personnel at higher levels, the National Laboratories, the Atomic Energy Commission, the Ministry of Irrigation and Power, the Meteorological Department and others have arranged for special facilities.

**Scientific Personnel.** The National Register for Scientific and Technical Personnel maintained by the Council of Scientific and Industrial Research, carries about 106,000 registrations of whom Indians abroad account for nearly 5000. Of the number registered with the Council, about 33,000 are post-graduates in science subjects or graduates in agriculture, and about 66,000 are engineers and technologists both at the degree and diploma levels, the rest being specialists in medical profession. It is estimated that the coverage in the National Register is about 80 per cent of the total number of scientists.

The "Scientists Pool" which has been maintained by the Council of Scientific and Industrial Research for the last three years for providing temporary placements for highly qualified scientists and others, especially those returning to India from foreign countries so far assisted the selection of 653 scientists and technologists. The following Table brings out the position of postgraduate scientists in India :

***Table 4 : Estimated additional scientific personnel***

| | total numbers in position in 1955 | additional personnel in Second Plan |
|---|---|---|
| Mathematics and Statistics | 5700 | 6300 |
| Physics | 4600 | 2200 |
| Chemistry | 7300 | 1700 |
| Botany | 2100 | 1400 |
| Zoology | 2300 | 1400 |
| Geology | 1300 | 1200 |
| total | 23300 | 14200 |

Enduring foundations for expansion of scientific education can be laid only through the provision of larger facilities for science education both in the secondary schools and at the university stage.

The demand for scientists comes from many different directions-science teachers, maintenance engineers, research scien- tists, etc. Out of 27,000 teachers required for colleges in the Third Plan, as many as 17,000 will be scientists. There has been marked in- crease in facilities for science education in universities as may be seen from the following Table :

*Table 5 : Facilities for science, education-enrolment*

| degree | 1950-51 | 1955-56 | 1960-61 |
|---|---|---|---|
| Bachelor of Science | 32600 | 52300 | 84000 |
| Master of Science | 3800 | 6500 | 11300 |
| Doctorate | 630 | 1120 | 2000 |
| total | 37030 | 59920 | 97300 |

By the end of the Third Plan, science as an elective subject will be available in 9,500 secondary schools out of a total of 21,800 and at the university stage facilities will be provided for additional enrolment of about 230,000 students in science out of a total of about 400,000 students.

The need for scientists for fundamental and applied research and employment of scientists in other fields will have to be reviewed con- tinuously during the Third Plan and increase in facilities considered in the light of such estimates.

## AGRICULTURE AND RURAL DEVELOPMENT

Programmes in agriculture and allied fields of development in the Third Plan entail a very considerable expansion in personnel. The necessary training facilities were developed to a large extent during the Second Plan, so that in most fields the demands at present anticipated are expected to be met with only a small increase in the facilities available. However, the possibility of the total demands under different heads increasing as the Plan proceeds has to be kept in view. Tables 6 and 7 below show the additional requirements of agricultural and allied personnel during the Third and Fourth Plans as at present estimated and the programme for expanding training facilities during the Third Plan :

5

# Natural Resources

## INTRODUCTION

Under its terms of reference, the Planning Commission was required to-

(i) make an assessment of the material, capital and human resources of the country including technical personnel and investigate the possibilities of augment- ing such of these resources as are found to be deficient in relation to the nation's requirements, and

(ii) formulate a Plan for the most effective and bal- anced utilisation of the country's resources.

Accordingly, the First Five Year Plan presented an account of the land, water, mineral and energy resources of the country on the basis of information then available. It drew attention to the main problems in each field and set out programmes for further surveys and investigations. It also offered suggestions for strengthening the organisations responsible for these surveys, providing them with personnel and equipment. and expanding programmes of training.

Over the past few years organisations dealing with the survey and utilisation of natural resources, such as the Indian Council of Agri- cultural Research, the Central Water and Power Commission, Central Board of Irrigation and Power, Geological Survey of India, Oil and Natural Gas Commission, Indian Bureau of Mines, Survey of India, Forest Research Institute Atomic Energy Commission, and the Council of Scientific and Industrial Research and its National Laboratories have been greatly expanded and have undertaken a series of new surveys and investigations. These surveys have resulted in a fuller assessment of the country's natural resources bringing to light the gaps in informa- tion relating to these resources as also their deficiencies in rela- tion to the nation's future requirements,

The objective of planning is to raise the standard of living of the people as a whole. The attainment of this objective involves the development on scientific lines of the nation's natural and human resources. Expanded demand for natural resources and materials has led to technological developments which have in part overcome limita- tions and thus increased the supply of resources.

The dynamic forces at work in creating shifts in the demand for and supply or natural resources necessitate their continuous study as well as reformulation of policies relating to them. Natural resources must be looked at in a coordinated manner and their investigation and utilisation planned for long-term needs. The extent to which resources have been studied and possibilities established ahead of needs is an important factor determining the rate at which the economy can grow.

With the formulation of the Third Five Year Plan, the stage has reached when, as a necessary condition of well-conceived long-term plans, a comprehensive view needs to be taken of the extent and quali- ty of the information available in respect of the country's main natural resources.

The principal gaps which exist, the surveys required in this connection, and the further steps needed in relation to specific long range objectives, such as irrigation, power, steel, coal,oil and minerals, land use and forest resources have to be iden- tified.

As stated earlier, over the next 15 years, population may increase by about 187 million. Increase in labour force is reckoned at about 70 million, of whom some two-thirds must be absorbed outside agriculture. It becomes, therefore, a matter of the greatest impor- tance that a high rate of economic 'growth is achieved and sustained during this period. Her natural resources give India a large poten- tial for agricultural and industrial production, and their rapid development is an essential condition for the achievement over the next two or three Plan periods, of a self-reliant and self-sustained economy which can provide to the mass of the people continually rising living standards and opportunities for gainful employment.

The long- term goals in national and per capita incomes and the development of agriculture, irrigation and power, and the provisional targets sug- gested earlier for industries like steel, aluminium, coat, oil refin- ing, fertilisers, cement and others can only be achieved in time if the nature and extent of the natural resources of the country and the essential requirements concerning their development are assessed and the necessary steps taken well in advance. For balanced development, it is equally necessary to assess availabilities, requirements and possibilities in relation to each of the principal regions within the country.

In the Chapters on irrigation and power, forests, industries, minerals and others, an attempt has been made to indicate the main directions in which further efforts are needed to ascertain more fully the resources of the country and the measures required for their more rapid development.

The object of the present Chapter is to set the problem of assessing and developing natural resources in the context of the Third and subsequent Plans and to explain briefly some of the implications in this respect of the growth of population and of intensive and largescale industialisation.

A unit for Natural Resources has been recently set up in the Planning Commission for studying problems relating to the assessment and development of natural resources and assisting the various agen- cies engaged in the survey and investigation of these resources in linking up their work closely with the requirements of the rapidly growing economy, and generally, helping in securing a common approach in various related fields.

This unit will be strengthened as its work develops. In collaboration with other organisations, it is hoped to arrange for coordinated studies of natural resources on a continuing basis, to specify gaps in the existing information, particularly from the aspect of long-term development, and to suggest suitable policies and measures for giving effect to them.

Against this background, it is proposed briefly to review recent developments and to indicate the problems that lie ahead in relation to the development of the land, water, mineral, energy and other resources of the country.

## LAND RESOURCES

The most important natural resource of the country is land, which is the base for agricultural production. While population grows, the land surface is fixed, and of this only a certain propor- tion is available for cultivation. Several aspects of the problem need to be studied.

Through irrigation and other measures of agricul- tural development, the productivity of land can be considerably increased. It is necessary to ascertain the extent to which land now lying waste can become available for cultivation. Increasing popula- tion also means withdrawal of areas now under farms for building houses.

Development of communications such as roads, railways, and airways may take up fertile land. Owing to rapid urbanisation and growth of large cities land is needed for parks and open spaces. Irrigation dams may submerge fertile areas. Industrial plants and other establishments also require substantial areas. In all these developments wherever fertile land can be saved efforts should be made to do so. This indicates the need for a comprehensive inventory of land and for greater refinement in land classification and continuous attention to land use.

**Land Utilisation.** The total geographical area of India is about 806 million acres, of which reporting area is about 721 million acres and net area sown is about 318 million acres. The broad fea- tures of the present pattern of land utilisation and that anticipated by the end of the Third Plan are set out in the Table below :

***Table 1 : Land utilisation in 1965-66 (area in million acres)***

| | 1955-56 | 1960-61 | 1965-66 |
|---|---|---|---|
| total reportingarea | 720.0 | 721.0 | 721.0 |
| forests | 125.6 | 131.0 | 132.0 |
| landunder miscellaneous tree crops and groves | 13.9 | 14.0 | 15.0 |
| permanent pastures and other grazing lands | 28.4 | 32.0 | 32.0 |
| culturable waste | 54.8 | 47.0 | 40.0 |
| barren and uncultivated land and land put to non-agricultural use | 118.7 | 114.0 | 114.0 |
| fallow lands other than current fallows | 30.9 | 28.0 | 26.0 |
| current fallows | 29.5 | 28.0 | 25.5 |
| not area shown | 318.2 | 327.0 | 335.0 |
| area sown more than once | 44.4 | 51.5 | 67.0 |
| gross area sown | 362.6 | 378.5 | 402.0 |

Availability per head of cultivable land in India is about 0.82 acres as against 0.42 in U.K., 0.48 in Germany, 0.17 in Japan, 0.50 in China, 2.68 in U.S.A. and 2.59 in U.S.S.R.

**Soil Surveys.** Until recently knowledge of soils in different parts of the country was inadequate and the necessary Organisation for soil surveys had not been established. Appraisal of soil resources, involving survey and classification of soils provides the basis for assessing their potentialities as well as their limitations for effec- tive exploitation and rational land use.The main object of soil surveys is to classify and man out of various types of soils, to know soil differences, and to coordinate knowledge of soils with a view to laying down standards of nomenclature, etc. With the aid of these surveys it becomes possible to prepare schemes for the better use of land and to plan, for soil conservation and irrigation and drainage works. In 1955 an all-India soil survey scheme was initiated at the Indian Agricultural Research Institute with a view to carrying out reconnaissance soil surveys leading to correlation of soils of different regions. Soil correlation work involves classification and laying down of nomenclature of soils on a uniform basis and also the preparation of soil survey reports and soil maps. In the field of soil surveys, State Governments are specially concerned with aspects relating to agriculture, forestry, irrigation, drainage, soil conser- vation, etc.

Since there are common soil problems covering more than one State and all States do not have their own soil survey organisa- tions, with a view to coordinating work on soils, it was felt that the best course would be to set up laboratories on a regional basis for the four major soil groups occuring in India, namely, (1) at Delhi, for the Alluvial Soil Region, (2) at Poona (now at Nagpur) for the Black Soil Region, (3) at Kharagpur (now at Calcutta) for the Red and Laterite Soil Region I, and (4) at Bangalore for the Red and Laterite Soil Region II. Three years after its inception, the scheme was integrated with the scheme for soil and land use planning drawn up by the Central Soil Conservation Board for the purpose of soil and land use survey in the catchment areas of six major river valley projects, namely, Machkund, Hirakud, Chambal, Bhakra Nangal, Kosi and Damodar, totalling about 78,000 square miles.

Surveys in the catchment areas aim at classifying lands into capability classes essentially from the point of view of adopting soil conservation measures with a view to minimising soil erosion, preserv- ing the top soil for cultivation and preventing sediment flowing into storage reservoirs, and thus increasing their life. Soil conservation work in the catchment areas involves detailed surveys in agricultural lands and reconnaissance surveys in other areas. The total area to be surveyed is about 500,000 square miles. By the beginning of 1961, an area of about 18,000 square miles had been covered by both detailed 'and reconnaissance surveys undertaken through the all-India scheme. Of this area, about 3000 square miles fall within the catchment areas of the river valley projects.

Soil survey organisations in the States have surveyed about 50,000 square miles. Under the all-India programme, about 23,000 square miles are to be surveyed during the Third Plan.

**Survey of Wastelands.** Agricultural production can be stepped up through extension of area under cultivation by cultivating waste lands, double cropping of single crop areas, and other measures of intensives farming. There is considerable scope for extending the gross area sown by double cropping. It is anticipated that the area sown more than once might increase from about 52 million acres in 1960-61 to about 67 million acres by 1965-66. According to the avail- able land utilisation statistics the area under culturable waste in 1955-56 amounted to about 55 million acres. In June 1959, the Govern- ment of India constituted a Committee to make a survey of land classified as "other uncultivated land excluding fallow lands" and "fallow lands other than current fallows" and to locate areas where large blocks of land are available for reclamation and resettlement.

The Committee has completed its survey of seven States. In these, the area of wasteland available for cultivation in blocks of 250 acre or more is reckoned at nearly a million acres. The Committee's findings regarding the present statistics of wastelands are of considerable importance. On the whole the existing data are not sufficiently reliable, and lands classified as culturable waste at the time of settlement often continue to be shown as such in the revenue records long after they have come under cultivation. In the view of the Committee, the mere collection of statistics under the head 'cultura- ble waste' can serve little purpose and detailed information should be available about the types of wastelands in each State, the ownership of such lands, their availability in sizeable blocks and the cost of reclamation measures. The Committee has, therefore, recommended that rapid reconnaissance surveys should be conducted for collecting such information.

To sum up, there are large gaps in the information at present available regarding land resources. To secure quick results it is necessary that land surveys using photogrammetric techniques (aerial photographs) should be undertaken, and data on and use, land improvement, reclamation of water-logged, saline and alkaline lands and productivity should be collected in a systematic manner with a view to drawing up further plans.

## FOREST RESOURCES

Out of the total geographical area of 1.26 million square miles, about 274,000 square miles or about 21.8 per cent of the area consists of forests. Due to variations in climatic conditions and differences in altitude a large variety of natural vegetation ranging from temperature to tropical is found in the forests of India. For- ests may be classified as follows :

*Table 2 : Classification of forests*

| | percentage |
|---|---|
| temperate forests | |
| coniferous | 3 |
| broad-leaved | 4 |
| tropical forests | |
| deciduous | 80 |
| evergreen | 12 |
| others | 1 |

The productivity of India's forests can be greatly in- creased. Forests are among the few renewable resources in nature which, if properly managed, could go on yielding at undiminished rate and for an indefinite period. There is shortage of timber and fire- wood, of raw materials for drugs, paper and pulp and of fodder for cattle.

Wood and other forest products are basic raw materials essential for 'industrial development. In the past no proper apprais- al of local forest resources was made and products such as paper or pulp, plywood, tannin, etc., were freely imported . With a view to developing such industries in the country, an appraisal of the posi- tion of such raw materials is a matter of importance. The consumption of industrial wood in India is as low as 0.6 cft. per capita per year as against 16.0 cft. in

France and 13.4 cft. in Japan. India's present requirements of industrial wood amount to 4.5 million tons and are estimated to be more than 9 million tons in 1975. As regards firewood resources, in the ordinary course, a demand of 100 million tons is anticipated by 1975.

It is essential that a sustained increase in production should be secured from year to year through injtensive development schemes, including selection of high yield areas, planting of quick- growing species, introduction of improved logging and processing techniques, development of communications and more generally, the linking of forest development with specific schemes of industrial development to be undertaken over the next few years. While the requirements and supplies of industrial wood are still more or less balanced, it is considered that over the next 10 or 15 years unless special steps are taken, acute shortages might be experienced. This calls for measures for the intensification of production, devel- opment of hill forests, improved utilisation of low grade timbers, economy in fuel wood consumption and systematic surveys of forest re- sources in relation to specific industries. It is also necessary to undertake a survey of forest lands, indicating areas which are badly eroded, those fit for natural regeneration and those where planting should be undertaken. In some areas, specially in Central and South India, there are natural forests with trees which 'have only fuel value. These areas can be covered with valuable planted forests. There is need too for obtaining data regarding forest resources in inaccessible areas.

## WATER RESOURCES

Water resources may be divided broadly into surface water and underground water. Their development has to be viewed in relation to the need to increase the productivity of land through irrigation, flood control, drainage and other means and also to domestic. and industrial requirements.

**Surface Water.** The annual rainfall over the entire country represents something more than 3000 million acre-feet of water. Of this amount, about 1000 million acre-feet are lost immediately due to evaporation and roughly 650 million acre-feet seep into the soil, leaving 1350 million acre-feet to flow into the river systems. The entire surface flow cannot be utilised because topography, flow char- acteristics, climate and soil conditions impose limits on usability. It has been estimated that only 450 million acre-feet can be harnessed for purposes of irrigation.

**Underground Water.** Of the 650 million acre-feet of water that seep down annually into the soil, about 350 million, acre-feet get absorbed in the top layers thereby contributing to soil moisture which is essential for the growth of vegetation. The remaining 300 million acre-feet percolate down into porous strata and represent the annual enrichment of underground water. The total storage underground at any particular time may be several times this amount, but it can be assessed only if a country-wide investigation is undertaken. The actual utilisation of underground water at present is less than 20 per cent of the annual enrichment. Over the past eight years, through a series of ground-water exploration projects, efforts have been made to establish areas favourable to the sinking of tube-wells. For the third Plan, a project including 500 exploratory borings has been accepted. With a view to facilitating the work of exploration and reducing the need for large-scale drilling, it is also proposed to carry out geo- physical investigations. In peninsular India such investigations would quickly de ermine the depth of the bed rock and are likely to give first indications of ground-water availability. A survey pro- gramme is also in hand in Andhra Pradesh for localising areas of underground water where filter points for extraction of water can be successfully drilled.

**Utilisation.** The major use of water is for irrigation and hydropower generation, but water is also used for public water supply, industrial and navigation purposes. Water supply for irrigation can be obtained both from surface and underground resources.

The Central Water and Power Commission initiated in 1954 a study of different basins in the country for assessing the ultimate potential of major and medium irrigation projects. For purposes of this study the country was divided into five principal zones covering groups of river basins, and for each river basin the topography, rainfall, intensity of cultivation, possible storage sites, irrigable areas, reservoir capacity and other relevant factors were examined. Studies in respect of four zones are almost complete, while the fifth has still to be taken up.

The first comprehensive attempt towards assessment of the minor irrigation potential was made in 1955 by the Minor Irrigation Committee set up by the Ministry of Food and Agriculture. Similar studies were later initiated by the Minor Irrigation Team of the Committee on Plan Projects. Some State Governments have also initiat- ed minor irrigation surveys. A tentative appraisal of the data from these surveys indicates that the total ultimate irrigation potential of minor irrigation projects may be about 75 million acres (gross).

It will be seen that there is considerable scope for increasing the ratio of irrigated area to cultivated area. By realising the entire potential for irrigation of 175 million acres (gross) over the next 20-25 years (by which time the cultivated area may increase to about 350 million acres) the proportion of irrigated lands may perhaps rise to 50 per cent. Correspondingly, the amount of water utilised may go up to 350-400 million acre-feet or 60 per cent of the annual supply from both surface and underground sources. That will leave adequate quantities of water for meeting public supply, indus- trial needs and the requirements of thermal power generation the demand for which is likely to rise steadily.

**Industrial Uses.** The major uses of water in industry are for cooling, processing and boiler feed. Industrial needs of water are increasing rapidly. Hence the need to pay attention to methods of conservation and re-use of water in industries has become urgent. Most of the water used for industrial purposes is renewable in the sense that it becomes available for refuse if properly reconditioned.

One of the important problems associated with industrialisa- tion and urbanisation is the pollution of available water supplies, specially rivers, by industrial effluents and trade waste. This leads, amongst others, to mortality of fish and contamination of drinking water. Proper disposal of these wastes is difficult and costly. The problems which arise in this connection are being studied by the All-India Institute of Hygiene and Public Health, the Indian Council of Medical Research and the Public Health Engineering Research Institute. There is need for coordinated surveys and experimental work. These should cover analysis of effluents, data on extent of pollution caused by them, development of methods for their treatment and, preparation of standards to which they should conform, before they can be discharged into rivers.

## FISHERIES

Inland fisheries.-Rivers and their tributaries, canals, takes, reservoirs, tanks and ponds with perennial water supply constitute a rich potential source of inland fisheries. Out of 1.4 million tons of annual catch about 300,000 tons are from inland water. In the first Plan over a million acres of inland waters were surveyed and 68,000 acres reclaimed. In the Second Plan about 340,000 acres of inland waters have been surveyed and an area of 720,000 acres stocked. The Third Plan includes proposals for the development of more than 50,000 acres of water area as demonstration fish farms, 1500 acres for estuarine fish culture and reclamation of about 1500-2000 acres of marshy and fallow lands for fish culture. An urgent need is a com- plete survey of waters which do not dry up during summer and which can be stocked with fish. An inventory of the existing waters as to type namely, ponds, reservoirs, lakes, rivers, etc. and the areas under each type should be prepared. This should be followed by a detailed inventory of the physical, chemical and biological features. When this work is completed, it will provide a sound basis for development of the inland fisheries resources

**Marine Fisheries.** Out of the total fish production of 1.4 million tons annually about 1.1 million tons are marine. Of the marine fisheries, the most important are the mackerel, sardines and prawns. India's need is estimated at about 4 million tons but the production rate is only about a quarter of requirements. The sea fisheries generally exploited are confined to 6-10 miles from the coast. India's marine fisheries resources have not been properly as- sessed and there is need for a comprehensive survey. The importance of this survey is underlined by the fact that the resources of the sea can supplement those of the land to a significant extent.

## MINERAL RESOURCES

Minerals play an important part in the industrial economy of the present day-some like coal and mineral oil are sources of energy, others are raw materials for industry, while a few are the ulti- mate source of synthetic substitutes for natural materials like rub- ber, timber cotton and others.

The country has fairly abundant reserves (in terms of volume) of coal, iron ore and mica, adequate supplies or ores of manganese, titanium and aluminium, raw materials for refractories and lime-stone, but there is deficiency in ores of copper, lead and zinc. There are no workable deposits of tin, nickel, molybdenum and elemental sulphur. Until recently, except for Digboi in Assam, mineral oil was not known to occur in other parts of the country.

**Coal.** Coal is India's most important mineral asset and is the main source of commercial energy. Reserves of coal estimated for seams of thickness 4 feet and above are of the order of 50,000 million tons, of which coking coal accounts for 5.6 per cent, or about 2800 million tons. Inferred reserves are placed at 80,000 million tons. In addition about 2073 million tons of lignite are estimated to be available.

The coking coal reserves are a matter of concern in future. For every ton of steel 2.2 tons of coal are required. The rapid increase in the output of steel visualised during the next 15 years will increase the demand for coking coal. There is need to conserve carefully the limited reserves of coking coal. The position in regard to non-coking coal is not unsatisfactory, but since the bulk of the resources are of the low grade, economy in the consumption of better grade coal is essential.

The overall coal resources are highly concentrated. About 80 per cent of the present supply comes from a group of mines in a 200mile section of Bihar and West Bengal, thereby making it necessary for coal to be hauled over distances of 400-1400 miles for consumption in Southern and Western India. Efforts are being made to increase production from coal fields outside Bihar and West Bengal—their production increased from 5.7 million tons in 1951 (16 per cent of the total) to 10.2 million tons (20 per cent of the total) in 1960. By the end of the Third Plan the output of coal outside Bihar and West Bengal is expected to increase to about 28 million tons or 29 per cent of the total production in the country.

Mineral oil and natural gas.-Next to coal, petroleum and natural gas are major sources of commercial energy. So far India has not developed any considerable domestic petroleum supplies. However, intensive exploration for oil is under way. New oil wells in Assam are expected to produce about 2.75 million tons of oil per annum. in the initial stages which is likely to increase by the end of the Third Plan. Considerable quantities of natural gas are found associated with petroleum in Assam and in addition there is non-associated natu- ral gas also. Plans have been made for utilising the associated natural gas. Recent drilling operations in Cambay and Ankaleswar areas have given encouraging results and the production from these areas may reach about 2.0 million tons by 1965-66.

The annual increase in the demand for petroleum products which was 4.5 per cent during the last decade is expected to rise to 10-11 per cent in the current decade. The total demand which was about 7.5 million tons in 1960 is expected to rise to over 11 million tons in 1965-66 involving a foreign exchange expenditure of over Rs. 50 crores for meeting the deficit of 5 million tons by imports. Household requirements (chiefly kerosene for lighting) represent about 25 per cent of the total consumption. The demand of the transport sector (diesel oil and gasoline) is more than 30 per cent. The share of industry is about 20 per cent mainly in the form of furnace oil. There has been a significant increase in the consumption of middle distillates comprising kerosene and diesel oil.

**Other Minerals.** Though the principal mineral regions have been ascertained and a broad indication obtained of the potential mineral wealth of the country, until recently no detailed investiga- tions had been undertaken for a quantitative and qualitative assess- ment of the country's mineral resources. With the initiation of the planned development of the country attention was paid to systematic and detailed surveys and investigations by the Geological Survey of India, Indian Bureau of Mines, National Laboratories and Atomic Energy Commission with a view to a quantitative and qualitative assessment of the reserves of the more important minerals and their proper utilisation and the adoption of a policy aimed at systematic exploitation of minerals with due regard to conservation.

As a result of surveys carried out during the last ten years, more information is now avail- able of the extent of mineral reserves and their quality. Estimated reserves of manganese ore have now gone up from 20 million tons to 180 million tons. The assessment of sulphur-containing pyrites in Amjor area (Bihar) opens up the prospect of meeting a substantial part of demand of sulphur from internal production. Reserves of copper ore, iron ore, chromite, bauxite, magnesite, gypsum, limestone, lead and zinc, etc. have now been assessed and the gaps between requirements and availability determined.

The National Laboratories have carried out investigations with a view to improving the quality of minerals, making them usable (through investigations on the washing of coal, manganese ore, copper ore, etc.), finding uses for materials which would otherwise be wasted (as in the utilisation of scrap and waste mica) and substituting scarce metals by metals available within the country (for instance, nickel- free stainless steel and coinage alloys and aluminised steel wires).

The Mines and Minerals (Regulation and Development) Act, 1948 which was subsequently amended and elaborated in 1957, and the rules framed thereunder have brought a measure of uniformity in regard to leasing of mineral properties and for ensuring systematic development of the mineral resources of the country. The Coal Mines Conservation and Safety Act, 1952 provides for the adoption and enforcement of methods of conservation in regard to coal.

Though in the recent past a considerable amount of work has been done in the study of mineral resources and in assessing reserves in quantitative and qualitative terms in particular areas, in the context of rapid industrial development of the country and the conse- quent increasing demand for mineral raw materials, exploration for and investigation of mineral deposits requires to be pursued with 'greater vigour in order to know more fully the minerals available and eventually their quality and quantity.

Apart from the urgent necessity of more intensive exploration for minerals, there is need for enforcement of measures for conservation. Measures for conservation in relation to minerals will mean mainly avoidance of waste in mining and processing and in a large sense the substitution of scarce materials by those which are abun- dantly available in the country. Avoidance of waste in mining re- quires that there should be no selective mining-the richer and the poorer grades should be worked together and then blended to obtain a marketable grade. Upgrading of low grade ores (e.g. beneficiation of manganese ore, coal, copper ore, etc.) and utilising byproducts of mining and processing, (e.g. sintering of iron ore fines and utilising washery middlings) are also measures of coservation.

## ENERGY

The demand for energy in India is growing rapidly due to industrialisation, increasing transport facilities and rising standards of living. India's consumption per head is still among the lowest in the world.

Pattern of production and consumption The total production of energy in India during 1960-61 was roughly of the order of 165 million tons of coal equivalent. The commercial sources of energy are coal, petroleum and falling water. Wind power and solar, geothermal and tidal energy may constitute future sources subject to appropriate technological developments. Nearly 61 per cent of the energy comes presently from non-commercial sources, such as cattle dung, wood, charcoal, farm wastes, etc. as will be apparent from the following Table. Amongst the non-commercial sources of energy, that from ani- mate effort has not been taken into account. This has been estimated to be equivalent to 76 million tons of coal per year.

**Non-commercial Services of Energy.** Dried cattle dung is the main Source of energy for cooking and heating throughout the rural area and in many urban households as well. It has been estimated that the amount of cattle dung annually available is 1200 million tons (wet weight) of which 400 million tons are used as fuel and 215 million tons as manure, the balance being wasted. On the basis of energy content, 400 million tons of dung is equivalent to 46 million tons of coal. Wood is used as fuel both for domestic purposes as well as by some industries either directly or in the form of charcoal. The fuelwood consumption of the country is estimated to be of the order of 60 million tons, which in terms of energy equivalent would be equal to roughly- 35 million tons of coal.

**Commercial Sources of Energy.** These include coal, mineral oil and natural gas which have been considered in the previous sec- tion, and electricity which is discussed below.

**Electric Power.** Large quantities of low grade coal and middlings will be available at collieries and washeries for generation of power. These locations are therefore well suited for coal-fired stations. Hydel stations take a long time to set LIP, involve relatively large outlays and are, by their very nature, located in relatively remote localities from which the power has to be transmitted over long distances.

Currently, the electric energy consumption in India is about 45 kWh per head of population. In 1950 it was 14 kWh and in 1958, 35 kWh and by 1965-66 this is expected to increase to about 95 kWh per capita. This rate of increase will need to be maintained for a long period. Compared to other countries India's consumption is extremely low. In Japan per capita consumption rose from 455 kWh in 1947 to 930 in 1958 ; in Italy during the same period it rose from 454 kWh to 928.

However, extensive surveys of individual project sites involving contouring, reservoir areas, flow characteristics, availability of local construction materials, etc., have to be undertaken before this potential can be more definitely assessed and harnessed. In the Third Plan 64 specific project sites are proposed to be investigated.

**Nuclear Energy.** For a self-sufficient atomic energy programme an adequate supply of fuel material is a prerequisite. It has been known for several decades that in the monazite sands found on the beaches of the Kerala and Madras coasts India has one of the largest deposits of thorium in the world, containing no less than 200,000 tons of thorium in a concentration of over 9 %.

As a result of the work of the Atomic Minerals Division, during the period of the Second Plan an even more extensive monazite deposit has been discovered in the State of Bihar which contains no less than 300,000 tons of thorium in a concentration of over 10%.

India thus has the largest known thorium reserves in the world equalling in amount the total world reserve of uranium. Several deposits of uranium also have been discovered in various parts of the country, which are still being proved by drilling. A deposit containing several thousand tons of uranium has, however, been established in Bihar and steps are being taken to open up a mine to produce a thousand tons of ore a day. Nuclear power plants are expected to make a progressive contribution towards meeting the growing demand for power.

Unconventional sources of energy.Attempts to convert primary forms of energy such as solar radiation, wind motion, tidal energy, heat of the earth and oceans, etc. are being made in different parts of the world. Of the several devices developed so far, solar house heating, solar batteries and wind power generators have proved reason- ably successful in many places. Tidal motion has also been harnessed in some countries.

In India, work has been done on the development of a solar cooker, a solar evaporator and prototype windmills. A great deal of research and experimentation and several years of development work go into every divice meant for catching the energy of the sun, wind or tides in an efficient and economical manner. Research schemes for tapping unconventional sources of energy should be developed.

## RESOURCES OF THE SEA

India has a coastline of about 3530 miles. a continental shelf of more than 10,000 square miles and a large number of gulfs and bays along the coast. This alone indicates the vast possibilities of marine resources in the form of marine algae, fish and other edible animals as well as minerals. Oceans are huge reservoirs of organic material and photosynthesis occurs in them at greater rate than in forests or grasslands.

The importance of marine fisheries has already been stressed. Marine algae (sea-weeds) are a promising source of food which still remains unexploited in India. Sea-weeds are also the source of agar, alternates, mucilages and iodine. Some of them can be used for making jams, jellies, etc. for human consumption.

Addition of sea-weeds to cattle feeds in other countries has proved remarkably beneficial due to the presence of trace elements which the farm ani- mals generally lack. Similarly, incorporation of sea-weed-cowdung compost to soil proved much more beneficial to crops than cowdung alone. A preliminary survey conducted by the Central Marine Fisheries Research Station, Mandapam, indicates that systematic exploitation of sea-weeds could be quite profitable. There is need for a comprehensive survey of the availability of economic sea-weeds on India's coastline and their utilisation.

Mineral resources from the sea bold considerable promise. of these, the most important is the common edible salt. Its production in 1958 was about 4.2 million tons valued at about Rs. 8.5 crores. At present very little use is being made of salt bitterns which are a source of magnesium chloride, potassium chloride and bromine.

Against a possible quantity of million tons, only 8000 tons of magnesium salts are recovered. Only a few hundred tons of potassium chloride are recovered against a possible total of 90,000 tons. Similarly, bromine is recovered to the extent of 25-30 tons against a possible total of several, thousand tons. The ocean is likely to become the major source for sodium, potassium, magnesium, bromine and chlorine. A recent development is the possibility of recovering manganese, cobalt, nickel, copper and thorium from nodules that occur on the deep sea floor. So far no surveys have been made to estimate the mineral resources of the ocean bed.

## SURVEYS AND PROGRAMME OF WORK

The Survey of India, the Botanical Survey and the Zoological Survey have been strengthened under the first two plans and have undertaken extensive surveys in their respective fields.

Thus, the Survey of India has carried out surveys in connection with the multi- purpose river valley projects, oil refineries, coalfields and the lead-zinc zones in Rajasthan. The Botanical Survey of India was en- gaged in exploring plant resources of the country. The Zoological survey has been engaged in collecting scientific information regarding animals, fish, birds, insects, etc. and its studies are of 'great importance in the fields of public health, agriculture and forestry.

The Council of Scientific and Industrial Research and the National Laboratories have undertaken a number of important surveys. Among these, mention may be made of studies of wind velocity, tanning materials to replace imported wattlebark, road materials, medicinal plants, raw materials for glass and ceramics, refractories, paper and pulp, and food and agricultural wastes and their utilisation.

Several surveys of a regional character have been undertaken in recent years and some are in progress. Under the auspices of the Planning Commission, the Indian Statistical Institute has carried out a pilot regional survey of Mysore and also a less elaborate survey of the State of Kerala. A diagnostic survey of the Damodar region is being carried out jointly by the Institute of Technology, Kharagpur and the Universities of Calcutta and Patna.

The survey is potentially of great importance for the planning and development of the Damodar Valley area'. The National Council of Applied Economic Research has, at the instance of the State Governments concerned, undertaken techno- economic surveys of the States of Andhra Pradesh, Assam, Bihar, Kera- la, Madhya Pradesh, Madras, Mysore, Orissa, Punjab, Rajasthan and West Bengal.

It has also completed for the Government of India surveys of the Union Territories of Himachal Pradesh, Manipur and Tripura. These surveys bring together a considerable body of information and will be of use as bench marks for later studies. They also indicate possibilities of development which need to be studied further. The survey of the metropolitan region of Delhi, completed recently, has value not only for the development of the region but also as a pioneering effort of interest to other large towns. A similar survey is proposed to be carried out for Calcutta.

Natural resources cover a most extensive field and, within the compass of a short chapter, it is not possible to do more than touch upon a few broad features of the subject. Over the past ten years, a great deal of new information regarding the country's natural resources has become available.

The principal organisations engaged in surveys of resources are now equipped with personnel and expertise to expand their activities even more rapidly in the future. States are also more fully seized of their own problems of resource develop- ment. Considerable numbers of highly trained scientists and technologists are already engaged in studies relating to resources. There is growing recognition of the need for conservation of natural resources in all fields, but in this direction much still remains to be done.

A great deal of valuable scientific research is being undertaken for resource location and resource utilisation in the National Laboratories, in the universities and in other research establishments. Technological changes are already transforming the economic life of the country.

With economic development, there will also be greater technological progress and many new possibilities will open up. The preparation of a long-term plan of economic development, stretching over the next fifteen years and more can serve as a common thread to hold together and help interpret the results of scientific research and the growing knowledge being gained of the country's resources. It will also point to gaps that exist and suggest new problems for study.

The task ahead is one of considerable magnitude and will call for continuous cooperation between the Planning Commission, the various research organisations of the Central Government, Departments in the States, leading institutions engaged in scientific and economic re- search and the universities. The potential for development of India's natural resources is vast; with systematic study and exploration of these resources and the increasing application of science and technol- ogy in their assessment and utilisation, the possibilites of economic growth may be enlarged far beyond the present anticipations.

# 6

# Land Reform

## OBJECTIVES FOR THE THIRD PLAN

Land reform programmes, which were given a place of special significance both in the First and in the Second Plan, have two specific objects. The first is to remove such impediments to increase in agricultural production as arise from the agrarian structure inherited from the past. This should help to create conditions for evolving as speedily as possible an agricultural economy with high levels of efficiency and productivity. The second object, which is closely related to the first, is to eliminate aft elements of exploitation and social injustice within the agrarian system, to provide security for the tiller of soil and assure equality of status and opportunity to all sections of the rural population.

The principal measures for securing these objectives were the abolition of intermediary or 'rent-receiving' tenures and the reform of tenancy, including regulation and reduction of rent and security of tenure. A further step to which tenancy reform led was the conferment of right of ownership on tenants.

In pursuance of the second object, in particular it was proposed that steps should be taken to reduce disparities in the ownership of land a policy widely accepted as being essential for the economic development of countries with limited areas of land and large population dependent on it. It was realised that with the existing pattern of distribution of agricultural holdings and the predominance of small farms, redistribution of land in excess of any given level of ceiling was not likely to make available any large results in the shape of surplus land for distribution. It was considered, however, that such reduction in disparities was a necessary condition for building up a progressive cooperative rural economy. At the same time, such redistribution of land as might be possible would, along with other measures which have been taken for resettlement on waste lands, afford a measure of opportunity to the landless section of the population, to whose problems special attention was drawn both in the First and in the Second Plan. It should be stressed that the princi- ples on which the scheme of land reform is based do not merely involve adjustments between the interests of different sections of the popula- tion which depend on land, but are part of, a wider social and econom- ic outlook which has to be, applied in some, measure to every part of the economy.

It will be seen that, with the implementation of a programme of land reform on the lines described above, the vast majority of cultivators in India would consist of peasant-proprietors.

They are to be encouraged and assisted in organising themselves in voluntary co-operative bodies for credit, marketing, processing and distribution and, with their consent, progressively also for produc- tion. To the extent such reorganisation is carried out at the village level, some of the difficulties arising from small and uneconomic holdings could be diminished and the weaker in each community could be assisted to raise their standards. It has always been stressed that as each phase of land reform is implemented, it will become possible to give fuller assistance, to cultivators in increasing agricultural production and in diversifying the village economy. Greater cohesion among cultivators and the strengthening of the village community will also lead to a larger local effort and more rapid economic and social progress.

As legislation has been enacted in one State after another, there has been greater understanding of the need for land reform and the purposes it is intended to achieve. The Bhoodan and Gramdan movements have greatly helped to create a favourable atmosphere for implementing progressive measures of land reform. Yet, the total impact of land reform has been less than had been hoped for. For this there are several reasons. In the first place, there has been too little recognition of land reform as a positive programme of develop- ment, and it has been only too often regarded as extraneous to the scheme of community development and the effort to increase agricultural production. Secondly, there has been insufficient attention to the administrative aspects of land reform. Frequently at the lower levels of the administration, collusion and evasion have gone unchecked, and there has been failure also to enlist the support and sanction of the village community in favour of effective enforcement of legal provi- sions. In the third place, it has not been sufficiently realised that the reform of land tenures and the early enforcement of ceilings are an essential foundation for the building up of the cooperative rural economy. While removing such shortcomings in the legislation or the rules as may come to notice, it is important that the land reform programme should be completed with the least delay, so as to eliminate any feeling of uncertainty arising from delays in implementation. This aspect has been specially stressed by the Panel on Land Reform constituted by the Planning Commission to assist in the study of proposals for the Third Plan.

## ABOLITION OF INTERMEDIARY TENURES

Work on the abolition of intermediary tenures like zamindaris, jagirs and inams, which covered more than 40% of the area of the country, has been fully carried out except for a few minor tenures such as those held by religious and charitable institutions and service inams. These reforms have brought more than 20 millions of tenants into direct relationship with the State and improved their social and economic position. As a result of the abolition of intermediary tenures, considerable areas of cultivable waste land and private forests came under the management of Government.

Several States with intermediary tenures did not possess the requisite revenue administration. Over the past few years, they have done much to strengthen their revenue agencies but there is need for further improvement, especially at the village level. There has been progress also in survey and settlement and in the preparation of records of rights, but much still remains to be done. Largely on account of the heavy burden thrown on the revenue administration, there has been a measure of delay in the assessment and payment of compensation to intermediaries. Out of a total amount of Rs. 670 crores (Rs. 520 crores as compensation and Rs. 150 crores for interest charges), so far compensation to the extent of only Rs. 164 crore has been paid, mainly in the form of bonds. It is important that in the course of the Third Five Year Plan, all the States concerned should arrange to issue the compensatory bonds still outstanding and complete records of rights and other administrative tasks arising from the abolition of intermediaries.

## REDUCTION OF RENTS

Ten years ago the coustomary level of rents commonly paid by tenants-at-will, non-occupancy tenants and share-croppers over the greater part of the country was one-half of the produce or more. In addition to rent, very frequently there were other payments which enhanced the burdens borne by tenants. The situation was reviewed at length in the First Five Year Plan which suggested that a rate of rent exceeding one-fourth or one-fifth of the produce would call for spe- cial justification.

Over the past few years, all States have enacted legislation for regulating rents which a landlord may receive. In some States, as in Gujarat, Maharashtra and Rajasthan, the maximum rent now stands at one-sixth of the produce. In Assam, Kerala, Orissa and Union Territories, the rent payable is about one-fourth of the produce or less. In several States, the normal level of rent is still about a third of the produce. It is to be hoped that in these States rents will be reduced to the level envisaged in the first two plans so as to facilitate more rapid improvement in the economic conditions of tenants.

In the early years of tenancy legislation, it was observed that reduced levels of rents-and indeed other conditions of tenancy- provided for by legislation were far from adequately enforced, and to a large extent customary rates of rent continued to prevail. Where arrangements for leasing land are arrived at between individual parties, variations from the norms set by legislation can occur for a variety of reasons, for instance, if the owner undertakes to provide seed or bullocks or pay for irrigation. In the beginning, there is also considerable ignorance on the part of tenants of the rights granted by legislation. Where there is pressure on land and the social and economic position of tenants in the village is weak, it becomes difficult for them to seek the protection of law. Moreover, resort to legal processes is costly and generally beyond the means of tenants. Thus, in many ways, despite the legislation, the scales are weighed in favour of the continuance of existing terms and conditions. Effective implementation of tenancy legislation, therefore, requires specially vigorous and sustained action on the part of governmental agencies. There must be special efforts not only to acquaint tenants with the rights due to them but also to bring about greater understanding on the part of the people of each area of the objects of land reforms and of the need to complete them without delay.

Although, in the past, rents have generally been paid as a proportion of the gross produce, with progress in the rural economy and larger use of money as the medium of exchange, it would be desira- ble, as a matter of policy, to hasten the transition from rents in kind to cash payments. With cultivators having to purchase a growing proportion of their requirements, such as fertilisers, implements etc., in cash, the change-over to cash rents is likely not only to reduce the burden on tenants, but also to promote investment in agri- culture.

As suggested in the Second Plan, commutation of rents in kind into cash payments might be facilitated if, with due regard to conditions of each district, rents could be declared as multiples of the prevailing land revenue assessment. Where this is not feasible, suitable norms could be proposed on the basis of other criteria. It would greatly assist the enforcement of rents prescribed by legislation if State Governments could make it obligatory on the part of owners to furnish receipts for the rents received by them and if, as is already the practice in some

States, tenants could deposit the rents due from them with the appropriate revenue officer, the land owner being advised accordingly.

## SECURITY OF TENURE

Legislation providing for security of tenure has been enacted in eleven States and for all the Union Territories. In four States Bills are before the legislature and will be enacted in the near future. Pending legislation, ejectment of tenants has been stayed. Legislation for security of tenure has three essential aims-.firstly, that ejectments do not take place except in accordance with the provisions of the law; secondly, that land may be resumed by an owner, if at all, for 'personal cultivation' only; and thirdly, that in the event of resumption the tenant is assured of a prescribed minimum area.

In the first phase of tenancy legislation it was perhaps inevitable that the provisions regulating the rights of owners and tenants should be somewhat elaborate. Such complexity comes in the way of making the legislation effective. In the light of the experi- ence gained, it is suggested that steps should be taken to simplify the existing legislation wherever possible, and tc strengthen or modify provisions which are in practice difficult to enforce.

As stated earlier, the impact of tenancy legislation on the welfare of tenants has been in practice less than was hoped for. One of the principal reasons for this is that in a number of States ejectments of tenants have taken place on a considerable scale under the plea of 'voluntary surrenders'. Two main recommendations on this subject were made in the Second Plan.

The first was that voluntary surrenders by tenants of lands held by them should not be regarded as valid unless they were duly registered by the revenue authorities. Secondly, in the event of surrender of tenancy, the land owner should be entitled to take possession of land only to the extent of his right of resumption permitted by law. On the whole, both legislation and administrative action have fallen short of these recommendations.

A few States have provided for registration of surrender of land by tenants. Registration of surrenders is essential and a provision on these lines should be a feature of tenancy legislation. The second lacunas in the existing legislation concerns the conditions applicable to surrenders. In two States effect has been given to the recommenda- tion in the Second Plan that resumption of land arising from a volun- tary surrender by the tenant should take place on conditions identical with those governing resumption for personal cultivation. In Maha- rashtra and Gujarat, the overall limit for resumption applies also to surrenders, but other conditions governing surrenders are different. As was pointed out in the Second Plan, most voluntary surrenders of tenancy are open to doubt as bonafide transactions. This has been confirmed by such enquiries and investigations as have been undertak- en. it is, therefore, important that early steps should be taken to remove legal and administrative deficiencies relating to the registration of 'voluntary surrenders' and resumption of land arising from them.

In most States legislation provides for a definition of 'personal cultivation' which is, as a rule, a necessary condition for resuming land from tenants. There are three elements in 'personal cultivation', namely, risk of cultivation, labour and personal super- vision. The obligation of the owner to bear the entire risk of culti- vation implies that wages will be paid in cash or in kind, but not as a share of the crop. While the expression 'labour' is generally defined to include 'labour by the owner or by a member of his family', this is not an obligatory element in personal cultivation'. In the Second Plan, the proposal was made that where land is resumed on grounds of 'personal cultivation', it would be desirable to provide for personal labour as a necessary ingredient, in the absence of which the ejected tenant should have the right of restoration. So far this suggestion has not found its way into the legislation undertaken by the States. A provision on these lines is desirable and would serve to make the legislation more effective. As an essential element in 'supervision', the Second Plan envisaged residence during the greater part of the agricultural season by an owner or a member of his family in the village where the land is situated or in a nearby village within a distance to be prescribed. The Panel on Land Reform has suggested that the condition of residence in these terms should apply during the period the main agricultural operations are undertaken. This suggestion should be considered by State Governments and the current definitions of 'personal supervision' modified to the extent necessary.

## RESUMPTION OF TENANCIES

The main recommendations in the Second Plan for regulating resumption of tenancies on grounds of personal cultivation were as follows :

(1) The area to be resumed should be declared within a certain period and should be demarcated in advance.

(2) Oweners with very small holdings, for instance, those having one-third of a family holding or less should be free to resume their entire land for personal cultivation. Those with holdings above this level might resume land for personal cultivation subject to a mini- mum area being left with the tenant.

(3) Right of- resumption may be exercised within a period of five years.

(4) Persons serving in the armed forces or those subject to disabilities, like widows, minors or those suffering from mental or physical infirmities etc., should be permitted to lease out land anti should have the right to resume land for perssonal cultivation when the disability ceases.

From the tenor of legislation enacted or under consideration, States fall broadly into four categories :

(a) those in which no resumption is permitted, as in Uttar Pradesh, Delhi and in respect of under-raiyats, West Bengal;

(b) those in which the right to resume a limited area for personal cultivation is allowed subject to the condition that a minimum area or a portion of the holding is left with the tenant, as in Bihar, Gujarat, Kerala, Madhya

Pradesh, Maharashtra, Mysore, Orissa, Rajasthan, Himachal Pradesh and Manipur;

(c) those in which the right to resume is subject to the tenant being given alternative land upto a pre- scribed limit for cultivation, the land being found by the State, as in Punjab and Assam, and

(d) those in which resumption is allowed up to the level of the ceiling without any minimum area being provided for the tenant, as in Andhra Pradesh and Ma- dras. Bargadars in West Bengal who are crop-sharers, are not regarded as tenants. They do not have the rights extended to under-raiyats, although strictly speaking they fall within the definition of 'tenant'.

Experience of the working of legislation relating, to re sumption on grounds of personal cultivation leads to certain broad conclusions. In the first place, whatever the conditions, the right to resume land creates uncertainty and tends to diminish the protection afforded by the legislation. Both in the First and in the Second Plan, it was contemplated that it would not be necessary to allow resumption beyond a period of five years. It is considered that except for owners holding land equivalent to a family holding or less, in view of the period which has already elapsed, there should be no further right of resumption. Further uncertainty for tenants would not be in the interest of agricultural development. In the second place, small owners, that is owners with a family holding or less, deserve special consideration.

As suggested in the Second Plan, owners with less than a basic holding (that is, one-third of a family holding) should be free to resume their entire area for personal cultivation and to lease out their lands. As regards owners whose holdings lie between a basic holding and a family holding, they may be permitted to resume for personal cultivation, within a specified period, one-half of the area held by the tenant but in no event less than a basic holding. Where a tenant is left without any land or with area smaller than a basic holding the Government should endeavour to find land for him to cultivate. The general aim should be to encourage small owners, and specially those among them with very small holdings, to enter into cooperative farming societies. Membership in a cooperative farming society would enable them to move to other work if they so desire. For such owners it would not be necessary to prescribe a period beyond which resumption for personal cultivation should not be permitted.

Provisions regarding resumption for personal cultivation could be abused if medium-sized owners were to act malafide and transfer their lands to relatives or others and so come within the definition of small owners. With a view to ensuring that the provisions for resumption are observed, legislation in Gujarat and Maharashtra was amended in 1957 so as to restrict resumption in respect of such land as stood in the name of a land holder or any of his ancestors in the record of rights on the 1st day of January, 1952.

In the legislation in Kerala which includes special provision for small holders, it has been provided that any transfers or partitions carried out after the 18th day of December, 1957, shall not entitle the land holder or the transferee to the benefit of the provisions for small holders. A condition on these lines would be generally desirable.

## RIGHTS OF OWNERSHIP FOR TENANTS

Security of tenure and reduction of rents are the first stage in tenancy reform; the goal is to confer rights of ownership on as. large a body of tenants as possible. In the Second Plan it was suggested that each State should have a programme for converting tenants of non-resumable areas into owners and putting an end to vestiges of the landlord-tenant relationship.

It was urged that instead of optional rights to tenants to purchase lands cultivated by them, all tenants of non-resumable areas should be brought into direct relationship with the State. For owners with holdings equivalent to a family holding or more, a period of five years within which the right of resumption could be exercised was proposed, and it was suggested that on the completion of this period, rights of ownership should be conferred on their tenants. Finally, as it was difficult to obtain precise information regarding the progress made in the transfer of ownership rights to tenants, the recommendation was made that States should arrange to compile regular annual returns.

In the course of the Second Plan, some progress has been made in the direction of providing ownership rights to tenants. In a few States as in Punjab, only optional right to purchase has been given to tenants. This is an unsatisfactory approach, for, as was observed in the Second Plan, where rights of purchase are optional, they are scarcely exercised. In a number of States, legislation provides for bringing tenants of non-resumable lands into direct rela- tionship with the Government. This may be achieved in one of the three ways :

(1) by declaring tenants as owners and requiring them to pay compensation to owners in suitable instalments, responsibility for recovering unpaid instalments as arrears of land revenue being accepted by Government;

(2) through the acquisition by Government of the rights of ownership on payment of compensation and transfer of ownership to tenants, compensation being recovered from them in suitable instalments; and

(3) through the acquisition by Government of the landlord's rights and bringing tenants into a direct relationship with the State, option being given to tenants to continue as such on payment of fair rent to the Government or to acquire full ownership on payment of the prescribed compensation.

The first of these courses has been followed in Gujarat, Maharashtra, Madhya Pradesh and Rajasthan, the second in Delhi and in respect of under-raiyats (without payment of compensation) in West Bengal, and the third in Kerala and Uttar Pradesh. In Madras, steps in favour of ownership rights for tenants have not yet been initiated. In Assam and Bihar, the right of ownership will be available only to the tenants of land-holders holding more than the ceiling area. As much of the legislation is quite recent. exact information regarding the extent to which ownership rights have been conferred on tenants is not available. It is understood that in Gujarat and Maharashtra, under legislation enacted by the former Bombay State, rights of owner- ship would accrue to 1.3 million tenants over an area of about 2.4 million acres. In Uttar Pradesh, about 1.5 million sub-tenants and tenants of home-farm lands, holding about 2 million acres, were brought into direct relationship with the State. In the Union Terri- tory of Delhi ownership of about 25,000 acres was transferred to about 18,000 tenants and subtenants.

It is recommended that in the course of the Third Plan, steps should be taken to complete the programme for conferring rights of ownership on the tenants of non-resumable lands. With the enforce- ment of ceilings on agricultural holdings, tenants of owners with lands above the limit of ceiling will. in the ordinary course, become owners of land. It has been suggested earlier that owners holding land exceeding a family holding, as prescribed in different States, should have no further rights of resumption. Tenants of such owners should also become owners of lands held by them. With this object, according to its legislation and other conditions, a State may either acquire the rights of ownership and transfer them to tenants or declare tenants as owners and require them to pay for their rights in instalments on terms prescribed by legislation. On the whole, it would be desirable for payments by tenants for acquisition of owner- ship to be made directly to Government rather than to the owners. This will ensure more effective implementation and will end the land- lord-tenant nexus.

The question arises whether Tights of ownership should also be conferred upon the tenants of small owners. This would be desira- ble, in principle to the extent of non-resumable lands held by such tenants. However, in view of the large number of petty owners in- volved. a uniform approach might not be feasible. The problem should be studied by States in the light of their conditions with a view to determining the action called for in this direction.

## CEILING ON AGRICULTURAL HOLDINGS

In the course of the Second Plan, there has been legislation for placing ceiling on agricultural holdings in Andhra Pradesh, Assam, Gujarat, Kerala, Madhya Pradesh, Maharashtra, Orissa, PEPSU territory in the Punjab, Rajasthan, Uttar Pradesh and

West Bengal and in, the Union Territories. Bills proposing, ceilings are at present before the State legislatures in Bihar, Madras and Mysore. In Punjab, out- side the area of the former PEPSU territory, the existing legislation permits the Government to utilise land in excess of the permissible area for the purpose of resettling tenants who have been ejected or may be ejected. Annexure I of this Chapter sets out in summary form information relating to the levels at which ceilings have been pre- scribed or proposed in different States. With the completion of legislation, essential task must be that of ensuring speedy and effec- tive implementation.

The question whether ceilings should apply to the holding of an individual owner or to the aggregate area held by the members of a family was considered in the Second Plan. As is to be expected, practice in this respect differs. In several States, as in Andhra Pradesh, Jammu and Kashmir, Orissa, Punjab, Uttar Pradesh and West Bengal the ceiling applies to individuals without any special provi- sion being made for joint Hindu families. In Madhya Pradesh, while the ceiling applies to individuals, in the case of a joint Hindu family each co-sharer is entitled to a separate ceiling area. In Assam, Gujarat, Kerala and Rajasthan, the ceiling applies to the aggregate area held by a family. the expression 'family' being defined in the" legislation. A similar approach has been adopted in the legislation now under consideration in Madras and Mysore. Thus dif- ferent States have applied ceiling to individuals or families as they considered appropriate to their conditions.

Once legislation has been enacted, amendments should aim primarily at eliminating deficiencies and facilitating implementation rather than at introducing fundamental changes in the principles underlying the legislation. In this context, the most important issue for consideration is the treatment of transfers of land on the part of land owners subject to ceilings. On the whole, it would be correct to say that, in recent years, transfers of lands have tended to defeat the aims of the legislation for ceilings and to reduce its impact on the rural economy. The question as to whether or not transfers should be disregarded and, if so, from what date, has been debated at length in every State. In the majority of States a date prior to the enact- ment of the legislation has been indicated. This may be the date of, the introduction of the Bill providing for ceilings or of its publication or other specified date. In several States transfers subsequent to this date are disregarded as in Assam, Gujarat, Kerala, Madras, Maharashtra, Rajasthan, Uttar Pradesh and West Bengal. In a few States, there is no such provision at all, as in Andhra Pradesh. In Madhya Pradesh and Orissa, legislation allows the owners of surplus lands to dispose of them to persons belonging to, certain prescribed categories even after the enactment of the legislation.

Since many of the transfers are apt to take place between members of the family, it has been suggested that the ceiling should apply invariably to the aggregate area held by a family rather than to individuals. However, in view of the fact that ceiling have been applied in several States to individual holdings and in others to the aggregate area held by a family, any attempt to remove deficiencies or weaknesses would have to fit into the pattern of the prevailing legis- lation. The question of transfers could perhaps be dealt with in the following manner

(1) Where legislation does not contain a provision for disregarding transfers, in view of the fact that transfers have taken place on a considerable scale, a suitable date subsequent to which transfers are disregarded may be proposed, if necessary, through an amending legis- lation. This date may be the date of the publication of the ceiling proposals or an earlier date as may be prescribed in view of the local conditions.

(2) In respect of transfers made after the specified date, a distinction may be made between (a) transfers among the members of a family, (b) benami transfers and other transfers which have not been made for valuable consideration and through a registered document, and (c) transfers made for valuable consideration through a registered document. Transfers coming under (a) and (b) can be disregarded. Transfers falling under (c) may need to be dealt with differently in view of the fact that

the transferees may be small owners or landless persons who may have purchased some land. It may be necessary to protect such transferees, at any rate, upto a prescribed limit, say, a family holding.

(3) There should be provision for a review of trans- fers by a competent authority on the lines suggested above.

## EXEMPTION FROM CEILING

The Second Plan envisaged exemption from ceilings for the following categories of farms :

(1) tea, coffee and rubber plantations;

(2) orchards where they constitute reasonably compact areas;

(3) specialised farms engaged in cattle-breeding, dairying, wool-raising, etc.;

(4) sugarcane farms operated by sugar factories; and

(5) efficiently managed farms which consist of compact blocks, on which heavy investment or permanent structur- al improvements have been made and whose breakup is likely to lead to a fall in production.

This recommendation was based on three main considerations. Firstly, in undertakings like plantations, industrial and agricultural work had to be closely integrated. Secondly, in certain specialised branches of agriculture such as horticulture, cattle-breeding, dairying, etc. investment has to be made on a long-term basis and several years elapse before the output could be realised. In the third place, it was thought that in safeguarding efficiently managed farms which consisted of compact blocks on which heavy investment or permanent structures had been made, risk of fall in production would be avoided.

In the legislation which has been enacted in the States, plantations have invariably been exempted from ceilings. There are provision also in favour of specialised farms. There has been some measure of variation in the approach to sugarcane farms operate by sugar factories and to efficiently managed farms. Legislation in several States (Andhra Pradesh, Assam,

Gujarat, Madhya Pradesh, Orissa, Punjab and Rajasthan) and proposals under consideration in some others (Bihar and Mysore) provide for the exemption of efficiently managed farms from ceilings.

Where the exemption exists, by and large it has still to be implemented, In Kerala, Madras, Maharashtra and Uttar Pradesh, exemption of efficiently managed farms from ceilings has not been envisaged. In Uttar Pradesh, the Government has taken power to operate the surplus lands of mechanised farms as State farms and to appoint suitable persons as managers on terms and conditions to be prescribed, preference being given to the existing holders of these farms if they are otherWise qualified.

As regards sugarcane farms operated by sugar factories, legislation in several States exempts them from the operation of ceilings, as in Andhra Pradesh, Assam, Madhya Pradesh, Orissa, Rajasthan and PEPSU area of Punjab and in the Bills at present under consideration in Bihar and Mysore. In three States, however, a different approach has been adopted. In Madras legislation provides for the setting up of a Sugar Factory Board to review whether individual factories should or should not be exempted from ceilings.

Considerations such as the requirements of the sugar factory and its financial structure have to be taken into account before final decisions are taken. In Uttar Pradesh, while there is no exemption from ceilings, provision relating to mechanised farms mentioned above would also apply to sugarcane farms operated by sugar factories.

In Maharashtra, sugarcane farms of the sugar factories are not exempted from ceilings but provision is made for maintaining the integrity of the farms in one or more compact blocks, for full and continued supply of raw material to sugar factories at a fair price, and for grant of surplus land to joint farming societies consisting, as far as possible, of persons who had previously leased their lands to the sugar factory, agricultural labourers employed on the farm, technical and other staff engaged by the factory for work on the farm, adjoining land holders who are small holders and landless workers.

The considerations urged in the Second Plan and the recommendations regarding the exemption from ceilings of efficiently managed farms and of sugarcane farms operated by sugar factories remain generally valid for the Third Plan and there are advantages in fol- lowing the course proposed. On the other hand, where a State, because of practical difficulties or other considerations, wishes to adopt a different course, certain conditions should be assure. These are, firstly, that the integrity of the farms should be maintained and their levels of efficiency ensured and, secondly, in the case of sugar factory farms satisfactory and continuous supply of the raw material to the factory concerned should be secured.

## SCHEMES OF RESETTLEMENT

Proposals to set ceilings on agricultural holdings were intended to serve two objects-firstly, to bring about reduction in disparities and pave the way to the development of a progressive cooperative rural economy and, secondly, to provide land for redistribution to the landless sections of the rural population. Far-reaching legislation has been enacted and although precise estimates are difficult to make, it would appear that the total area of surplus lands likely to be available for distribution to the landless might be considerably less than what had been hoped for at one time. At the present stage in land reform the most important consideration is that such lands as can be made available by each State as a result of the implementation of its ceilings legislation should be allotted with lest possible delay. Along with these lands, waste lands and, where possible, land available through Bhoodan should be pooled and system- atic schemes of resettlement speedily implemented.

In providing land care should be taken to make available the necessary credit and other facilities, so that those settled on the land may develop high stand- ards of cultivation. It was contemplated in the Second Plan that in the settlement of land acquired in consequence of the application of ceilings, tenants displaced as a result of resumption of land for personal cultivation, farmers with uneconomic holdings and landless workers should receive preference. It was also proposed that settle- ments should be made, as tar as possible, on cooperative lines. Generally, the legislation which has been enacted follows these recom- mendations. It was also proposed in the Second Plan that farmers with uneconomic holdings should be admitted into cooperatives constituted with surplus lands if they also agreed to pool their lands. In taking action along these lines the necessary financial and technical assistance should be provided as envisaged in the programme for the development of cooperative farming proposed for the Third Plan.

## CONSOLIDATION OF HOLDINGS

Progress in the consolidation of holdings has been recorded in Punjab, Uttar Pradesh, Maharashtra, Gujarat and Madhya Pradesh. In other States, there has been comparatively little advance during the Second Plan. By the end of 1959-60 about 23 million acres had been consolidated and work was in hand over another 13 million acres. According to indications given by States, the total area likely to be taken up for consolidation in the Third Plan is about 30 million acres.

With a view to making experience in consolidation of holding available to all States, two special studies were prepared by the Planning Commission four years ago. One of these explained the meth- ods which had been developed in different parts of the country and the problems which had been encountered . The second study set out suggestions for speedy execution of the programme of consolidation. Although consolidation of holdings has been regarded as an integral part of the agricultural production programme, in practice the two pro- grammes are not always co-ordinated. Except where consolidation of holdings is already being undertaken on a large scale, in view of the limitations of trained personnel, it would appear desirable to concen- trate consolidation work in areas which are already receiving irriga- tion or are likely to come under irrigation. The Planning Commission propose to study more closely how best the factors which come in the way of extension of the consolidation programme in the southern and eastern parts of the country can be over-come and what changes and adaptations in the present methods and system of consolidation are called for in these areas.

## LAND MANAGEMENT LEGISLATION

The place to be assigned to land management legislation and the manner in which it should be applied need to be considered in the light of developments during the first two plans. In the First Plan, while land management legislation was intended to be general in scope, its specific applications were to be in relation to farms held by substantial owners. In the proposals in the Second Plan the object was that land management legislation should provide for standards of efficient cultivation and management which would permit objective and qualitative judgments.

If farms could be classified into certain grades, those above the average could receive suitable encouragement, while those falling below the average could be assisted to come up to higher standards. For certain purposes the legislation could provide for sanctions. Legislation regarding land management Union Territory and even in these it has not been actually implemented. A large number of enactments exist in the States for certain specific agricultural purposes such as utilisation of waste lands, adoption of improved seeds, control of pests and diseases, etc. Much of this legislation is fairly old and needs to be reviewed in relation e present development programmes for agriculture and the extension services which have been brought into existence in the community development blocks. While it will be of value to bring together the best experience in land management practices for the guidance of farmers, cooperatives and panchyats, the question of enforcing legislative sanctions and of the role of panchayats and panchayat samitis has to be studied further in consultation with the States and in the light of the experience gained by them in working the existing enactments.

## PROBLEMS OF IMPLEMENTATION

Problems arising in the implementation of land reform legislation enacted in States have been studied by the Panel on Land reform and the urgent tasks to be performed have been listed separately in respect of abolition of intermediaries, tenancy reforms and ceilings. The Panel has laid particular stress on the preparation of correct and up-to-date records of right and on the need to strengthen the revenue administration. Records or rights have been brought up-to-date in several areas, but in some of them there is need for a more intensive programme of work.

In several States, record of rights do not provide information regarding tenants, sub-tenants and crop-sharers, and as such implementation of the legislation itself suffers. Expenditure incurred on cadastral surveys and in the preparation and correction of records of rights has been included in the plans of some States and is eligible for Central assistance. Provisions made for these purposes would need to augmented as the work proceeds.

A number of surveys of land reform have been undertaken in different parts of the country through the Research Programmes Commit- tee of the Planning Commission. They bring out the problems encoun- tered in enforcing the legislation. In view of the wide scope of the legislation which has been enacted and differences in conditions, it is desirable to extend these studies on a systematic basis. For this purpose the assistance of universities and leading research centres should be fully availed of. The aim should be to cover different areas in accordance with a general scheme to arrange for the evaluation of land reforms both in the transitional phase and from the aspect of long-term economic and social effects.

The planning Commission has under preparation a report on the progress of land reform which bring enacted in different States. This study will also set out data regarding land holdings and cultivation collected at the census organised in 1954-55, which have been summa- rised in Annexure II of this chapter.

## EXPLANATORY NOTE

As recommended in the First Plan, a census of land holdings and cultivation was carried out in 1954-55 in all States except Assam, West Bengal and Jammu and Kashmir and the Union

Territories of Manipur an Tripura. In Assam and West Bengal, the State Governments had al- ready collected certain data regarding land holdings. West Bengal had already enacted legislation for ceilings, in Assam a Bill had been passed and in Jammu & Kashmir a ceiling had been imposed earlier. A new census was not considered necessary in these States. In Manipur and Tripura the proposal to conduct the census was dropped due to lack of trained personnel and difficulties of terrain.

The census was based on completed enumeration of all holdings in the former States of Andhra, Bombay, Madhya Pradesh, Madras, Hyderabad, Madhya Bharat, Saurashtra, Ajmer, Bhopal and Kutch. In Punjab and in the former States of Mysore, Coorg, Delhi Himachal Pradesh and Vindhya Pradesh, with a view to expediting the census, the enumeration was restricted to holdings of 10 acres and above. However, estimates of holdings below 10 acres were also made. In Bihar. Orissa, Rajasthan, Uttar Pradesh and in the former State of Travancore-Cochin sample surveys were under taken.

The data relate generally to the year 1953-54. The main con- cepts employed in teh census were the following:

(1) The census related to agricultural land comprised in owners' holdings, agricultural land being defined as the cultivable area, comprised in a holding, including groves and pastures. Unoccupied area such as forest land and other uncultivable land, was to be excluded. Land held in urban areas was also outside the scope of the census.

(2) The expression 'area owned' was defined so as to include lands held by owners as well as those held under occupancy (permanent and heritable) rights. Land owned by a person 'A' but held under rights of occupancy by a person 'B' was thus included in 'B's holding and exclud- ed from 'A's holding. It was further agreed that persons who did not posses permanent and heritable rights de jure but enjoyed them for all practical purposes, should also be treated as owners.

(3) The entire agricultural land by a person as owner throughout the State constituted a single holding. In

the case of joint holdings, the share of each co-sharer was treated as a separate holdings.

(4) Area under 'personal cultivation' was defined as the difference between 'area owned' and 'area leased'. The 'area leased'represents land let out to a tenant in which he has not acquired permanent and heritable rights.

To the extent they were available at the time, the results of the land census data were presented in summary form in the Second Five Year Plan. The data were subsequently retabulated for the States as reorganised in 1956. In this form they are set out in the tables which follow except for Bihar and Orissa. The Bihar government felt that the data collected in the sample survey did not represent even approximately a correct picture of ownership and cultivation. The data received from Orissa were incomplete.

## LABOUR POLICY

LABOUR policy in India has been evolving in response to the specific needs of the situation in relation to industry and the working class and has to suit the requirements of a planned economy. A body of principles and practices has grown up as a product of joint consulta- tion in which representatives of Government, the working class and employers have been participating at various, levels. The legislation and other measures adopted by Government in this field represent the consensus of opinion of the parties vitally concerned and thus acquire the strength and character of a national policy, operating on a volun- tary basis. Joint committees have been set up to assist in the formu- lation of policies as well as their implementation. At the apex of this tripartite machinery is the Indian Labour Conference.

## RECENT DEVELOPMENTS

The structure of industrial relations has been designed for the purpose of securing peace in industry and a fair deal for the workers. When the efforts of the parties fail to secure an amicable settlement of industrial disputes, the Government has assumed powers of intervention. Provision has been made for conciliation of disputes and for enabling the State to, refer unresolved differences to tribu- nals set up for the purpose. Stoppages of work after such a reference and any contravention of awards and agreements have been made illegal. This system has helped to check the growth of industrial unrest and has brought for the working class a measure of advance and a sense of security which could not otherwise have been achieved. At the same time, the spirit of litigation grew and, delays attendant on legal processes gave rise to widespread dissatisfaction. In the course of the Second Five Year Plan a new approach was, therefore, introduced to counteract the unhealthy trends and gave a more positive orientation to industrial relations, based on moral rather than legal sanctions. The stress now is on prevention of unrest by timely action at the appropriate stages and giving adequate attention to root causes. This involves a basic change in the attitudes and outlook of the parties and the new set of readjustments in their mutual relations.

A Code of Discipline in Industry, which applies both to the public and to the private sector, has been accepted voluntarily by all the Central organisations of employers and workers and has been in operation since the middle of 1958. The Code lays down specific obligations for the management and the workers with the object of promoting constructive cooperation between their representatives at all levels, avoiding stoppages as well as litigation, securing settle- ment of disputes and grievances by mutual negotiations, conciliation and voluntary arbitration, facilitating the free growth of trade unions and eliminating all forms of corcion and violence in industrial relations.

The Code provides that a regular grievance procedure be laid down in all undertakings and complaints should receive prompt attention. The legal means of redress and the normal channels should be fully availed of and there should be no direct, arbitrary or unilater- al action on either side. Under the Code, management and workers have agreed to avoid litigation lock-outs, sit-down and stay-in strikes. There will be no recourse to intimidation, victimisation or 'go-slow'. The unions have also agreed not to engage in any form of physical duress and to discourage unfair practices such as negligence of duty, careless operation, damage to property, interference with or disturbance to normal work and insubordination. The employers have to allow full freedom to workers in the formation of trade unions) and to abide by the criteria adopted for determining which union has a better claim to recognition. A union guilty of a breach of the Code of Discipline loses its right to such recognition. Both sides are pledged to the scrupulous and prompt implementation of awards, agreements settlements and decisions. Organisations of employers as well as workers Pave bound themselves to express disapproval and take appropriate action against officers, office-bearers and workers who violate the letter or spirit of the Code.

It is obvious that a new concept with such far-reaching aims, in a difficult field, requires a considerable period of earnest endeavour before it gets firmly established in practice. The results so far achieved are, however, encouraging both in terms of the reduc- tion of man-days lost owing to stoppages and in bringing about a general improvement in the climate of industrial relations. The number of man-days lost declined steadily and significantly from 47 lakh during January-June 1958, the six months prior to the introduction of the Code, to 19 lakh during July-December, 1960. The Code has also been successful in creating an awareness amongst the employers and workers of their obligations towards each other ; the desire to settle disputes mutually without recourse to the wasteful methods of trial of strength and litigation is steadily growing.

The deplorable consequences of inter-union rivalry both for industry and for the workers are well-known. They have been mitigated to some extent by the Code of Conduct which was drawn up and accepted by the representatives of workers' organisations three years ago. The Code provides that every employee shall have the freedom and right to join a union of his choice. Ignorance and backwardness of workers shall not be exploited by any Organisation. Casteism, communalism and provincialism shall be eschewed by all unions and there shall be no violence, coercion, intimidation or personal vilification in inter- union dealings. It is enjoined that there shall be unreserved accept- ance of and respect for democratic functioning of trade unions and all Central organisations shall combat the formation and continuance of company unions.

The failure to implement awards and agreements has been a common complaint on both sides and if this were to continue, the Codes would be bereft of all meaning and purpose. A machinery for implemen- tation and evaluation has, therefore, been set up at the Centre and in the States to ensure observance by the parties of the obligations arising from the Codes and from laws and agreements.

Two lines of advance during the period of the Second Plan deserve special mention because of their great significance as ele- ments of labour policy and for the reason of the great promise they hold for the future. In the first place to give the workers a sense of belonging and to stimulate their interest in higher productivity, a form of workers' participation in management was evolved during the Second Plan. A small beginning was made in this direction on an experimental basis and Joint Management Councils have been set up so far in 23 units. The Council has the right to obtain information regarding the working of the undertaking and has direct administrative responsibility for matters concerning workers' welfare, training and allied matters.

Its main function is to bring about mutual consulta- tion between employers and workers over many important issues which affect industrial relations. In a seminar held in March, 1960, repre- sentatives of employers, workers, State Governments and others con- cerned reviewed their experience of the working of the Joint Councils and the solutions they had evoked for specific problems. Keeping in view the short duration of the experiment, its results have been found to be satisfactory and heartening. Secondly, after completion of the preparatory stage, the programme of workers' education has made a good start and is being widely appreciated. The scheme comprises the training of teacher-administrators and worker-teachers. The latter, on returning to their establishments on the completion of their train- ing, start unit-level classes for the rank and file of the workers. According to an independent appraisal of the working of this scheme, these courses have helped to raise the self-confidence of the workers, increased their ability to take advantage of protective labour laws, reduced their dependence upon outsiders and inculcated in them an urge for material and economic welfare. A beginning was made in sponsoring investigations on labour problems through independent research insti- tutions with Government support.

## APPROACH AND OUTLOOK

The coming years should witness the fuller impact of the ideas which have been tried and found useful during the Second Plan period. The Third Five Year Plan has to make its own contribution towards the evolution of labour policy and the realisation of Its basic aims. It has always to be kept in view that the measures that are adopted must serve adequately the immediate and long-term ends of planned economic development. Economic progress has to be rapid enough to attain a level of full employment, and secure a rising standard of living for the people. The fruits of progress should be shared in an equitable manner and the economic and social Organisation which is being created must be in keeping with the concept of a so- cialist society. In the implementation of these objectives the work- ing class has an important role and a great responsibility, and these will grow with the rising tempo of industrialisation, The large expansion of the public sector which is occurring and is being envisaged will make a qualitative difference in the tasks set for the labour movement and will facilitate the transformation of the social structure on the lines of the socialist pattern in view.

The implications of this approach are manifold. Economic activity has not to be con- ceived of solely in terms of output and return ; the principal test of this would be the good of all those who are engaged in it. the quality and growth of the individual human being and the service and happiness of the entire community. The surpluses that are generated are a social product, to which neither the employer nor the working class can lay an exclusive claim ; their distribution has to be according to the worth of the contribution of each, subject to the requirements of further development and the interests of all the sections of society, in particular the satisfaction of the basic needs of all its members. While jobs and functions may vary, all are workers of different grades. Those of the lowest rank and their children should be fortified in the faith that they are free to equip themselves to be able to rise to the highest Positions and that the worker and management are joined in partnership to strive for common ends. Thus, a new type of community is being created in which individuals and groups are moved more by a sense of mutual obligations than the spirit of acquis- itiveness or the making of private gains at the expense of the general well-being.

## INDUSTRIAL RELATION

The development of industrial relations in the Third Five Year Plan rests on the foundations created by the working of the Code of Discipline which has stood the strain of the test during the last three years. A full awareness of the obligations under the Code of Discipline has to extend to all the constituents of the Central organ- isations of employers and workers, and it has to become more and more a living force in the day-to-day conduct of industrial relations. The sanctions on which the Code is based have to be reinforced, relying on the consent of the parties, for this purpose.

Ways will be found for increasing the application of the principal of voluntary arbitration in resolving differences between workers and employers. Steps will be taken to remove certain hin- drances in the way of a fuller recourse to voluntary arbitration. The same protection should be extended to proceedings in this case, as is now applicable to compulsory adjudication. Government should take the initiative in drawing up panels of arbitrators on a regional and industry-wise basis. Employers should show much greater readiness to submit disputes to arbitration than they have done hitherto. This has to be the normal practice, in preference to a recourse to adjudication, as an important obligation accepted by the parties under the Code.

The law provides for the establishment of Works Committees at the plant level in order to develop harmonious relations between employers and workers. According to a recent assessment, the system has proved its capacity to render substantial help in composing dif- ferences between the parties though, owing to lack of earnest effort, the Committees are not functioning effectively in some units. The decision to demarcate the functions of Works Committees, as distinct from those of trade unions. will remove an obstacle in the way of the successful functioning of the Committees. It is, thus. essential that Works Committees are strengthened and made an active agency for the democratic administration of labour matters.

**Joint Management Councils.** A major programme for the period of the Third Five Year Plan will be the progressive extension of the scheme of Joint Management Councils to new industries and units so that, in the course of a few years. it may become a. normal feature of the industrial system. As it develops, workers' participation may become a highly significant step in the adaptation of the private sector to fit into the framework of a socialist order.

It can serve to bridge the gulf between labour and management. create better mutual understanding and facilitate the adoption, on both sides. of an objec- tive approach towards the problems of industry and the workers. The success or failure of an undertaking is not the concern of management alone. For the peaceful evolution of the economic system on a demo- cratic basis, it is essential that workers' participation in manage- ment should be accepted as a fundamental principle and an urgent need, In course of time, management cadres should arise out of the working class itself. This will greatly help to promote social mobility which is an important ingredient of a socialist system.

Joint Management Council should be set-up in all establish- ments in the public as well as the private sector in which conditions favourable to the success of the scheme exist. A primary test of eligibility is the presence of goodwill on both the sides. Wherever a representative union exists, a Council should come into being as a matter of course. An intensive programme of workers' education will be undertaken in all the establishments where such Councils are set up.

**Workers' Education.** The programme of workers' education which Government has undertaken through a semi-autonomous Board is being run with the cooperation of all the employers' and workers' organisations. A largescale expansion of this scheme is visualised for the period of the Third Plan. It is intended to diversify the programme and secure fuller association of workers' representatives and their organisations. The complementary question of management training in labour matters is also receiving consideration.

The spread of literacy among the workers is an indispensable precondition for the success of the various programmes that are being undertaken. The benefit of literacy should be made available to as large a number of workers as possible in the next few years, particu- larly to those below the age of forty.

**Trade Unions.** There is need for a considerable re-adaptation in the outlook functions and practices of trade unions to suit the conditions which have arisen and are emerging. They have to be ac- cepted as an essential part of the apparatus of industrial and econom- ic administration of the country and should be prepared for the dis- charge of the responsibilities which attach to this position. Trade union leadership has to grow progressively out of the ranks of the workers. and this process will be greatly accelerated as the programme of workers' education gathers momentum. At present, the trade unions are in most cases labouring under the handicap of insufficient re-sources and are not in a position to obtain all the help and guidance that they need.

The basis for recognition of unions adopted as a part of the Code of Discipline, will nave the way for the growth, of a strong and healthy trade unionism in the country. A union can claim recogni- tion, if it has a continuing membership of at least 15 percent of the workers in the establishment over a period of six months and will be entitled to be recognised as a representative union for an industry or a local area. if it has membership of at least 25 per cent of workers. Where, there are several unions in an industry or establishment. the union with the largest membership will be recognised. Once a union has been recognised, there should be no change in its position r a period of two years, if it has been adhering to the provisions of the Code of Discipline.

The personnel of the industrial relations machinery calls for greater attention in respect of selection as well as training. It is necessary to ensure that the quality and equipment of conciliators and tribunals are adequate for the complex tasks which now confront them . It is proposed to institute a suitable training programme for this purpose.

## WAGES AND SOCIAL SECURITY

The Government has assumed responsibility for securing a minimum wage for certain sections of workers, in industry and agriculture, who are economically weak and stand in need of protection. Towards this end the Minimum Wages Act provides for the fixation and revision of wage rates in these occupations. These measures have not proved effective in many cases. For better implementation of the law, the machinery for inspection has to be strengthened. Wage determina- tion in major industries is left to the process of collective bargaining, conciliation, arbitration and adjudication. The Second Plan recommended the setting up of Wage Boards as the most suitable method of settling wage disputes where large areas of industry are concerned. This has so far been applied to the cotton and jute textiles, cement, sugar and plantation industries; and will be extended to other industries according to circumstances. It has been decided to appoint a Board soon for the iron and steel industry. The representatives of employers and workers have agreed that unanimous recommendations of a wage board should be implemented fully. An encouraging trend has been noticed in the coal mining industry where employers and workers have agreed to set up a bipartite committee to examine the entire question of wage revision in the industry; alternative wage-fixing machinery will be considered only if the bipartite committee fails to arrive at a settlement.

Some broad principles of wage determination have been laid down in the Report of the Fair Wages Committee. On the basis of agreement between the parties, the Indian Labour

Conference had indicated the content of the need-based minimum wage for guidance in the settlement of wage disputes. This has been reviewed and it has been agreed that the nutritional requirements of a working class family may be re-examined in the light of the most authoritative scientific data on the subject. Apart from the minimum wage, care should be taken in fixing fair wages for different classes of workers, that adequate incentives are provided for the acquisition and development of skills and for improvements in output and quality. There are, however, wide disparities between the wages of the working class, on the one hand, and the salaries at the higher management levels, on the other.

Owing to the uncertainty attaching to it, the question of bonus has become a source of friction and dispute. It has been decided to appoint a Commission which will include representatives of both parties to study the problems connected with bonus claims and to evolve guiding principles and norms for the payment of bonus.

**Social Security.** The Employees' State Insurance Scheme has mow been implemented in more than a hundred centres covering about 17 lakh industrial workers. During the Third Plan period, the scheme will be extended to all centres where there is concentration of five hundred or more industrial workers, bringing the total coverage to about 30 lakh workers. Medical care and treatment including hospital- isation and midwifery services will be extended to the families of insured persons in all centres where the scheme is in operation. The preventive aspects will also receive greater attention. A great deal of leeway remains to be made up in the provision of separate hospital accommodation for the insured workers. The construction of new hospi- tals and dispensaries will be speeded up so as to add at least 6000 hospital beds during the period of the Third Plan.

The Employees' Provident Fund Scheme, which now covers 58 industries/establishments will be further extended. The employment limit for coverage under the scheme has already been lowered from 50 to 20. The Provident Fund Organisation has completed a survey of other industries and during the

Third Plan the scheme will be extended to such industries among these as are able to bear the financial burden. The proposals to enhance the rate of contribution to the provident fund from 6 1/4 to 8 1/3 per cent has been already accepted by Government in principle, but in view of the varying capacity of different industries, a Technical Committee has been constituted to ascertain which industries are not capable of bearing the additional liability. It is also proposed to bring employees of commercial establishments within the purview of the scheme.

A Study Group on Social Security had recommended the integration of existing social security schemes and the conversion of the various Provident Fund schemes into a statutory scheme for old age, invalidity and survivorship pension-cum-gratuity. Urgent consideration has, now to be given to the various aspects of the question of integration, so that the entire scheme takes shape as early as possible.

The social security approach has so far extended mainly to wage earners in organised industry. There are some groups whose condition calls for closer attention on the part of the community. In the past, on account of the traditional values associated with the small community and the joint family, a great deal, of relief was available to those who were unable to provide for themselves. For a long period to come, in one form or another, the community. the group and the family must continue to be the main sources of assistance. Progres- sively, however, the State and local bodies, both urban and rural, will need to participate in schemes undertaken by way of social assistance and social security. Even at this stage, it would be desira- ble to make a modest beginning in respect of three groups of persons- the physically handicapped, old persons unable to work, and women and children where they are altogether lacking in the means of liveli- hood and support. Assistance for them will have to come from volun- tary and charitable organisations, municipal bodies, Panchayat Samitis and panchayats and voluntary organisations. With a view to enabling these organisations to develop their activities with the help of local communities, and giving them a little support, it might be useful, to constitute a small relief and assistance fund. Details of the propos- al should be considered further in cooperation with States and volun- tary organisations.

## WORKING CONDITIONS, SAFETY AND WELFARE

Under various laws, a comprehensive code has been developed to ensure satisfactory working conditions, safety of person and the provision of a variety of facilities to promote the welfare of the workers. Steps, however, have to be taken to make the implementation of the statutory provisions more effective. The improvement of work- ing conditions call result in greater productive efficiency on the part of the workers. Every effort should be made to keep abreast of the modern developments in these and various other aspects relating to the human factor in industry. Towards this end, the activities of the the Central Labour Institutes and the three Regional Labour Insti- tutes should be developed to provide a comprehensive service to indus- try through training, education and research. The problem of safety should receive greater attention. A Standing Advisory Committee will be set up to promote measures for bringing down the incidence of accidents in factories. State Governments have to strengthen the inspectorates provided for the administration of factory laws. Both in factories and in mines, a great deal of scope remains for reducing hazards by education of the workers in safety-consciousness and the setting up of safety committees. Steps are being taken in pursuance of the recommendations of the Mines Safety Conference and its various committees, and intensive studies are in progress concerning various aspects or the problem of safety in all mines.

A National Mine Safety Council is proposed to be set up regarding safety education and propa- ganda in the mining industry In view of the rapid expansion of the output of mines and the increase in depths and mechanisation to which it leads, it has become imperative that there should be greater vigi-lance and stricter enforcement of rules and regulations. The building and construction industry is a similar field ill which rapid pro- grammes of expansion call for greater attention to safety standards. while the Central and State Public Works Departments are among the major employing authorities, a significant amount of building and construction work is in private hands. Working conditions at con- struction sites are very different from those in factories, primarily because of the purely "temporary" basis upon which most of the work is organised. The question of separate safety legislation for building and construction workers is under examination. Industrial hygiene surveys undertaken so far have disclosed that exposure to occupational disease has been increasing. The surveys Should cover the remaining industries and prompt remedial action should be taken in each case. Special welfare funds have been constituted for financing welfare measures for workers in the coal and mica mining industries. They are meeting very real needs. Similar funds are proposed to be created for workers in the manganese and iron ore mines. Workers' Cooperatives. Some progress has been made in the formation of miners' cooperative societies through the help of the Coal Mines Welfare Fund Organisation. A few workers' cooperative housing societies also exist in some industrial centres. On the whole cooperation has not made much headway so far as the working class is concerned. It will derive immense benefit from the extension of cooperative activity in various forms. Campaigns should be undertaken for setting up cooperative credit societies and cooperative consumers stores. it is hoped that trade unions and voluntary organisations will evince greater interest and initiative in running such cooperatives.

**Industrial Housing.** Although the Subsidised Industrial Housing Scheme has been in operation for some years, the situation in respect of the housing of industrial workers has not improved and, in several centres, it has even deteriorated. The present approach to the problem has been found to be wholly inadequate and new ways will have to be devised immediately so that the workers may be assured of minimum standards in respect of living conditions within a reasonable period in the interest of their health and efficiency. Towards the same end, facilities for recreation and sports will have to be greatly. enlarged for all sections of the workers.

**Other Problems.** With the help of studies which are now in progress regarding contract labour, it will be possible to select occupations in which contract labour will not be permitted and, where abolition is not feasible, to decide on the steps which can be taken to safeguard fully the interests of contract workers. While consider- able improvement has occurred in the living and working conditions of employees in large and organised industries owing both to State activ- ity and trade union action, a great deal of leeway remains to be made up in respect of the workers engaged in agriculture and unorganised industries. Their conditions should become, a matter of special concern to the Government as well as to the organ- isations of labour.

## EMPLOYMENT AND TRAINING SCHEMES

A large increase in the demand for craftsmen will have to be met during the Third Plan. By the end of the Second Plan period, there were 166 industrial training institutes with 42,000 training seats. It is intended to increase the, number of these institutes to a total of 318 by the end of the Third Plan with an additional 58,000 seats, raising the training capacity to 1 lakh craftsmen and an esti- mated out-turn of 2 lakh craftsmen during the Plan period. Adequate in-plant training facilities will also be provided. Separate facili- ties have been organised for the training of educated youth in the techiques of management so that such of them as have the inclination and aptitude for undertaking business responsibilities on their own or through cooperatives, will be provided with wider employment opportunities.

The capacity of the three existing Central Training Institutes for Craft Instructors will be raised from 512 to 976 seats and three other Central Institutes will be set up during the Third Plan period. As against 2000 in the Second Plan, 7800 instructors will be trained during the Third Plan. Separate arrangements are being made to train women craft instructors.

During the Second Plan, little progress has been registered under the apprenticeship training scheme, which has so far been carried out on a voluntary basis. It has now been decided to place the scheme on a compulsory footing and a Bill on the subject is proposed to be introduced in Parliament. A target of 14,000 seats has been set for the apprenticeship training programme. The target for the pro- gramme of evening classes for industrial workers is to raise the present 3,000 seats to 15,000 seats during the Third Plan.

One hundred employment exchanges will be opened during the Third Plan with the object of providing at least one exchange in each district. It is also intended to increase the number of rural employ- ment exchanges and strengthen the organisation of the State Employment Directorates. An effective start has been made with the Employment Market Information programme; the scheme now covers all public sector establishments and private sector units in 150 areas. The scheme will be extended to all areas covered by employment exchanges. Similar provision has been made for expanding the programme of Youth Employ- ment Service. Youth Counselling and collection and analysis of occu- pation information undertaken by the exchanges.

Closures of establishments have occurred to a varying extent in certain industries during the last few years. Where unfavourable market conditions develop, marginal units are affected severely unless steps are taken in advance to safeguard their position. In several cases, the collapse follows a prolonged period of neglect and misman- agement. The workers, who are thrown out of employment, often fail to find avenues for absorption in other units in the same industry. It often happens that besides losing their jobs these workers are de- prived of arrears of wages and even the collections in respect of Provident Fund or Employees' State Insurance cannot be recovered from the employers. As a result, the workers have to face acute distress.

It becomes evident that having regard to the human aspect, and for the purpose of preventing a sense of demoralisation among other workers, steps will have to be taken to afford a measure of relief and assistance to retrenched workers who are thus reduced to a state of helplessness. In a fully developed form such a scheme has to be on a contributory basis, with adequate support from the Government, and besides assistance and relief to the retrenched workers, its functions might include:

(1) help to industrial units which are temporarily in financial difficulties but have otherwise a reputation for efficiency and good management;

(2) taking over units for temporary management; and

(3) financing, in suitable cases, co-operative ven- tures of workers threatened by closures.

A start has, however, to be made immediately, and it has now been decided to draw up a scheme of a limited scope to furnish such assistance as is practicable in the existing circumstances. This will be in the form of loans to tide over the immediate difficulties and facilities for retraining for alternative occupations and for transfer to other places where work may be available. A small financial provision has been made in the Plan for this purpose.

**PRODUCTIVITY**

Industry is being called upon to meet, as rapidly as possible, the claims on behalf of the workers for a living wage, better living and working conditions, the needed volume of employment opportunities and a fuller measure of social security. It must yield a reasonable return on capital and provide for capital formation on an adequate scale. Neither the exercise of their organised strength in industrial conflicts, nor laws and the intervention of the State can help the workers much in realising their aspirations. Their gains can arise only out of the strength and dynamism of the economy, the only enduring basis of which is a rising level of productivity. No in- crease in profits which does not come out of improvements in produc- tivity but has its origin in current scarcity and the stresses of development, can be regarded as a sign of prosperity. Productivity has many facets and it suffers because of the one-sided and rigid approach which is frequently adopted in dealing with it both by the employers and the workers. Rationalisation of effort in every direction is the true basis of productivity, The term has often been wrongly associated with increase in workloads and added strain on workers in order to swell the volume of private gains.

Large gains in productivity and an appreciable reduction in unit costs can be secured in many cases without causing any detriment to the health of the workers and without incurring any large outlays.

Greater responsibility in this respect rests on the management which should provide the most efficient equipment, correct conditions and methods of work, adequate training and suitable psychological and material incentives for the workers. For several purposes, it will be more helpful to take the working group as unit of activity rather than the individual worker, and the scheme of incentives should be aimed, at the group no less than at the individual.

The industry, trade unions and the Government should together ensure that every worker whether employed already or freshly recruited receives adequate training to acquire the requisite skill and efficiency. By proper organisation, it should be possible to supply the essential needs of the workers at reasonable cost without unduly increasing the burden on industry.

Management has to give the lead by bringing about the maximum rationalisation in its own sphere and eliminating all unjustifiable practices which at present act as disincentives in drawing the best out of the workers. The vicious circle of poverty and unemployment and low productivity can be broken only by a tremendous stress on the maximum possible contribution being made by all the participants in the processes of production. For the workers no real advance in their standard of living is possible without a steady increase in productivity, because any increase in wages generally, beyond certain narrow limits, would otherwise be nullified by a rise in prices. Workers have, therefore, to insist on and not resist the progress of rationalisation in their own interest and in the larger interest of the country.

The pace of development as well as the volume of employment rests to a considerable extent on the capacity to export in the face of increasing competition. This can be achieved primarily through higher productivity and a measure of sacrifice by the employer, the worker and the rest of the community.

Vital reforms cannot be secured without the cooperation and goodwill of the workers. They can be brought about by creating a proper understanding and the provision of the necessary safeguards in the interests of the workers. The greatest anxiety experienced by the workers is with regard to the stability of employment. The agreement regarding rationalisation at the national level guarantees to the workers security in their existing jobs. The scope for rationalisa- tion can be considerably extended if effective arrangements are made for retraining and transfer to other jobs on the basis of the workers' consent. The workers can be expected to respond. A favourable environment for this should be created. This process will be helped greatly by the agreement reached at a seminar organised by the National Productivity Council, which provides an initial basis for cooperation for higher productivity.

The formulation of the Code of Efficiency and Welfare will now be taken up for consideration by the Indian Labour Conference. Greater attention will also have to be given to the training of management at various levels in the important aspects of employer-employee relations. Systematic studies will have to be undertaken for determining the individual wage differentials and the manner in which wages should be linked to productivity. In this connection, the work of the Training-Within-Industry Centre in introducing T.W.I. and other techniques for improving the managerial and supervisory skills and that of the Productivity Centre in training in the higher productivity techniques and in carrying out field inves- tigations like job evaluation and work load studies have helped in stimulating the interest of both management and workers. Further development in this field can be of considerable assistance in evolv- ing rational wage policies.

## RESEARCH

Government undertakes special programmes of studies and surveys of aspects such as working and living conditions, family budgets, wage census, index of earnings, patterns of absenteeism, productivity, etc. There will be further extension of this activity during the period of the Third Five Year Plan.

The inadequacy of reliable data on labour matters available at present and the need for sustained and objective research on a systematic basis were discussed at a Conference on Labour Research held in September, 1960. It was agreed that, to begin with, a small Central Committee for coordinating labour research, comprising, representatives of Government, employers' and workers' organisations, universities and institutions interested in the subject may be consti- tuted. It should be the function of this body to make a survey of the existing agencies in the field and their physical resources, identify the gaps, explore possibilities of filling up the same, determine priorities, allocate research schemes to the various agencies in order to avoid overlapping, stimulate research work in the labour field and recommend means of utilising the results of such research. It is intended to provide for research in labour matters some new institutional facilities outside the set-up of the Government. It will have the association and assistance of organisations of workers and employers as well as others.

7

# Organisation of Public

## ENTERPRISES

The Industrial Policy Resolution of April, 1956, recognising the need of rapid industrialisation for promoting the accelerated growth of the economy, emphasised the key role of the public sector in setting up new industrial undertakings in the following words :

"The adoption of the socialist pattern of society as a national objective, as well as the need for planned and rapid development, required that all industries of basic and strategic importance, or in the nature of public utility services should be in the public sector. Other industries which are essential and require investment on a scale which only the State, in present circumstances, could provide, have also to be in the public sector."

A number of basic industries which require large investments and extensive collaboration with foreign firms or governments and which could be undertaken only on the assurance of future prospects, with no immediate gain in sight, would not normally be started if reliance was to be placed entirely on private enterprise. As the need for establishing these industries is urgent and insistent in the present phase of the country's development, it is inevitable that the scope of the public sector should be large. Moreover, in the case of industries where for technological reasons, the plants have to be large, requiring big investments, by organising them in the public sector, undue concentration of economic and industrial power in private hands can be prevented. Rapid expansion of the public sector would materially con- tribute to increasing public savings for investment, making it possi- ble thereby to increase the rate of growth. The particular advantage of the expansion of the public sector from this point of view is that a possible conflict between efficiency and the distribution of income is, to a large extent, eliminated. Increased profits, which in the private sector would create inequalities (and possible conspicuous and wasteful consumption), in the public sector can be directly used for capital accumulation. By efficient conduct of enterprises and follow- ing a rational and economically sound price policy for its products and services, the public sector undertakings ought to secure adequate return on capital employed and contribute their full share to the increase in the portion of national resources devoted to investment.

As a direct consequence of the objective of working towards the realisation of a socialist pattern of society, there will be large expansion of the public sector in a wide range of activities, covering fields as varied as mining and manufacturing, generation and distribu- tion of electric power, construction, transport and communications, irrigation, banking and insurance, trade, social services, etc. Extended operations in all these fields will call for the development of appropriate organisations and, as experience is gained in their working, it will be possible to make them progressively more efficient and effective. Although the discussion in this Chapter is primarily with reference to industrial undertakings, most of the considerations have applicability to a wider field.

During the last few years a number of major industrial undertakings have been established in the public sector. Several more are due to come in existence in the course of the Third Plan. Indeed, an increasingly large number of new enterprises will be established during each subsequent Plan period. So far, however, the main thought has been on initiating new projects and finding financial resources for them. It was getting things started which counted. The time has now come to give close attention to the question of how best to manage these enterprises so that they become efficient producers, capable of yielding substantial surpluses which will provide for future expan- sion, and set an example of careful planning, good management and cordial worker and management relationship.

As soon as a new project has been established, in fact much earlier, it is of utmost importance to give proper attention to its effective management. No matter how well the project has been conceived and the plant engineered, it will ultimately succeed or fail on the strength of its management. Before attempting an analysis of certain shortcomings of management and seeking to identify areas calling for remedial action, the present position regarding the organ- isation of public enterprises in the manufacturing field may be brief- ly described.

Public enterprises in the manufacturing field have been organised in three forms. Some of them like the Chittaranjan Locomotive Works are administered departmentally; there are a few which are corporations constituted by a statute; but the majority are joint stock companies established under the Companies Act, although some- times designated as corporations. The important enterprises of the Centre have been listed in the Annexure which shows under each administrative Ministry, the name of the enterprise, the year of its establishment and its legal status.

The usual practice till recently was to establish each manufacturing unit as an independent company. Where it was felt that some special coordination was necessary between certain enterprises either because they were in the same field of operation or because they had special commercial or technical relations with each other, it was sought to be achieved by having a number of common Directors. Moreover, in the case of enterprises under the same Ministry, there was little difficulty of coordination because even the Chairman of the Board and some of the Directors were the same on account of the fact that directorships in many cases were held by certain officials ex-officio.

It has now been recognised that proliferation of special organisations of such number and variety as to be unmanageable should be avoided and there should be a definite policy of consolidating these organisations so as to bring together enterprises functioning broadly in the same field. This would enable provision of common facilities to individual units, which otherwise might be well beyond their means, and lead to overall economy and efficiency. For example, number of enterprises grouped together and working in the same field and pooling their resources can maintain an organisation of adequate side both for purchase and sale, with a net-work of branch offices on a large enough scale; can set up facilities for scientific and technological research; establish design and development organisation undertake technical training programmes and institute suitable systems of personnel selection and recruitment on a common basis. Also as enterprises in the group will be largely concerned with the same type of problems, interchange of experience will be very profitable with a view to arriving at common solutions. Bringing together of several manufacturing units under the same company in this manner should not, however, lead to excessive centralisation on the part of the Board of Directors or intervention in the day-to-day activities of the individ- ual constituent production units; otherwise, the General Manager of the undertaking will not have the necessary authority and initiative to ensure the smooth and efficient conduct of the enterprise.

The awareness of these possibilities is reflected in the recent tendency to form large companies such as the Hindustan Steel Limited, the Heavy Engineering Corporation, the Heavy Electricals Limited, the Hindustan Insecticides Limited, the Fertiliser Corporation, the National Coal Development Corporation, etc., each of which controls, or is intended to control, a number of separate undertak- ings in steel, machine building, chemicals, fertilisers, coal mining, etc.

Till some years ago, in the earlier stages, projects were handled departmentally. Later, a decision was taken that government enterprises of a commercial nature should be organised as companies. At present in the case of most of the new projects, such as the Heavy Machinery Project at Ranchi, a company is formed to see that project through from the very outset, including the stage of construction. Also existing companies are being encouraged to establish new units in their field as illustrated by Hindustan Steel Limited being assigned the responsibility of establishing the Alloy and Tool Steels Plant at Durgapur and the new integrated steel works at Bokaro, and the Hindustan Machine Tools Company being charged with the responsibility of bringing into existence one or more machine too] factories.

It has become necessary now to give serious thought to the establishment of specialised agencies for designing and construction. These agencies would be able to undertake large works in connection with industrial development and to gain and preserve valuable experi- ence of actual construction which could be put to use in the construc- tion of similar succeeding projects. A start has been made with the establishment of design and construction organisations in Hindustan Steel Limited and Sindri Fertilisers Limited.

The successful operation of large industrial enterprises is a relatively new challenge. Efficient conduct of industrial and business enterprises requires that operational decisions should be prompt. They need not always be right for most such decisions are reversible and can be corrected later. Far greater delegation of authority and flexibility of operation is necessary to enable the management of the enterprise to produce results. If an enterprise does not have real autonomy it is not likely to be effective.

Lack of delegation within the enterprise is another common failure. Even as the general manager does not enjoy sufficient au- thority to manage effectively, there is often a failure by him and other management stall in the hierarchy to delegate authority to others down the line, who cannot do their jobs properly without the necessary authority. The lack of delegation of authority is usually accompanied by a failure to define responsibilities and duties. Nobody can operate confidently or effectively or be held responsible for results unless he knows what he is supposed to do and has the authority to do it.

Another important factor which determines the success of an enterprise is whether there are enough experienced men in positions of management. A good plant can appear to operate, and in fact can operate in an uneconomic way, without enough management staff, but if their number is not sufficient, an enterprise will be handicapped by high production cost, low output, high wastage, mechanical and processing difficulties and break-downs.

Lack of quality of managerial personnel is another, factor prejudicing the success of an enterprise. Besides, there being too few experienced persons in managerial posts, often the key positions as general managers, production managers, maintenance superintendents, etc., are held by people who do not have the requi- site training and experience to do their jobs effectively. '

The consciousness of profit and cost is also not as widespread as is necessary. The purpose of management should be to secure economic efficiency; cost consciousness is necessary to achieve the desired results. But even the most cost-conscious manager cannot control costs unless he knows what they are, and this is not feasible without the use of cost accounting and other management techniques which are not being used very widely. There are deficiencies also in selection of personnel, their training, and in securing maximum work from them while giving them maximum satisfaction.

Some important aspects, calling for suitable action. are discussed below :

**Public Accountability.** Democratic control of publicly owned industries is very important. At the same time it is generally agreed that a public enterprise, if it is to be run successfully, must possess a sufficient degree of autonomy from Government and Parliament. When day-to-day decisions of a public enterprise become the subject of parliamentary interpellations and discussions, the Ministers will find it necessary to ask for advance knowledge and approval of all decisions. Moreover, exposed to constant public scrutiny, the management will be afraid of making the day-to-day decisions necessary in commercial undertakings. and an ostensibly autonomous enterprise will be virtually stifled by red tape and bureaucracy. The need has, therefore. been felt for a Committee of Parliament which would enable informed parliamentary criticism to be brought to bear on public enterprises. This

Committee would keep itself continuously informed regarding the working of public enterprises. It may be useful if membership of the Committee is for a period of about three years so as to give time to members to master complex facts and to ensure some continuity. This will also result in a growing number of members of Parliament taking a specialised interest in these matters. As Parliament would be assured of necessary vigilance by the Committee, individual members would count on the judgment of the members of the Committee for proper and periodic evaluation of the public enterprises.

**Nature and Functions of the Board of Directors.** The main function of the Board should be to, lay down the broad policies and the general objectives of the undertakings. Subject to the policies laid down. the Managing Director or the General Manager should have full authority and lie should be held responsible for achieving the necessary results. Secretaries to the Ministries should not be ap- pointed as Chairmen or Directors. It may, however, be useful, in the initial stages, to appoint one or two directors from amongst govern- ment officials who are actually dealing with the project in the admin- istrative Ministry concerned and in the Finance Ministry. They will function like any other Director within the constitution of the Compa- ny and will be bound by its rules and regulations. In respect of subjects reserved for the Government, they will be able to explain to the Board of Directors the thinking within the Government and, when matters are referred to Government, they will be able to explain the views of the Board of Directors.

The Managing Director and/or Chairman should be appointed by the Government and, except in the case of very small concerns, should be full-time. Other Directors may be full-time or part-time according to the requirements of the undertaking.

Membership of the Board should be on the basis of ability, experience and administrative competence, and should be open not only to the employees of the public undertakings but also to persons from outside. Having been selected to serve on the Board, all Directors must identify themselves with the interest of the undertaking.

The Board of Directors should have adequate powers to make appointments and to fix salaries. However, to avoid the risk of migration of personnel from one public sector undertaking to another if different scales of pay are adopted by them for posts of similar nature, it may be necessary to indicate to the Board broadly the basic scales of pay for different categories of posts. It should, however, be open to the Board to fix specific pays for specific jobs.

The powers of the Board for sanctioning of capital works will have to be considerably enhanced as the limits stipulated in the case of some of the big undertakings appear to be too low at present. The financial limits will have to be comparatively high in the case of big undertakings and could be more modest in the case of smaller undertakings. The reference to the Government for expenditure sanc- tion should be reduced to the minimum so that within, the frame-work of certain rules and limits, the Board of Directors should be free to proceed with the operations of the plant or the execution of a project.

Of late, there has been an attempt to form large companies under which are brought together separate undertakings of allied character. The constitution of such large companies has been consid- ered desirable from the point of view of providing certain common facilities to individual units in the interest of overall economy and efficiency. The wider delegation of power from the Ministry to the Company should be accompanied by sufficient delegation of authority by the Company to the General Managers of the individual undertakings. The defects of excessive centralisation would remain and the operation of individual undertakings would he adversely affected if the requisite authority and autonomy are withheld from the men on the spot who have to run the undertaking.

Managing Director/General Manager.The leadership, guidance and the main driving force must come from the Managing Director/ General Manager. He must be selected on the basis of technical competence, administrative ability and quality of leadership. He must be able to see clearly what is going on and to know which department is not working satisfactorily and must have the requisite knowledge and authority to help the departmental managers to put it right. He must enjoy real autonomy within the frame work of general rules laid down and must be held responsible for the results. Day-to-day decisions should be his concern. It must be recognised that some mistakes will occur, for these are inevitable when decisions have to be taken quick- ly in the interest of efficiency. The flexibility of operations will be possible only if he enjoys a reasonable degree of freedom from being called upon to explain to a number of different people at dif- ferent times why certain decisions were taken and why departures had to be made from particular rules. For the proper discharge of his responsibilities, the General Manager should remain in charge of an undertaking for a reasonably long period so that he has an intimate knowledge of the problems and possibilities of his enterprise. Quick changes of appointments must, therefore, be avoided. At the same time, his security of tenure should depend on performance. If he succeeds, he will naturally be continued in office and receive encour- agement if he fails he must expect to be superseded.

**The role of Financial Adviser.** All companies should be provided with an internal Financial Adviser who should function subject to the authority of the General Manager. In case of difference of opinion, it should be quite open to the General Manager to overrule the advice of the Financial Adviser, but there should be a convention that such cases should be brought to the notice of the Board by the General Manager at the next Board meeting.

The Financial Adviser should concern himself with problems of financial management rather than devote exclusive attention to those of control of expenditure. For this purpose it would be neces- sary to arrange for orientation of Financial Advisers in the princi- ples and practices of financial management either before Joining an undertaking or through refresher courses. This is required particularly for Financial Advisers who may be drawn from the usual channels available for this purpose at present.

**Supporting Management.** The General Manager should have enough supporting management staff to provide adequate control,' supervision, direction and training for all employees. This staff should be selected and appointed by the General Manager. subject to Board approval, and should be responsible only to him or to some one authorised by him. He should delegate and define adequate authority to them and then hold them responsible for performance.

**Building up of Management Cadres.** The efficient functioning of the enterprises will depend greatly on two important factors bearing on personnel management, namely training for positions of responsibility in the organisation and development of personnel to serve as second line for eventual selection to key appointments. Managerial personnel for key appointments should not only be technically qualified but they should also develop an "all plant" outlook. The manner in which this should be done will depend on the particular circumstances of each enterprise, which may use specially devised courses and other practical ways such as giving opportunities to selected persons for proving their managerial capacity in suitable posts.

**Advance Planning.** Planning, that is deciding in advance what is to be done, is a precondition for the success of an enterprise. It provides the basis for organisation, assembling resources. direction and control. An able manager is one who can say with an assurance based on detailed planning what products he would produce during the next month and the year, how many men and of what qualifications he would need and what would be the expense thereof, which materials and in what quantities would be required, what the spoilage would be and can state in similar specific terms the results he plans to achieve in other phases of his operation.

The plans for a given enterprise should fall into a hierarchy. A general objective is accompanied by a whole series of successively more detailed plans, each designed to implement the general plan of which it is a part. There have to be similarly gener- al plans for longer periods. say five years, annual operational plans and budgets and detailed day-to-day programmes of individual depart- ments.

The preparation of advance costs, operation and capital budgets will greatly reduce the need for making references to the administrative Ministry and strengthen the autonomy and flexibility of the enterprises. All enterprises, in their own interest, should, therefore, build suitable machinery for this purpose.

Advance planning provides an opportunity for seeing that each part fits in with the other and is directed towards the overall purpose. When bottlenecks or weak spots are uncovered by careful and realistic advance Planning, there is often time to find a remedy before the event occurs. whereas expensive breakdowns may be unavoid- able if corrective action is not initiated until overwhelmed by a crisis. Moreover, trouble is often more easily corrected in its early stages than after a crisis has developed. Thus, for example. preven- tive maintenance systematically carried out avoids expensive repairs and replacements and shutting down of plants later. The existence of a detailed plan provides the impetus for developing more efficient methods and procedures and also facilitates delegation of authority.

Setting up of specific goals and subgoals is an inseparable part of the whole planning process. A wide variety of operating standards and 'norms' need to be set up to express the anticipated results of the more detailed plan. These may include norms for use of raw materials power and fuel inputs of labour; overhead expenses; targets of output, both in terms of quantity and quality; tasks for training, etc, Comparable data from other similar plants in the coun- try and outside are often found of value in this connection. An operational budget of the enterprise, carefully prepared from this point of view, could serve as the goal towards which all activities are directed. Many benefits follow from such practice. It makes purposeful and integrated planning easier; it helps the executive and the operators to concentrate on the essentials and contribute to the constant vigilance that is necessary to keep the enterprise from unproductive activities; the accumulation of operational data and norms useful for planning provides the basis for building. realistic pro- grammes in future; and, most important of all; the setting up of specific goals and norms is an essential condition for administrative control, that is, the securing of results in accordance with plans. Standards and norms are vital if appraisal is to have any validity. Also the recognition and acceptance of specific and clearly defined objectives and standards play an important part in the motivation of individual effort.

**Incentives.** An enterprise which has worked realistic 'norms' of performance would find it easy to introduce systems of wage incentives, which play an important part in raising labour productivity, reducing costs and improving quality. These systems fall into three broad categories :

(1) wages regulated on piece work,

(2) a basic wage for an agreed output to which is added a bonus proportionate to addi- tional output, and

(3) a bonus payable on the output of a group, each member of which draws a separate basic wage.

The applicability of any system depends to a large extent on the specific situation of an enterprise and has to be worked out in relation to its requirements. All that can be said is that incentive wage system should be intro- duced on the largest possible scale for the mutual benefit of the workers anti the industry.

**Research Departments.** It is necessary to maintain adequately staffed Research and Development Departments in the public undertakings which should constantly endeavour to improve the product quality and operational and technical efficiency through scientific studies. The recommendations of such departments should be implemented speedily. Innovations and new ideas should be suitably rewarded and publicised.

There should be frequent exchange of technical and managerial experience between different public enterprises so that all benefit from the common pool of experience. Inter-plant visits will be useful in this connection.

**Personnel Relations.** The enterprises of the public sector have a special obligation to follow labour policies which are condu- cive to securing and keeping a competent working force at a reasonable cost. This requires a suitable wage policy with incentives, careful selection of personnel, organised training to improve the skills of workers at all levels, opportunities for workers to attain higher positions as their ability improves, active encouragement of workers to make suggestions to improve the operations of the enterprise and recognition of useful ideas by suitable rewards, a grievance procedure to settle small problems before they become large, and generally an attitude towards the workers which will encourage added effort and initiative and give the employees satisfaction, a sense of participa- tion and feeling of loyalty to the enterprise and pride for its achievement.

**Surpluses and their Utilisation.** When public enterprises run efficiently and follow a proper price policy for their goods and services, the results of their operations must be reflected in larger earnings and surpluses. In a developing economy, these constitute a ready and increasingly important source for financing investment either for the expansion of the enterprises which yield these sur- pluses or elsewhere in the economy. It is, therefore, incumbent on public enterprises to produce efficiently and to accumulate surpluses which should be earmarked for further development.

It is not enough for an enterprise to operate efficiently and carry out its assigned task satisfactorily. It must assume responsibility for continuously improving its performance and for initiating and planning its growth and expansion. The management of a public enterprise should not merely carry out plans approved by Gov- ernment, but must in fact be closely concerned with and be largely responsible for preparing the plans for further development and for securing the requisite resources.

A brief review like the one attempted here must of necessity leave many gaps. It is not the purpose to prescribe detailed opera- tional recommendations for each enterprise but to touch upon some significant aspects to which greater attention needs to be given. Many of the enterprises in the public sector have already adopted policies and management techniques which have enabled them to produce remarkable results in relatively short time. The record of public enterprises, considering their relatively recent origin. is very creditable. The deficiencies of management to which attention has been drawn are as characteristic of enterprises in the private sector as in the public sector. Striving for constant improvement must be a common goal for all.

### *List of major public enterprises of the Centre in the field of manufacturing and mining*

### *[With authorised capital of Rs. 5 million and above]*

| | Ministry/Enterprise | year of establishment |
|---|---|---|
| | *Commerce and Industry* | |
| 1 | Indian Drugs and Pharmaceuticals Ltd. | 1961 |
| 2 | Heavy Electricals Ltd. | 1956 |
| 3 | Heavy Engineering Corporation Ltd. | 1958 |
| 4 | Hindustan Antibiotics Ltd. | 1954 |
| 5 | Hindustan Cables Ltd. | 1952 |
| 6 | Hindustan Insecticides Ltd. | 1954 |
| 7 | Hindustan Machine Tools Ltd. | 1953 |
| 8 | Hindustan Organic Chemicals Ltd. | 1960 |
| 9 | Hindustan Salt Company Ltd. | 1958 |
| 10 | Nahan Foundry Ltd. | 1952 |
| 11 | Hindustan Chemical and Fertilisers Ltd. | 1956 |
| 12 | National Instruments Ltd. | 1957 |
| 13 | National Newsprint and Paper Mills Ltd. | 1947 |
| 14 | Sindri Fertilisers and Chemicals Ltd. | 1951 |
| 15 | Praga Tools Corporation Ltd. | 1943 |
| 16 . | Hindustan Photo Films Manufacturing Company Ltd. | 1960 |
| | *Defence* | |
| 17 | Bharat Electronics Ltd. | 1954 |
| 18 | Prototype Machine Tool Factory* | 1953 |
| 19 | Hindustan Aircraft Ltd. | 1940 |
| | *Department of Automic Energy* | |
| 20 | Indian Rare Earths Ltd. | 1950 |
| | *Finance* | |
| 21 | Silver Refinery, Calcutta* | 1952 |
| | *Railways* | |

| | | |
|---|---|---|
| 22 | Chittaranjan Locomotive Works* | 1948 |
| 23 | integral Coach Factory* | 1952 |
| | *Steel, Mines and Fuel* | |
| 24 | Hindustan Steel Ltd. | 1953 |
| 25 | Indian Refineries Ltd. | 1958 |
| 26 | National Coal Development Corporation Ltd. | 1956 |
| 27 | National Mineral Development Corporation Ltd. | 1958 |
| 28 | Neiveli Lignite Corporation Ltd. | 1956 |
| 29 | Singareni Collieries Company Ltd, | 1920 |
| 30 | Oil and Natural Gas Commission | 1956 |
| | *Transport and Communications* | |
| 31 | Indian Telephone Industries Ltd. | 1948 |
| 32 | Hindustan Shipyard Ltd. | 1952 |
| 33 | Hindustan Teleprinters Ltd. | 1960 |
| | *Works, Housing and Supply* | |
| 34 | Hindustan Housing Factory Ltd. | 1953 |

* Departmental undertaking. ** Statutory corporation,

All others are companies registered under the Companies Act.

# 8

# Public Cooperation and Participation

## APPROACH

Public cooperation has been recognised as an essential condition for the success of our Plans. Its role and contribution have to be judged in relation to the social and economic objectives that the country is seeking to achieve. For a developing country, which cherishes its democratic values, the people's part in the attainment of these objectives is of supreme importance. The peaceful struggle for freedom and the tradition of constructive work associated with it had marked out for the people a decisive role in the tasks of planned development initiated ten years ago.

Shramdan, the contribution of the people to local works and amenities, and their participation in the community development movement are among the ways in which their support has been enlisted in the tasks of national development. It is evident, however, that the possibilities of full involvement of the people in the processes of change and growth are not being realised to a sufficient degree.

In the context of democracy, administration is effective in the measure it is based in its day-to-day working on the participation and support of the people. In the activities in which official agencies are engaged there is a large sphere in which the cooperation of the people can be sought and secured to achieve a degree of success which would otherwise not be possible. These tasks should be identified precisely and the obligations and responsibilities of the people in relation thereto made known clearly.

The people in the rural areas are now coming into their own. Direct responsibility for the administration of their affairs is being passed on to them as panchayati raj gets established in one State after another. The transformation now occurring at the base in the country-side, and emerging from panchayati raj, is intended to facilitate the fuller play of the energy and initiative of the people in dealing with the tasks which lie close to them in the villages of the Country. Conditions are being created for a fuller use of the manpower and other resources in order to secure more rapid development in every direction. This will also widen very much the opportunities for public participation.

The concept of public cooperation is related, in its wider aspect, to the much larger sphere of voluntary action in which the initiative and organisational responsibility rest completely with the people and their leaders, and does not rely on legal sanctions or the power of the State for achieving its aims. So vast are the unsatisfied needs of the people that all the investments in the public and private sectors together can, at this stage, only make a limited provision for them. Properly organised voluntary effort may go far towards augmenting the facilities available to the community for helping the weakest and the most needy to a somewhat better life. The wherewithal for this has to come from time, energy and other resources of millions of people for whom voluntary organisations can find constructive channels suited to the varying conditions in the country. Everyone can contribute something. But the greater obligation in this regard lies on those who are better placed. Applied on a mass scale, as was done in the construction of the Kosi project, the results of public participation in terms of savings of both time and money can be tremendous. Material gains to the nation from this source can be widespread and large. What has been achieved so far on this account is, however, of small proportions. There should. therefore, be an early appraisal of the activity in this field to remove hindrances in the way of a much more massive advance.

The transition from a state of economic and social stagnation and the initial period of advance are attended with social and political hazards, especially in the case of a country where political freedom is of recent occurrence. The new awakening brings to the fore pressing claims and expectations but the sense of duty and obligations lags behind. The development process also imposes a measure of sacrifice and forbearance. When the democratic structure and values have to be preserved, these strains and stresses become greatly accentuated. To counteract this and to create a social and political climate conducive to smoth progress must be the primary concern of a developing nation. In this field, social action has a pre-eminent role.

Uneven distribution of the fruits of progress, which is associated to an extent with the early stages of development in a democratic society, gives rise to a sense of deep resentment and frustration. This is greatly heightened by the spectacle of fortuitous incomes and gains from anti-social activities. Sharp conflicts, which stem from narrow sectional and regional interests, have arisen in India occasionally. It is not possible to provide full satisfaction for the rising expectations of various sections and regions at this stage. At the same time, there are forces at work which exploit all kinds of discontents and tensions, and pose a threat to the solidarity of the nation. While action has to be taken at political and administrative levels to curb these tendencies, the most effective means of combating this evil is for the community itself to strengthen its own defences and repel from within the attacks on the integrity of the nation.

This protective strength can come chiefly from voluntary service and constructive activities organised by the people. themselves. Explosive situations do not develop suddenly and when outbursts occur they are only symptoms of a malaise which has existed and grown over a period of time. Remedies applied at the moment can have only a limited efficacy. Wrong influences and destructive trends have to be neutralised constantly by positive forces that should be generated within the community all the time. This is, in the first instance, a task of widespread social enlightenment Appeals made at the last moment are usually not heeded, It is through the quiet influence of voluntary workers. steadily engaged in acts of selfless service into which a large section of the community is drawn, that the voice of reason can prevail. Constructive work and comradeship in unselfish activity are a sure basis for progressive and healthy group life in a community which is exposed to a variety of disturbing impacts. In the circumstances of our country, these facts and considerations invest social action and public cooperation with a deep significance.

## PUBLIC COOPERATION IN THE FIRST TWO PLANS

The distinctive feature of public cooperation programmes is the presence of the contribution of voluntary service on a considerable scale. This became available in the earlier years chiefly for construction of roads and school buildings, drinking water schemes and other local works to provide simple amenities for the people.

Over the past decade voluntary contributions in the community development programmes, in cash, kind and service, have been estimated at about Rs. 100 crores. The people's quota in local development works amounted nearly to Rs. 15 crores out of a total expenditure of Rs. 33 crores. Welfare programmes of the Central Social Welfare Board and those relating to the welfare of backward classes and emergency relief schemes were implemented largely through voluntary organisations. The intensive area scheme of the Khadi and Village Industries Commission bases itself to a considerable extent on people's own effort and local resources for creating additional employment opportunities through village industries. The midday meal and school improvement schemes in Madras are being executed with a large measure of support from the people. Bhoodan and gramdan movements, in which the Sarva Seva Sangh workers are actively engaged, are an outstanding demonstration of the potentialities which reside in voluntary action stimulated by high ideoalism and a missionary zeal. The University Planning Forums have succeeded in drawing a large num- ber of teachers and students with various socioeconomic programmes such as small savings, literacy, slum clearance and improvement and construction schemes involving voluntary work.

It was realised at the time of the formulation of the First Five Year Plan that for rapid progress public cooperation will have to be enlisted on a very large scale in every aspect of development The Bharat Sevak Samaj was formed to provide a common platform with the object of drawing out the available unused time and energy of the people and directing them into various fields of social and economic activity. The Samaj has adopted a comprehensive programme and has branches all over the country. It has a large cadre of trained workers. Its association with the Kosi project during 1955-59 has brought forth evidence of the large possibilities of reducing cost, improving quality of performance and speeding up completion of various projects through public participation. Against the original estimates of Rs. 11.5 crores, the actual expenditure on the Kosi embankment scheme came down to Rs. 6.5 crores.

The work was completed in 1958 against target date of 1960, i.e. 2 years in advance. The Samaj has taken part on a smaller scale in the construction of several other irrigation and flood protection projects. Encouraged by its experience it has set up a Construction Service with branches in several States. It has undertaken construction of a variety of public works. The Organisation of works camps for students and youth of the country in connection with the Labour and Social Service Camps scheme of the Ministry of Education has become a major activity of the Samaj in which the contribution of the people is becoming available in an increasing measure. A specific approach has now been worked out in respect of activities in the rural areas. A group of villages is selected as the field of activity of two or three trained social workers whose task it is to develop, in an integrated manner, people's programmes on the basis of a plan for the area. The Lok Karya Kshetra aims at developing new resources for the area and creating local leadership. This programme receives assistance from the State and is now being shared by other voluntary organisations. To create social awakening and disseminate information about the problems of the country and the various Plan programmes, the Samaj has set up Jan Jagran (social enlightenment) centres. This is an assisted activity which is now becoming an integral part of the Lok Karya Kshetra programme. In the urban areas, the Samaj has given special attention to the problems of the slum-dwellers and has been running a number of night shelters for the homeless.

There are several other organisations which are functioning at the national level and have done valuable work in attending to the specific needs or sections of the community. Considerable progress has been made in the coordination of the activities of these bodies. The National Advisory Committee on Public Cooperation makes a periodical review of the progress in the field of public cooperation and lays down lines of guidance. Among the organisations who are members of this Committee are All India Cooperative Union, All India Women's Conference, Bharat Sadhu Samaj, Bharat Scouts and Guides, Bharat Sevak Samaj, Bharatiya Adim Jati Sangh, Bharatiya Grameen Mahila Sangh, Central Social Welfare Board, Gandhi Samarak Nidhi, Harijan Sevak Sangh, Indian Conference of Social Work, Indian Council for Child Welfare, Indian Red Cross Society, National Cadet Corps and Auxiliary Cadet Corps and Sarva Seva Sangh.

## PRIORITIES AND PROGRAMMES

**Welfare.** With so much poverty and ignorance in the country, there is no limit to the scope of voluntary service in mitigating the hardships of the under privileged and in creating a better environment for them. In view of the present limitations of personnel and resources some consideration of priorities becomes inevitable.

A great deal still remains to be done to promote healthy habits and clean surroundings in rural as well as urban areas. Concerted volun- tary action can produce gratifying results in this sphere without much cost. Services can be rendered to patients in hospitals and to the ailing persons who cannot be looked after in their homes. The spread of literacy can be greatly accelerated through voluntary help. To bring about social reforms and to rid the community of social evils and anti-social activities, the sanctions of law can have only a minor role, and the brunt of the challenge must be borne by voluntary organisations.

**Socio-economic Programmes.** The emphasis of voluntary service is now shifting from welfare, in the restricted sense, to the realisation of broader socioeconomic aims. Voluntary organisations can play a very useful part in creating the climate and conditions favourable to smoth and effective functioning of panchayats and cooperatives. In rural areas, the two outstanding tasks are to assist in the fuller utilisation of the material and manpower resources so that both production and the opportunities for gainful employment may increase continuously. For this purpose, voluntary workers have to give to the community development organisations all the assistance they can.* In towns and cities voluntary service should be directed chiefly towards improving the slums and creating better living conditions for those who must live there. Organised self-help must be the basis of this and the other activities undertaken by voluntary agencies. The cooperative movement in its many phases is a field parexcellence which can absorb services of a large number of social workers. The building up of a network of service cooperatives in rural areas and cooperative consumer stores in urban areas is an urgent national need which should receive immediate attention.

**Construction.** Construction activity in the bigger projects as well as smaller and local works will remain the largest avenue for voluntary effort towards the utilisation of idle manpower. In villages, voluntary agencies will be encouraged and helped to take up construction work directly or through labour cooperatives. This will lead to reduction of cost, observance of satisfactory standards of work, a better deal for the construction workers and the promotion of honest dealings in the working of the construction industry. Excessive dependence on contractors will be avoided and additional resources will become available for the programmes of the voluntary organisations. A Committee set up in the Planning Commission has made the following recommendations to enable the voluntary organisations like the Bharat Sevak Samaj to undertake construction work on a large scale :

(a) It should be the effort of the official agencies to give maximum assistance to voluntary organisations. As far as possible, a certain proportion of the available work should be set apart for them and extended as their capacity develops.

(b) Continuous flow of work should be ensured. The project authorities should indicate well in time the magnitude, types and specific works that can be awarded to such organisations. They should be given preference over the private contractors and, where possible, given works on a negotiated basis.

(c) Works may be awarded at workable rates on (i) 'work-order' basis; and (ii) the basis of schedule of rates increased or decreased by a percentage decided by a competent authority. The schedule of rates should be kept uptodate.

(d) Delay should be avoided and prompt payment ensured. Powers may be delegated to the Superintending and executive Engineers and 'on account' payments may be authorised for works completed.

(e) Technical personnel may be deputed by the State Governments and the Central Ministeries to assist the voluntary organisations.

(f) Loan assistance should be given for working capital and purchase of equipment.

(g) Subject to proper assessment of their capacity, the voluntary organisations may be considered for all kinds of earth-work and simple masonry works. They may be given major structures if and when they are adequately equipped with technical manpower and necessary mechanical equipment. They may also be encouraged in undertaking contracts for supply of building material in bulk quantity.

Better understanding of our Plans.For enlisting widespread participation and voluntary effort in the reconstruction of social and economic life, understanding and appreciation of the significance, objectives and priorities of the Third Plan will be of considerable help. This is by no means an easy task in view of the growing complexity of the economy and of the many problems to be faced. On the other hand, as a result of the first two Plans and the awakening to which they have led, there is much greater ability to grasp the nature of the problems, the limitations within which solutions have to be found and the need to bear larger burdens for achieving rapid economic development. In the last resort, the Plan becomes meaningful in terms of the tasks it sets and the opportunities it provides to individuals, local communities and different sections of the population. As part of the programme for strengthening public cooperation and participation during the Third Plan, it is proposed to intensify the existing arrangements for bringing home the implications of rapid development and carrying the message of the Plan to the masses throughout the country.

**Wider Aims.** There are certain higher tasks which are related to the basic needs, ideals and goals of the nation. In the present circumstances they create special obligations for the people. The foremost need now is that the attitudes of the people and the pattern of conduct, which prevail in the community should be in harmony with the national purposes. There are three constituents of this pattern which may be regarded as the most essential in this context. In the first place, love of the nation and faith in its great destiny should become the dominant feeling in every heart. By common consent, whatever tends to impair the integrity and unity of the country should be held up to public censure. There should be a growing understanding of what kind of behaviour will hurt the cause of national unity and with what consequences. Dedicated workers can in a hundred ways help to project the image of a strong and united nation in the consciousness of every citizen. They can create the realisation how important and indispensable the united endeavour of the people is for every thing of value which the individuals and groups in the country can seek and aspire after.

Voluntary organisations with links in different parts of the country can help to create a sense of oneness and a common outlook by engaging the people in simple activities of service to the community which are performed all over the country as a great national programme. Secondly, it is envisaged that progressive socialisation and cooperative growth should be the basis of the social and economic order that is being created in this country. Thirdly, it should be remembered that it is only on the basis of right living that a strong nation and a just social order can be built. Every one will have to work for the good life which all can share. A society in which many must suffer so that a few may prosper is to be disfavoured.

To bring this about basic changes are needed in the habits and outlook of the people which may reflect a keen appreciation of social justice and our common humanity. Certain norms of behaviour, with accent on restraint, discipline and consideration for others, have to be cultivated and woven into the fabric of national character. Stress should be laid on the observance of 'Sadachar' (moral and social standards) in political and social relations and in all our business and economic activities. When social change of a large order has to be achieved in a relatively short period, the people's part in respect of scale and intensity of effort has to be such as to impart to it the character of a mass movement. Here is a limitless horizon and the widest scope for voluntary service through people's organisations. It should be realised that what is confronting us now is the call of a revolution to which people's mind must get attuned. The idealism and patriotic devotion of the people will find their highest expression in the service of this revolution.

## ORGANISATION AND TECHNIQUES

Since so much is expected of public cooperation and participation through voluntary organisations, it is important that they should grow in strength and dimensions so as to be capable of discharging their self-imposed obligations adequately. This will depend very much on the extent to which they inspire confidence by the proper and efficient execution of the programmes they undertake and the contribution they make to the satisfaction of the felt needs of the people. The spare time and other resources placed at their disposal must be put to the most effective use. This points to the need for advance planning, a proper assessment of requirements, training of personnel, systematic execution and adequate supervision and evaluation.

Voluntary organisations should establish a relationship of intimate collaboration with local bodies and for certain purposes act as agencies of the panchayats, municipalities, etc. The programmes which call for cooperation of the people may be framed jointly and the role and place of voluntary organisations should be clearly specified.

Official agencies should provide them with assistance and facilities to the maximum extent but their direction and control must be scrupulously left to the leadership of voluntary organisations: In this way alone, these organisations can acquire a national character and make an appeal to citizens irrespective of their political affiliations. In response, to local needs small units of voluntary workers are formed in many places. They should be encouraged and helped by the larger bodies to enable them to make a more effective contribution. This assistance may take the form of training of the workers, guidance and provision of various facilities.

Spontaneous development of activities on a voluntary basis is welcome but there is a danger of duplication and frittering away of valuable energy and resources. Voluntary organisations should, therefore, develop a common approach, work in close collaboration and specialise in certain fields for which they are best equipped. A measure of coordination has already been achieved. This may usefully be extended to cover a variety of activities including training, research, pilot projects, pooling of information and experience. publication of journals and guiding material and dealing with official 2agencies.

Voluntary activities have so far drawn their sustenance from individuals and such assistance as the State has been able to furnish. A strong base for voluntary service can be created if it can derive support from a large number of institutions and establishments in the field of education, entertainment. business, journalism, etc. They can help in raising funds through collection drives and charity shows. They may also accept responsibility for some specific jobs. They can render much useful service by permitting the use of their accommodation, equipment and other facilities, outside working hours for programmes and activities of voluntary organisations.

The personnel for voluntary organisations, has to be drawn from all walks of life specially from amongst social workers, teachers, members of various professions, members of Legislatures and local bodies and public servants. Persons retired from active service, either in civil occupations or the army, have given a good account of themselves in this field, and can be drawn into these activities in much larger numbers. The mainstay of this movement will have to be the youth of the country who can be enlisted and trained for activities aiming at their own welfare and the common good.

After a period of trial and experimentation, the concept of Lok Karya has been evolved to impart to non-official voluntary action the required degree of planning and continuity. The Lok Karya Kshetra, which corresponds to the area of an N.E.S. Block, would offer a common platform for voluntary bodies and bring about an integration of their various activities at the field level. The study of Lok Karya Kshetras undertaken by the Programme Evaluation Organisation has shown that workers in this programme are able in a special measure to bring intimate knowledge of the people and their problems to the task of mobilising local resources and manpower and overcoming such barriers to development as ignorance, factions and inadequate facilities for extension work in the villages. The approach is now being extended to urban areas also.

University Planning Forums are expected to play an increasing role during the Third Plan in bringing universities and colleges into closer contact with the larger community and in enabling teachers and students to contribute towards national development in constructive programmes undertaken in collaboration with panchayati raj institutions, municipal bodies and voluntary organisations. Studies and surveys undertaken during the Second Plan by teams constituted by planning forums have afforded useful opportunities to students and youth to gain insight into social and economic problems and valuable suggestions have been thrown up at seminars organised by planning forums from time to time. These and other activities will be further developed during the Third Plan. It is also hoped that planning forums may be able to organise Plan information centres which will help students to identify themselves more and more with the goals for which the nation will strive during the Third and subsequent Plans.

## TRAINING, RESEARCH AND EVALUATION

The tasks before the workers engaged in activities relating to public participation are by no means simple or easy. Their primary concern is to change the outlook of the people, win their confidence and stimulate them into new endeavour. They are faced with consider- able inertia and conflicting social forces at work. Complex social conditions and problems are encountered. To be able to do their part reasonably well, these workers must receive intensive training of a special kind. This aspect had been largely neglected till recently, when for the workers of the Lok Karya Kshetra programme, training facilities were provided on a regular basis. Training of part-time and whole-time workers from the village upward should be undertaken on systematic lines, so that they may be enabled to carry out their duties with an amount of skill and understanding.

To create a sound basis for training programmes and to develop suitable methods and techniques of public participation, the current experience should be subjected at intervals, to close study and analysis. Group discussions should also be organised for this purpose. There is a large scope for research into dynamics of social change, the attitudes of various groups towards problems and programmes placed before them, and the effectiveness of techniques employed for securing cooperation and participation of the people. Pilot projects to test new ideas should be taken up in different parts of the country. Facilities should be provided for evaluation of the activities of the voluntary organisations. The results of these studies and experiments should be embodied in suitable literature and guidance material.

# 9

# Community Development

## INTRODUCTION

When the first set of community projects were taken up nearly nine years ago, community development was described as the method and rural extension as the agency through which the transformation of the social and economic life of villages was to be initiated. During the intervening years the tasks to be accomplished by the community development movement and the national priorities to be realised through it have come to be more precisely defined. At the same time, the concept of rural extension has broadened into that of Panchayati Raj, that is to say, the development of a set of interconnected democratic and popular institutions at the village, block and district levels in which the representatives of the people in the Village Panchayats, Panchayat Samitis and Zila Parishads and co-operative organisations function with the support and assistance of the various development agencies of Government working together as a team. One of the principal tasks in the Third Plan will be to ensure the growth and working of Panchayati Raj institutions so as to enable each area to realise its maximum development potential on the basis of local man- power and other resources, co-operative self-help and community effort, and effective use of the available resources and personnel.

## REVIEW OF DEVELOPMENT

The community development programme now serves over 3,100 development blocks comprising about 370,000 villages. Of these, about 880 blocks have completed more than five years and entered the second stage of the community development programme. By October, 1963, the programme will extend over the entire rural area of the country. The total outlay on community development in the first two Plans has been about Rs. 240 crores. The Third Plan provides for a total outlay of Rs. 294 crores, in addition to about Rs. 28 crores for Panchayats.

In the course of the Second Plan, three important developments occurred in the community development programme. At the beginning of the Plan, work had been taken up in 950 development blocks of which about 370 were under the community projects scheme and about 580 under the national extension scheme. In the scheme of organisation prevailing at the time, every block was first taken up in the national extension service scheme, for which a programme budget of Rs. 450,000 was allotted. After a period, which extended from one to two years, a proportion of the national extension projects were taken up under the community development scheme for which the budget allotment was Rs. 15 lakhs. In this way the national extension and community development aspects were regarded as related phases of the same programme. The review undertaken in 1957 by the Study Team set up by the Committee on Plan Projects, led to the adoption of a single scheme of community development which was spread over two stages, each of five years. The first stage envisages a block budget of Rs. 12 lakhs, and the second of Rs. 5 lakhs. With these changes it was also decided to extend the period for covering the entire rural area by three years, from October, 1960 to October, 1963.

The second major development concerns the introduction of Panchayati Raj. For many years, the establishment of democratic institutions at the district and block levels, in addition to panchayats at the village level, was felt to be an essential and inevitable step if rural development was to proceed not only rapidly but largely on the basis of local effort and resources, This approach was broadly indicated in the First Plan. The Second Plan clearly visualised a well organised democratic structure of administration within the district in which the village panchayat would be organically linked with popular organisations at higher levels. Pending further study, the Plan offered interim proposals for setting up district development councils and also development committees in the blocks. The recommendations of the Study Team set up by the Committee on Plan Projects in favour of a system of 'democratic decentralisation' were considered by the National Development Council in January, 1958. The Council emphasised that the foundation of any democratic structure had to be democracy in the village. The two institutions which made effective village democracy possible were the village panchayat and the village cooperative.

The first step in any area should, therefore, be to establish the network of institutions needed at the village level. Democratic institutions at the district, block and village levels should be viewed as parts of one connected structure of development administration within the district. The Council, therefore, affirmed the objective of introducing democratic institutions at the district and block levels and suggested that each State should work out the structure which suited its conditions best. During the past three years, legislation for the introduction of Panchayati Raj has been enacted in Andhra Pradesh, Assam, Madras. Mysore, Orissa. Punjab and Rajasthan. In Madhya Pradesh and Uttar Pradesh legislation has been passed by the State Legislatures. In Bihar legislation is under consideration, and in Maharashtra and Gujarat proposals have been drawn up by special committees and their reports are being considered. These developments are the fruition of the general approach which has been regarded for the past ten years as basic to rural development under democratic conditions and constitute a most significant step forward.

A third aspect of community development work which has assumed considerable importance is the proposal that, along with the district, the block should serve as a unit of planning and development. It was suggested that in the following fields proposals for the Third Plan should be drawn up by States on the basis of district and block plans :

(1) agriculture, including minor irrigation, soil conservation, village forests, animal husbandry, dairying, etc. ;

(2) development of cooperatives;

(3) village industries;

(4) elementary education, specially provision of school buildings for local communities;

(5) rural water supply and the programme of minimum rural amenities, including construction of approach roads linking each village to the nearest road or rail-head; and

(6) works programmes for the fuller utilisation of manpower resources in rural areas.

Although efforts were made in several States to prepare block plans specially in agriculture, in the main, the plans of States have been prepared independently of local plans. The inference to be drawn from this is that much more effort will be needed before local plans can become a distinctive stage in the initial preparation of a Five Year Plan. In the present context of the Third Plan as formulated, what is important is that local plans should be worked out as a means for the more effective implementation of the State Plan.

Within the general framework of the district plan, the block plan is intended to include all social and economic activities undertaken within the block which call for (a) planning initiated locally at the block and village levels, and (b) coordination with the plans of various Departments which are implemented within the block. The following are the principal types of activities which will fall within the block plan :

(i) items in the schematic budget of the community development block according to the stage reached;

(ii) items included in the budgets of different Departments which can be executed through the block organisation:

(iii) works undertaken by the local community or beneficiaries in accordance with the obligations laid down by law;

(iv) works involving unskilled and semi-skilled labour undertaken in the block; and

(v) other activities undertaken in the block or by the block Organisation with a view to securing greater contribution from local communities in respect of development schemes in different fields.

The three aspects described above, namely, the extension functions of the community development organisation, introduction of democratic institutions, and the preparation and implementation of area and village plans, are closely related. For carrying out extension activities, each development block has a body of village level workers and a team of technical specialists in agriculture, animal husbandry, cooperation, rural industries and other fields functioning together under the leadership of the Block Development Officer. Supported and guided by senior specialists at the district level, these extension cadres serve the Panchayat Samitis in the Block and Panchayats and Gram Sabhas in the villages. They have to assist the elected representatives in preparing and implementing technically sound block and village plans on the basis of the widest possible participation on the part of local communities and the maximum use of local manpower and other resources.

## AGRICULTURAL EXTENSION

The principal extension functions entrusted to the community development organisation fall within the fields of agriculture, animal husbandry, cooperation and rural industries. It is to these that village level workers are expected to devote the bulk of their time and energy. In the Third Plan, the tasks to be accomplished in the fields of agriculture and cooperation are of formidable dimension. Agricultural production has to be raised by about 90 per cent, and large programmes of minor irrigation, utilisation of irrigation from both large and small irrigation schemes, soil conservation and dry farming, application of fertilisers and development of local manurial resources have to be carried out in the blocks. The programme for cooperation envisages a threefold increase in agricultural credit through cooperative agencies. Increase in agricultural production can only be achieved with the most intensive effort that can be organised at the village level. Increase in cooperative credit also demands the strengthening of the cooperative movement at the base, bringing all families in the village into the cooperative, and ensuring that credit is linked both with production and with marketing.

Thus, the basic problem in the rebuilding of the rural economy at present is the organisation of the agricultural effort at the village level. In the measure in which progress is achieved in mobilising the village community for increasing production, every other problem in the rural areas becomes easier of solution and more intensive development can be undertaken in other directions, specially rural industry and the provision of social services. The growth of agricultural production is of such critical importance that, in the immediate context of the Third Plan, the principal test to be met by the community development movement must be its practical effectiveness as an agricultural extension agency. It is, therefore, essential for the community development Organisation to take all steps necessary to strengthen itself in this respect, and to accept responsibility for achieving the targets of agricultural production on the basis of the largest possible local effort. At the same time, it is incumbent on the Agriculture Departments and other Departments concerned with agricul- tural production that they must place at the disposal of the community development organisation at the district and block levels, the necessary expert supervision and guidance and the supplies, trained manpower and other resources needed.

## VILLAGE PRODUCTION PLANS

The principal means for involving all cultivators in the village in the agricultural effort and mobilising effectively the resources of the local community is the. village production plan. The main elements in agricultural production programme at the village level are :

(i) full utilisation of irrigation facilities, including maintenance of field channels in good condition by the beneficiaries, repairs and maintenance of community irrigation works and economy in the use of water;

(ii) increase in the area under multiple cropping;

(iii) multiplication in the village of improved seed and its distribution to all cultivators;

(iv) supply of fertilisers;

(v) programme for composting and green manures;

(vi) adoption of improved agricultural practices, such as, soil conservation, contour-bunding, dry farming, drainage, land reclamation, plant protection, etc. ;

(vii) programme for new minor irrigation works to be undertaken in the village, both through community participation and on an individual basis;

(viii) programme for the introduction of improved agricultural implements;

(ix) programme for increasing the production of vegetables and fruits;

(x) programme for the development of poultry, fish and dairy products,

(xi) animal husbandry, e.g. maintenance of stud bulls and castration of scrub bulls, etc. ; and

(xii) programme for the development of the village fuel plantations and pastures.

The village production plan includes two main groups of programmes, namely; (a) supply of credit, fertilisers, improved seed, assistance for plant protection. minor irrigation, etc. for which a measure of assistance has to come from outside the village, and (b) programmes such as the digging of field channels for utilising irriga- tion from large projects, maintenance of bunds and field channels, contour bunding, digging and maintenance of village tanks, development and utilisation of local manurial resources, village fuel plantations, etc, which call for effort on the part of the village community or the beneficiaries.

The success of the village production plan will largely depend on the efficient organisation of supplies, credit, etc. and the quality of the technical advice given by extension workers. In the measure in which these services are provided, there will be greater enthusiasm and cooperation from the village community in the second group of programmes mentioned above.

In June, 1960, the Ministry of Community Development and Cooperation forwarded proposals to State Governments on these lines, and a number of States have since issued similar instructions. It cannot, however, be said that village production plans are yet established as a normal method of work in agricultural development or that the various practical problems involved have been resolved. In the field of extension, by far the most important task to be undertaken in pursuance of the Third Plan is to give effect to the idea of working out village production plans so as to draw all the cultivators into the common effort and, at the same time, to make, available to individual farmers in an efficient and organised manner the credit, supplies and other assistance needed. The Third Plan devotes considerable resources to minor irrigation and soil conservation, supplies of fertilisers on a large scale have been assured, and resources have been provided for plant protection, improved agricultural implements and other schemes. The programme for setting up seed farms is in an advanced stage and it should now be somewhat easier to arrange for the multiplication in the village of the quantities of improved seed required. Thus, the Third Plan provides for the various factors required for the successful execution of village production plans.

## PANCHAYATI RAJ

The establishment of democratic institutions at the district and block levels and the role assigned to the Gram Sabha and the Village Panchayat constitute fundamental and far-reaching changes in the structure of district administration and in the pattern of rural development. Their significance lies in the fact that, subject to guidance and supervision by the State Government, the responsibility for the implementation of rural development programmes will now belong to the Block Panchayat Samiti working with Panchayats in the villages and the Zila Parishad at the district level. These institutions have not been at work long enough to permit more than a preliminary statement of the problems which are likely to require careful attention, In considering these, certain aspects deserve to be stressed. The primary object of Panchayati Raj is to enable the people of each area to achieve intensive and continuous development in the interest of the entire population. The elected representatives should be encouraged to value the development of Panchayati Raj as offering new avenues of service to the people rather than opportunities for the exercise of authority. The concept of Panchayati Raj is not limited to the non-official and democratic organisations associated with it. Representing, as it does. a distinct level of responsibility and functions within the general scheme of administration, Panchayati Raj comprehends both the democratic institutions and the extension services through which development programmes are executed.

Extension personnel at the block and village levels, although functioning within the jurisdiction of the Panchayat Samiti, form part of a larger administrative and technical network, which extends to the district and even beyond it. It is vital to the permanent success of Panchayati Raj that the integrity of the structure of technical and administrative services provided by Government and their ability to fulfil the duties and responsibilities cast upon them should be fully ensured, while their knowledge and experience are made available to the elected bodies at the district and block levels. It is also of the highest importance that there should be clear recognition of the distinct role of federal cooperative organisations functioning at the State and district levels, as in the field of banking, marketing , processing, distribution and education and training. Large obligations are undertaken by various cooperative organisations and they should be enabled to fulfil them in accordance with the approach and principles of the cooperative movement. The economic development of rural areas is still in its beginnings and large possibilities lie ahead. It is the object of the new institutions and relationships now being established to help each area to realise these possibilities to the utmost limits of its resources. From this aspect the following are among the main tests by which the success of Panchayati Raj will need to be measured from time to time :

(1) agricultural production as the highest national priority during the Third Plan;

(2) development of rural industry;

(3) development of cooperative institutions;

(4) full utilisation of the local manpower and other resources;

(5) development of facilities for education and audlt literacy;

(6) optimum utilisation of resources available to Panchayati Raj institutions such as finance, personnel, technical assistance and other facilities from higher levels, and efforts by them to raise their own resources;

(7) assistance to the economically weaker sections of the village community;

(8) progressive dispersal of authority and initiative with special emphasis on the role of voluntary organisations;

(9) understanding and harmony between elected representatives and public servants to be achieved through comprehensive training in education and a clear demarcation of duties and responsibilities, and progressive increase in competence both among officials and non-officials, and

(10) cohesion and mutual self-help within the community.

From the limited experience gained so far, the following suggestions are offered for ensuring the effective and successful working of Panchayati Raj Institutions:

(1) while developing institutions at the higher levels. the greatest stress should continue to be Laid on the work of the Gram Sabha and the Panchayat at the village level. It is at the village level that the efforts of the people have to be mobilised and there is the largest scope for securing community action. Both on the part of the Gram Sabha and the Village Panchayat the approach of unanimity or near unanimity should be encouraged, so that various activities are undertaken with the general consent and goodwill of the community.

(2) technical officers at the district level should endeavour to make their advice and assistance available to extension officers at the block level and to the Panchayat Samitis for the initial preparation of programmes and schemes before decisions are taken. In turn, Panchayat Samitis should seek and welcome such assistance since

a considerable proportion of extension personnel at the block level are necessarily without adequate experience, but can render better service if they receive the necessary guidance and help from officials at the district level.

(3) the manner in which the block extension team, comprising the Block Development Officer and Extension Officers in different fields of development, functions is of the highest importance for the success of Panchayati Raj. To assist the Panchayat Samiti effectively, these officials must continue to function as a team, the Block Development Officer providing the necessary co-ordination and leadership, and Extension Officers in different fields participating actively in formulating programmes and schemes for the consideration of the Panchayat Samiti and its Standing Committees, executing them impartially in accordance with the rules, and ensuring that the supplies and services needed are organised efficiently. Adequate supervision over the work of the village level workers is essential. Care should be taken to see that the Block Development Officer and the Extension Officers undertake extensive touring within the block and are not tied up excessively with discussions at headquarters.

(4) in the work of Panchayat Samitis, the main stress should be on the preparation and implementation of carefully considered block plans. These, alongwith village plans, provide the essential means for securing intensive and continuous development. Block and village plans, which are technically well-conceived, will go a long way to counteract ad hoc decisions and local pressures.

(5) the introduction of Panchayati Raj enhances greatly the responsibility of the technical departments at the State level. They should transmit the best guidance and experience available in each field of development, provide for adequate training programmes for the elected represen- tatives, and assist them generally in fulfilling the onerous responsibilities which Panchayati Raj places on them.

(6) the Collector of the district will continue to have a large share of responsibility in facilitating the success of Panchayati Raj Institutions. He has the duty of ensuring coordination at the district level between the Zila Parishad and the technical officers in different fields, close contacts between the latter and the Panchayat Samitis and Extension Officers at the block level, and a continuing flow of technical advice and guidance from departments at the State level. An important aspect of the Collector's work will be to assist democratic institutions and the public services in developing the right conventions in day-today work and in administrative relation- ship based on recognition of their distinctive contribution in fulfilling common objectives.

For the effective implementation of the programme of community development, several technical Departments have to work together in a coordinated manner. If the vast majority of cultivators are to be assisted to utilise the results of research and to practise scientific agriculture, adequate assistance in the form of technical advice and supplies of improved implements, seeds, fertilisers and credit must reach them at the right time.

It is essential for the success of these complex but vital programmes that the responsibility of all official agencies and organisations concerned should be properly defined and there should be no ambiguity in the responsibility of the higher technical officers to provide the necessary guidance and supervision. In other words, in these matters, an uninterrupted line of responsibility reaching down to the village units should be assured.

While the responsibility of the official agency is defined and enforced as above, the functions of non-official leaders should be:

(i) to mobilise public participation and promote the acceptance of programmes by the people.

(ii) to assist village panchayats and cooperatives in their work;

(iii) to assist in training programmes for village leaders and others;

(iv) to organise programmes for the benefit of the community, using local man-power resources, and

(v) to promote the welfare of the weaker sections.

## RATIONALISATION OF DISTRICT ADMINISTRATION

The introduction of Panchayati Raj raises the wider question of the reorganisation of district administration. It is not generally realised that over the past decade changes in district administration have been somewhat haphazard. When the community development programme was taken up, the extension organisation had to be superimposed on the traditional district administration without adequate connecting links. The consequence is that in many districts the following organisations are working on parallel lines with their activities largely uncoordinated :

(i) the revenue administration which looks after certain specified development functions, such as taccavi advances, recoveries, etc. ;

(ii) the established Development Departments at the district, taluka and other levels,

(iii) the community development organisation with block officers and village level workers, linked at the village level with panchayats and cooperatives; and

(iv) Local Boards (where these have not yet been abolished).

With the introduction of Panchayati Raj, the functions of Panchayat Samitis include both community development activities and several activities hitherto entrusted to Local Boards. In the nature of things, there is still considerable overlapping which calls for some measure of rationalisation in district administration and fresh definition of functions and relationships.

## WEAKER SECTIONS AND THE PROBLEM OF EMPLOYMENT

From time to time evaluation reports on the community development programme have drawn attention to the fact that the benefits did not reach the less privileged sections if the village community in adequate measure. Recent studies report a degree of improvement in this respect. A study group set up by the Ministry of Community Development and Cooperation is at present engaged in considering how far and in what manner the community development pro- gramme can promote the economic development and welfare of the weaker sections of the community. The problem should be seen in the broader context of development within the rural economy. The welfare of weaker sections is closely related to that of the village community as a whole, and in a sense a large part of the village community consists of those who may be described as being economically weak. The main weaknesses of the present village economy are low income, low productivity and lack of continuous employment. Without the rural economy as a whole growing rapidly enough, it is difficult to solve the problem either of the community in the village or of its weaker sections. The essential aim must be to bring about a more productive agricultural economy and a larger range of non- agricultural occupations in the village so as to increase production and employment and, at the same time, much greater attention should be given in all activities to the needs of the less privileged sections.

In the efforts which have been made over the past three years to secure greater coordination between the community development and Gramdan movements, their common objectives have been emphasised. These include the acceptance by the village community of responsi- bility for the welfare, employment and livelihood of all its members. This is of the greatest importance from the point of view of the weaker sections in the village.

The block organisation can render useful service by assisting the implementation of the land reform legislation which has been al- ready enacted by creating public opinion and educating the people in their rights and obligations. Other measures which the block organisation can take to the immediate advantage of the weaker sections of the population are to increase subsidiary employment in the villages, raise the productivity of village industries and of village artisans, organise labour cooperatives, and promote the fullest possible utilisation of the manpower resources of the area. The programme of rural works leading to employment opportunities by the last year of the Third Plan for about 2.5 million persons specially during the slack agricultural seasons, will be implemented to a large extent through community development organisations. The programme will be extended first to areas with heavy pressure of population and considerable under-employment, and later to other areas. This programme should afford an opportunity of the highest value not only for providing additional employment, but also for implementing the community development programme with fresh emphasis on the maximum possible utilisation of local manpower resources and effort and participation on the part of local communities.

# 10

# Agricultural Labour

## REVIEW OF PROGRESS

To bring about improvements in the economic conditions of agricultural labourers and to remove the social disabilities from which they have suffered in the past are among the major tasks of planned development. The two principal problems are the place of agricultural labour in the future rural economy and provision of work. In the past the village economy was rooted in a scheme of stratification largely based on caste and occupation. As a result of various measures of social reform and the efforts made since Independence, the social handicaps associated with agricultural labourers, and with backward classes generally, have greatly diminished. At the same time, the economic problems of these sections of the population, especially the need for larger opportunities for work, have been thrown into sharper relief. It is one of the primary objects of the Five Year Plans to ensure fuller opportunities for work and a better living to all sections of the rural community and, in particular, to assist agricultural labourers and the backward classes to come up to the level of the rest. Their problems undoubtedly constitute a challenge, and the obligation rests upon the community as a whole to find satisfactory solutions for them.

The size of the problem of agricultural labour varies from region to region, depending on such factors as pressure of population, availability of land for cultivation, differences in the extent of irrigation and double cropping, fertility of lnad, cropping patterns and opportunities available for seasonal migration and for employment outside agriculture. However, the broad features can be discerned from the results of the two all-India Agricultural Labour Enquiries undertaken in 1950-51 and 1956-57 and the surveys of the Programme Evaluation Organisation. The concepts in the two Agricultural Labour Enquiries were different to some extent and the data are not wholly comparable. Generalisations for the, country as a whole have also several limitations. What both Enquiries bring out is the enormous size of the problem, the widespread underemployment that exists, and the fact that increase in population has borne harshly on this section of the population. These general conclusions are also reflected in the results of bench mark surveys undertaken by the Programme Evaluation Organisation.

The problem of agricultural labourers is part of the wider problem of unemployment and under-employment in rural areas. Even though, with the development of agriculture and irrigation, there has been increase in production and in the total volume of work, this is shared among much larger numbers. Those sections of the rural population who are landless and are not actual cultivators have benefited much less than others; in some areas their conditions may have actually worsened. The basic problems of the rural economy are low income, low productivity and lack of continuous employment. To the extent these problems are solved through the more intensive programmes of development to be implemented in the Third Plan, the economic conditions and prospects of agricultural labourers should also improve. It has, however, been always realised that the various programmes for the development of the rural economy, which are undertaken in the interest of the rural population as a whole must be supplemented in several directions by special measures for assisting agricultural labourers in improving their living conditions and obtaining a fair share of the wider opportunities which are now being developed in the villages through the community development and other programmes.

The First Five Year Plan included proposals for the settlement of agricultural labour and protection against ejectment from homesteads. Not much progress was made in schemes for land resettlement. The Minimum Wages Act, 1948, was applied to employment in agriculture. Experience shows that levels of agricultural wages are bound up to a considerable extent with increases in levels of agricultural productivity and the greater use of money as the medium of exchange. Accordingly, it was decided that in enforcing minimum wages, the first attention should be given to low wage pockets in different States, and these should be identified,

In the Second Five Year Plan, in addition to programmes of development, in agriculture and irrigation and the expansion of the community development programme, Rs. 200 crores were provided for the development of village and small industries. In rural programmes high priority was suggested for schemes intended to benefit the weaker sections of the population like agricultural labourers and artisans and others. The Plan also envisaged a number of special schemes for the benefit of agricultural labourers, including schemes for resettlement, grant of house-sites, formation of labour cooperatives, etc. In September, 1957, the National Development Council proposed that from lands obtained through the application of agricultural ceilings and those donated in Bhoodan and Gramdan, a programme for resettling 300,000 families of landless workers should be undertaken. Legislation regarding ceilings was still in its early stages, and the scheme could not be implemented in the form proposed. However, individual States continued with the resettlement schemes which they had formulated, and, a number of these were assisted by the Central Government. In some States, notably Punjab, Bombay, Andhra Pradesh and Bihar, labour cooperatives were promoted,

About 10,000 families were settled in Bihar on Bhoodan lands under two schemes for which the Central Government provided assistance. Assistance was also provided for developing a number of Gramdan villages in Orissa. Of the total area of 4.4 million acres donated as Bhoodan, about 900,000 acres have been distributed so far. Difficulties regarding the title to the lands donated and other procedural and organisational matters account for the slow progress.

During the Second Plan, a number of State Governments took steps to provide house-sites free or on a subsidised basis to landless agricultural labourers and protected them from forced ejectment. In Andhra Pradesh, house-sites granted to bona fide applicants, preference being given to those who own no sites. In Madhya Pradesh, land for house-sites is net aside generally in the village abadi and, if there is some Government land , it is allotted free of any premium and assessment. In Madras, Government wastelands in the villages are assigned to persons without houses. Where Government lands are not available for assignment as house-sites to 'Harijans' and others, the sites on which they are actually living or some other suitable sites are acquired and assigned free of cost to those who do not own a house or a house-site. The Government of Maharashtra have directed that ordinarily the provision of house-sites should take precedence over other uses of land situated close to the village. It is further provided that house-sites required by agricultural families should be granted by the Collector to agriculturists upto two gunthas in area and up to the value of Rs. 200. In Mysore, if no Government land is available for the grant of house-sites, private land is acquired on payment of compensation and allotted to the agriculturists for house- sites. In the Punjab, schemes have been formulated under which subsidies are given to landless persons for purchase of land and for securing suitable house-sites.

## PROGRAMMES IN THE THIRD PLAN

It is apparent from the experience of the first two Plans that while special schemes in the interest of agricultural labourers are useful, they can touch only the fringe of the problem. Ultimately, it is by achieving rapid and intensive development in the rural areas as part of the process of economic development for the country as a whole that the landless sections of the population can be substantially benefited. The Third Plan provides for large investments in the development of the rural economy. The total outlays in the public sector on agriculture, community development and irrigation will amount to over Rs. 1700 crores. Agricultural production is expected to increase by about 30 per cent. About 20 million acres of land will be benefited by irrigation and 11 million acres of agricultural land will come under soil conservation.

In the village and small industries programme, there is a total provision of Rs. 92 crores for khadi, ambar khadi and village industries and small scale industries and industrial estates will be extended to rural areas. All towns and villages with population exceeding 5000 and nearly 50 per cent of villages with a population range of 2000 to 5000 are expected to be electrified. If effective use is made of these facilities considerable additional employment will be created. The village and small industry programme as a whole is estimated to provide part-time employment or fuller employment for 8 million persons and whole-time employment for about 900,000 persons. Given full implementation of the Plan, these figures are by no means the limit of what can be achieved.

Through the extension of educational facilities to the entire age group 6-11 years and the development of other social services, some of the handicaps of the weaker sections will diminish. A village water supply programme at a total cost of Rs. 35 crores is being taken up with the object of providing good drinking water in all villages by the end of the Third Plan. The Plan includes programmes estimated to cost Rs. 114 crores for the welfare of backward classes. A considerable part of this amount will benefit agricultural workers.

In the, community development programme, the emphasis must always be on undertaking development which will benefit the weaker sections. Under the village housing project scheme, Rs. 5 crores have been allotted for the acquisition of land in villages foe allotment as house-sites to agricultural labourers. Thus, to a very large extent it is through the effective implementation of these various programmes and ensuring that their benefits reach the agricultural labourers and the backward sections generally that the conditions will improve. In a word, the Plan itself, implemented efficiently and with close attention to its basic social and economic aims, is the largest part of the answer to the problem of agricultural labourers and the weaker sections of the rural community.

The plans of States provide for about Rs. 4 crores for resettlement schemes. It may be expected that when surplus lands become available as a result of the imposition of ceilings, such additional resources as are required for their settlement by landless persons and others will be made available by the States through the annual plans. In addition at the Centre a sum of Rs. 8 crores has been allocated for resettle- ment schemes for landless labourers. A committee set up by the Government of India has recently surveyed lands classified as "other uncultivated lands excluding fallow lands" and "fallow lands other than current fallows", and has identified nearly a million acres of land in blocks of over 250 acres. When blocks of less than 250 acres are surveyed by district authorities, further areas should become available. These, together with the land to be reclaimed under agricultural programmes are expected to amount to about 4 million acres. The Central Advisory Committee on Agricultural Labour recently set up by the Planning Commission visualises that efforts will be made to settle about 700,000 families of landless labourers in the course of the Third Plan over an area of 5 million acres. This goal should be kept in view and lands suitable for resettlement identified to make such a programme feasible. In this connection, it will be necessary to extend surveys of lands fit for settlement to the block and village level. Wherever there is opportunity for settlement, this should be utilised, even though only a small number of families may be benefited in each case. Where land is allotted, steps should be taken to provide credit and other assistance, so that the persons settled are able to rehabilitate themselves effectively.

In some ways the most significant development proposed in the Third Plan. whose benefits will go largely to agricultural labour, is the programme for undertaking works projects in rural areas which has been described earlier in the Chapter on "Employment and Manpower". Under this programme, it is hoped to provide additional wage-employment in rural areas for about 100 days in the year, specially during the slack agricultural seasons, for about 2.5 million persons by the last year of the Plan. The programme will specially concentrate on schemes for agricultural development like irrigation, flood control, land reclamation, afforestation and soil conservation, road development projects, provision of rural amenities and village housing projects. In the rural works programme. labour co-operatives and other construction organisations will have a large role. They will be expected to carry stocks of tools, obtain contracts, organise the necessary cadres and work closely with panchayat samitis and panchayats. A permanent solution to the problem of under-employment can be achieved only when scientific agriculture comes to be universally adopted and the rural economic structure is greatly strengthened and diversified. Efforts in these directions will also be intensified during the Third Plan. Meanwhile, the large-scale programme of rural works will provide considerable relief and will help to accelerate the pace of development in rural areas.

In a real sense, the problems of agricultural labour are to be traced to the long period of stagnation in the rural economy and the persistence of a rigid social structure largely based on caste. These basic deficiencies are being gradually removed, and the processes of social and technological change have to be hastened. Successive Five Year Plans seek to harness the natural resources of the country, increase production and employment, and provide greater amenities to rural areas. Reorganisation of the rural economy along co-operative lines and emphasis on the role and obligations of the community are intended not merely to raise agricultural productivity and diversify the rural economic structure but, equally, to bring about as rapidly as may be possible an integrated society in which there will be equal opportunity for every member of the community irrespective of caste or status. In other words, in the structure of the rural economy which the Five Year Plans attempt to build up, agricultural labourers will participate fully and on equal terms with others, and will achieve effective economic and social equality with the rest of the rural population. A close watch on the progress actually achieved in these directions should be maintained through special studies and evaluation and review by the Central Advisory Committee on Agricultural Labour and similar bodies proposed to be set up in the States.

# 11

# Irrigation and Power

Irrigation and power have been among the most significant fields of development since the beginning of the First Plan. Expansion of irrigation, from large as well as small projects, is an essential condition for diversifying agriculture and increasing crop yields. The development of power is a prerequisite for carrying out large industrial programmes. River valley projects like Bhakra-Nangal, Hirakud, Chambal. Tungabhadra, Nagarjunasagar and the D.V.C., which provide both irrigation and power, have, along with other programmes of development, a leading role in establishing higher levels of well- being in the regions served by them. Thus, large-scale development of irrigation and power, helps to re-build the agricultural economy and to pave the way for the rapid industrialisation of the country.

## IRRIGATION

The available river water resources of the country were computed in 1950 at about 1356 million acre feet, of which it is estimated that because of physiographical conditions, only about 450 million acre feet can be used for irrigation. Up to 1951, about 76 million acre feet, i.e. about 17 per cent of the usable flow or 5.6 per cent of the total annual flow, had been utilised. By the end of the Second Plan, it is estimated that about 120 million acre feet representing about 27 per cent of the usable flow or 8.9 per cent of the total annual flow will be utilised. An additional 40 million acre feet are likely to be used in the Third Plan, bringing the proportion to about 36 per cent of the usable flow.

Substantial supplies are available from ground water sources. No inventory of these resources has been prepared so far, but a Ground Water Exploration Project was started in 1953 to carry out exploratory drillings in areas which held out promise of ground water availability, namely, inland river basins, coastal fringes, etc. Generally sneaking, the Indo-Gangetic basin. the Sabarmati basin and coastal area in Madras and Andhra Pradesh offer favourable scope for ground water development. Ground water can be utilised for irrigating areas which cannot be economically irrigated by canals, or which are susceptible to water-logging.

Land utilisation at the end of the First Plan was as follows:

| | (million acres) |
|---|---|
| gross area | 806 |
| culturable area | 476 |
| net area sown | 318 |
| area sown more than once | 45 |
| total cropped area | 363 |
| net area irrigated*: | |
| government canals | 19.8 |
| private canals | 3.4 |
| tanks | 10.9 |
| tubewells and other wells | 16.7 |
| other sources | 5.4 |
| total 56.2 say | 56 |
| area irrigated more than once | 7 |
| gross area irrigated** | 63 |

At the beginning of the First Plan, the area irrigated from all sources was 51.5 million acres, of which 22 million acres were irrigated from large and medium projects. It has been estimated that by the end of the Fifth Plan (1975-76), it might be possible to bring about 85 million acres (gross) under irrigation from large and medium projects including multipurpose projects. In formulating proposals for the Third Plan, this long-range goal has been kept in view. The overall ultimate irrigation potentialities from major @ and medium irrigation projects are expected to be about 100 million acres (gross) and from minor irrirgation including small tanks, tubewells, open wells, etc., about 75 million acres (gross).

Major and medium schemes benefit large and extensive areas, give more assured protection in years of scarcity and also can often be designed to serve a multiplicity of purposes. Minor schemes require comparatively small outlays, yield quick results and can be executed speedily with local resources. But the protection afforded by them is liable to be substantially cut short in drought years when protection is needed most. In particular, tanks fail to store water when there is failure of rainfall in the locality. Balanced development of major and medium irrigation schemes and minor irrigation schemes is essential as they from part of a composite irrigation programme. Each area has to be served by the kind of schemes for which it is best suited, and which will give the best results at minimum cost.

Development of irrigation.-The progress of irrigation up to the end of the First and Second Plans and the targets for the Third Plan.

## FIRST AND SECOND PLAN SCHEMES

The aggregate estimated cost of major and medium irrigation schemes included in the First and Second Plans is of the order of Rs. 1,400 crores, and on full development, they are expected to irrigate about 38 million acres. By the end of the First Plan. an outlay of Rs. 380 crores had been incurred on these schemes. The outlay on them in the Second Plan is estimated at Rs. 370 crores. In the Third Plan, these schemes will require a total outlay of about Rs. 436 crores, leaving a balance of about Rs. 214 crores for the Fourth Plan. Some of the projects such as the Rajasthan Canal, Gandak, Ukai, Narmada, Nagarjunasagar, etc., will continue beyond the Third Plan.

Irrigation benefits accruing from the First and Second Plan schemes, at the end of the First Plan, and during the Second Plan are given in the Table below:

In the Second Plan, it was proposed to bring under irrigation an additional area of 12 million acres from major and medium projects. When the Plan was reviewed in 1958, this was reduced to 10.4 million acres. The additional utilisation, as now estimated by States, is expected to be 6.9 million acres (gross). As against the outlay originally envisaged for the Second Plan, the actual outlay is about Rs. 370 crores. In several States, the programmes lagged behind on account of inadequacy of technical personnel. In some cases, progress was retarded owing to short supplies of essential materials, such as steel, cement, coal, etc. Also, in the past, under pressure of local or regional demands, some projects have been commenced despite incomplete investigations and inadequate surveys, and this has resulted in these projects lingering on with consequent delay in accrual of benefits from them. Increases in wages and costs of materials have also led to a reduction in the physical achievement anticipated from the outlay. There has been an improvement in the pace of utilisation in the Second Plan as will be seen from Table 2. Larger results, however, could have been achieved if greater attention had been given to the timely excavation of field channels** and demonstration to the cultivators, in advance, of improved techniques of agriculture and the most suitable cropping pattern to be adopted on irrigation facilities becoming available. In the course of the prepa- ration of the Third Plan, considerable emphasis has been placed on the strengthening of technical organisations and on taking such other steps as would ensure that progress during the Plan period is not hampered.

## PROGRAMME FOR THE THIRD PLAN

It is essential to secure maximum benefits in the shortest time from the large investments that are being made on irrigation projects. It is also important to ensure that the benefits which accrue from these projects are not diminished through deterioration of land due to water-logging and inadequate drainage or other causes. Emphasis has, therefore, been given in the Third Plan to the following categories of schemes :

(1) completion of continuing schemes of the Second Plan right up to the cultivators' fields, i.e., including field channels ;

(2) drainage and anti-waterlogging schemes and

(3) medium irrigation projects.

The total irrigation potential remaining to be utilised at the end of the Second Plan is 3.2 million acres. During the Third Plan, additional irrigation potential of about 13.8 million acres is expected to be created from continuing schemes and 2.4 million acres from new schemes of the Third Plan. The total utilisation in the Third Plan period is expected to be 12.8 million acres (gross). The State-wise distribution of irrigation pontential and utilisation is shown in Annexure I, in making, this assessment, the States have generally assumed full utilisation within a period of five years in the case of major projects, and within two to three years in the case of medium projects, from the time water becomes available at outlets of channels. It should be possible in several projects, through closer coordination of efforts in connected fields to do better.

The cost of the irrigation and flood control programme during the Third Plan is Rs. 661 crores. This includes Rs. 436 crores for irrigation projects carried over from the Second Plan, Rs. 164 crores for new projects and Rs. 61 crores for flood control, drainage, anti- waterlogging and anti-sea-erosion schemes. The State-wise distribution is given in Annexures II and III. The new projects to be commenced during the Third Plan include:

(1) about 95 new medium irrigation schemes which will be of value both for agricultural and for regional development ;

(2) storage schemes on the Beas in the Punjab undertaken as a result of the conclusion of The Indus Water Treaty 1960; and

(3) schemes representing the irrigation component of multi-purpose projects taken up primarily for power development, and those necessitated by irrigation programmes undertaken in neighbouring States, for instance, work on the Gandak Project in Uttar Pradesh.

The position in regard to phasing of expenditure on First, Second and Third Plan irrigation schemes.

Flood-control, drainage, anti-waterlogging and anti-sea-erosion schemes.-Flood control, drainage and anti-water-logging are closely related to irrigation, and have to be viewed together in drawing up comprehensive development plans. At the time of the preparation of the Second Plan, sufficient data had not been collected for preparing detailed proposals for flood control for inclusion in the Plans of States. The flood control programme was, in fact, taken up on an emergency basis, and was, therefore, treated as a Centrally sponsored programme. The flood control programme is now well under way and considerable progress has been made in surveys and investigations. In the Third Plan, therefore, flood control schemes, together with drainage, anti-waterlogging and anti-sea-erosion schemes form part of the Plans of States.

The importance of providing adequate drainage in irrigated areas to prevent their deterioration by rising ground water table and consequent waterlogged conditions has already been emphasised earlier. The cost of drainage works in irrigated areas in the case of continuing and new schemes has to be included in the project costs of these irrigation schemes. Waterlogging in certain parts of the country, particularly in the Punjab, has become serious, and anti- waterlogging measures such as drains, lining of irrigation channels in selected reaches, and other steps to depress the ground water table, have to be taken up in the Third Plan on an extensive scale. Similarly, anti-sea-erosion measures in certain coastal reaches, such as Kerala have to be given due attention. An outlay of Rs. 60 crores was provided in the Second Plan for flood control schemes. The actual expenditure is about Rs. 48 crores. In the Third Plan, flood control, drainage, anti-waterlogging and anti-sea-erosion schemes involving an outlay of Rs. 61 crores have been provided for in the Plans of States.

The programme for Irrigation. in the Third Plan, which includes flood control, drainage, anti-waterlogging and anti-sea- erosion, entails a total estimated outlay of Rs. 661 crores.

Soil conservation in river valley catchments.-Large sums of money are being invested in creating storage reservoirs for irrigation and power generation. It is important that the life of these reservoirs is not unduly shortened by excessive flows of silt and sediment from the catchment areas. Also, soil cover in the catchment area has to be conserved. These considerations make it imperative that adequate soil conservation measures comprising afforestation, contour bunding, terracing, gully plugging, construction of check dams, regulation of grazing prevention of shifting cultivation, etc., should be undertaken in these catchments. Taking only the larger river valley projects, viz. Bhakra-Nangal, D.V.C., Hirakud, Chambal and Machkund, the total catchment area for these is about 37 million acres, of which more than 15 million acres require soil conservation measures.

The programme has also to be extended to other river valleys. In the projects mentioned above, an area of about 1.4 lakh acres has been covered by soil conservation programme undertaken up to the end of the Second Plan at a cost of about Re. 1 crore. In the Third Plan, an outlay of Rs. 11 crores has been provided under "Agriculture" for soil conservation works in river valley areas and about a million acres of catchment area are expected to be covered. The programme of soil conservation is necessarily of a longterm character to be completed over four or five Plan periods. Administrative responsibility for this programme at the Centre rests with the Ministry of Food and Agriculture and the Central Water and Power Commission have set up a special unit for examining and advising on soil conservation schemes for river valley catchments received from the State Governments. The establishment of River Boards, to which reference is made later, will facilitate speedy implementation of the soil conservation programme. It will be one of their main functions to coordinate programmes of afforestation and control of soil erosion in inter-State river valleys.

Phasing of projects.-It is of utmost importance that projects should be correctly phased. This will lead to economy in construction costs and will also make it possible to secure the maximum use of irrigation facilities created, even before the actual completion of each project. It will also prevent unnecessary locking up of capital on items of work in advance of actual need. There are four aspects connected with planning for irrigation works which are interlinked and these should be appropriately coordinated from the time a project is first approved. These are :

(1) construction of the dam or barrage for storing or diverting water;

(2) construction of the canal and distributary system ending with definite and convenient points of offtake for individual villages ;

(3) completion by beneficiaries, according to a time schedule coordinated with (2) above. of field chanels in every village so as to irrigate the entire area to be served by the project as water becomes available in the canals; and

(4) adoption of improved agricultural practices and new crop patterns, so that the maximum agricultural output is secured from efficient use of irrigation facilities.

Careful coordination in planning and execution between these different stages will ensure that phase by phase under each project effective results are obtained.

## FINANCIAL RETURNS

Irrigation works constructed in recent years and those under construction at present, are much more expensive than works built in the past, partly on account of higher costs of labour and materials and partly on account of the more difficult and, therefore, more expensive means of making supplies available. viz., high dams, etc. For this reason, and also on account of the increased cost of maintenance and operation of old and new projects, adequate returns are not being secured. In consequence, irrigation systems are at present working at a loss in almost all States. The Second Finance Commission drew attention to the deterioration which had occurred in the net receipts from irrigation projects. The position has even worsened in recent years. Special steps to bring about substantial improvements in financial returns are, therefore, urgently called for along the following lines :

(1) speeding up utilisation of irrigation faci- lities created by irrigation projects;

(2) revision of water rates and introduction of compulsory water cess;

(3) recovery of betterment levy ; and

(4) economy in the use of irrigation supplies.

Utilisation of irrigation involves efforts by a number of departments, each of which has a distinct contribution to make, e.g. Irrigation, Revenue, Agriculture, Community Development, Cooperation, etc. Besides proper phasing of the construction programme of each project, including construction of field channels, a large number of other developmental activities have to be carried out simultaneously for speeding up utilisation. These aspects are considered further later in the chapter.

**Water Rates.** Water rates should ordinarily cover working expenses and debt charges and, outside scarcity areas, irrigation schemes should not involve loss to general revenues. The existing water rates in most States are relatively low. While there has been considerable increase in the value of crops produced as a result of irrigation, and maintenance costs have also greatly increased, there has not been commensurate increase in the water rates. On the whole, therefore, these require upward revision. Further, in States, where water charges are optional, there should be a compulsory water cess leviable on the entire area for which irrigation facilities are provided, irrespective of whether water is taken by cultivators or not This itself will be a factor in inducing cultivators to make timely use of water, thereby promoting increased crop yields.

**Betterment Levy and Flood Cess.** Legislation for betterment levy has already been enacted in all States except Uttar Pradesh, West Bengal and Jammu and Kashmir. Recoveries at the prescribed rates are spread over a period of 15 to 20 years and commence two or three years after irrigation waters become available. Almost everywhere, enforcement of the legislation has lagged behind, and the actual realisations in the Second Plan are expected to be only Rs. 3.5 crores against the initial estimate of Rs. 47 crores. As regards flood-

cess, the Governments of Andhra Pradesh, Assam, Bihar, Jammu and Kashmir, Kerala and Mysore have enacted the necessary legislation, while the question is under consideration in Madhya Pradesh, Maharashtra, Gujarat, Orissa, Punjab, Rajasthan, Uttar Pradesh and West Bengal. Madras does not have any serious flood problems. Promotion of necessary legislation in the remaining States and enforcement of legislation where it has already been passed, are essential steps to be taken to reach the estimate of Rs. 39 crores from betterment levy and flood cess during the Third Plan.

It is important that when an irrigation or a flood control project is proposed for a new area, the State authorities should place the broad outlines and advantages of the scheme before the agriculturists of that area, in particular, the structure of water rates, betterment levy, flood cess, etc., which have to be paid by the beneficiaries. Such education of public opinion is likely to result in quicker utilisation of irrigation and will also prepare the ground for acceptance of water rates and betterment levy by beneficiaries when the project materialises.

**Evaluation of Benefits.** While the financial return of an irrigation project is an important consideration, it does not by itself provide an adequate criterion for assessing the overall benefits of the project. In order to get an idea of the various benefits which accrue from irrigation projects, the Research Programme Committee, at the instance of the Planning Commission, initiated evaluation studies for five major irrigation works-Gang Ganal in Rajasthan, Sarda Canal in U.P., Tribeni Canal in Bihar, Damodar Canal in West Bengal and Cauvery Mettur Project in Madras. These evaluation studies suggest that while several of the indirect benefits of irri- gation cannot be assessed in precise quantitative terms, among the principal benefits to be taken into account, apart from the finacial returns to Government, are more extensive utilisation of land and other resources; adoption of a better cropping pattern and a shift to more valuable crops ; creation of conditions favourable to fresh investment or an increase in productive investment in farm business , increase in farm productivity and stabilisation or enhancement of farm incomes; increased employment opportunities for labour; and stimulus to industry, especially processing industries, and to trade and transport. The studies also provide useful information on various aspects of irrigation development.

## UTILISATION OF IRRIGATION

In consequence of the lags which occurred in the utilisation of irrigation during the First and Second Plans, the Planning Commission has given much attention to the subject over the past two or three years. The following are the principal measures needed for securing speedy benefits from irrigation projects :

(1) It is essential that there should be synchro- nisation in the programmes for the construction of head-works, canals, distributaries, water courses and field channels so as to ensure that as far as possible the irrigation waters can be passed down to the cultivators' fields about the same time as they become available at the head-works. The synchronisation of the construction programmes, except for field channels, is the direct responsibility of the project authorities;

(2) For speedy utilisation of these irrigation facilities, development blocks should be set up over the entire area to be served by an irrigation project as soon as possible after a project has been approved;

(3) In order to eliminate delay in the excavation of water-courses and field channels, their alignment should be marked out by the project authorities on village maps, and these maps should be supplied to the district and block authorities for getting the field channels excavated by the beneficiaries in good time. It is necessary to ensure that at the same, time as the canal system is ready, the excavation of field channels by the beneficiaries is also completed. Acting as agents of Government, Panchayat Samitis and Village Panchayats should be empowered to carry out the works and recover costs in case of default:

(4) A large number of other developmental activities have to be carried out simultaneously. These include soil

surveys, setting up of experimental farms for determining and evolving new cropping patterns, varities of crops, etc. and farms for demonstrating scientific irrigation practices, particularly the economical use of water. It is necesary that officials of Irrigation departments should be well acquainted with agricultural practices and with the problems of cultivators. Arrangements should, therefore, be made to impart in-service training to them for a few months. This knowledge will assist them in improving both the preparation and the operation of irrigation schemes;

(5) Economy in the use of water is a most important consideration. Distribution of water from canals on area basis, as practised at presents is not conducive to economy in the use of water. Distribution on volumetric basis is not practicable as metered outlets are expensive, and, even if installed are liable to be tampered with. The Agriculture Department has to advise on irrigation practices suited to different crops and conditions of cultivation and should undertake the necessary investigations in each area. The water in canals saved in this manner could be utilised for more intensive irrigation and for providing water to new areas. Intensive educational work should be undertaken by the community development organisation at the block and village levels ;

(6) It is also essential for the Departments concerned to undertake advance planning in their respective fields, for instance, for the supply of improved seeds and fertilisers and development of local manurial resources, provision of larger credit and marketing facilities, establishment of warehouses and godowns and improvement of·communications in. the areas commanded by irrigation projects. This will make it possible for cultivators to realise optimum benefits from irrigation, thereby increasing their net income ;

(7) Concessional water rates are allowed in several States in the initial two or three years of a new irrigation

project. This is a useful promotional measure and helps in speedy development of irrigation.

To ensure that planning in the various fields mentioned above is undertaken by the Departments concerned simultaneously with the planning of construction operations by the Irrigation Department, Development Committees consisting of representatives of all the Departments concerned are being set up by State Governments. There should be close consultation between different Departments from the earliest stage , and each Department's Programme should embody within it, in respect of every important irrigation project, adequate provision for carrying out its specific responsibilities At the district level, the Collector should coordinate the work of the various Departments in order to ensure speedy utilisation of irrigation facilities from irrigation schemes serving the district.

## INVESTIGATION, RESEARCH AND DESIGN

River valley projects require elaborate investigations. For integrated development of water and land resources of the country on a planned basis, and to ensure continuity in the development of water resources, adequate information regarding technological possibilities namely, suitable project sites, hydrological data, irrigable areas, etc. for all feasible projects in a river basin should be available in advance, so that projects can be selected properly and given ap- propriate priority. Master plans for the longterm development of irrigation should be prepared in each State to bring out clearly the ultimate potentialities of various irrigation and multi-purpose schemes. Although special investigation units have already been set up in almost all the States, adequate progress in the investigation and preparation of projects has not been made, even in respect of projects included in the Second Plan. It is essential that in the Third Plan there should be much greater emphasis on thorough investigation of schemes. including soil surveys of the commanded area, and completion of project reports in all important respects. For this purpose, investigation units in the States should be strengthened. Schemes, which may be proposed for consideration in the Fourth Plan by the State Governments, should be thoroughly investigated well in time, and project reports prepared for them in the course of the Third Plan itself. Certain improvements in the preparation and presentation of project reports have been recently introduced. These specify various technical, financial and other aspects which should be dealt with ade- quately in project reports before decisions are taken and construction is undertaken.

To supplement the efforts of States in preparing their master plans for irrigation, preliminary studies for suitable projects sites in different river basins in the country are being carried out from contour maps by the Central Water and Power Commission.

These are made available to States for comment before being finalised. Field investigations and surveys in respect of these schemes would normally have to be carried out by the State Governments to decide which of the schemes should receive relative priority for carrying out detailed in- vestigations and preparation of project reports. The Central Water and Power Commission have completed preliminary studies for certain river basins, viz. Chambal, Ramganga, Sone, Tambaraparni and Vaigai rivers, etc. Studies for other important river basins are in different stages of progress and are expected to be completed during the Third Plan period.

Research-Research in the field of irrigation and hydraulic engineering is being conducted in Central Water and Power Research Station at Poona and fifteen other research stations in the States. These stations are engaged in research in applied engineering, on problems connected with irrigation works, hydraulics and soils, etc. as well as fundamental research. With the larger programmes of development now being undertaken, the activities of these organisations have also been expanding.

The basic research carried out under the Second Plan included such problems as turbulence, cavitation in hydraulic structures, design of channels, engineering properties of soils, air entrainment in concrete, sub-soil flow, sedimentation in streams and reservoirs, river protection works, instrumentation, etc. The research programmes are coordinated by the Central Board of Irrigation an Power. In the Third Plan, the programme of irrigation research is being broadened to include, amongst others, the following new problems:

(1) utilisation of isotopes in sub-soil investigations;

(2) development of techniques in pre-cast hydraulic structures;

(3) minimising loss of head through improvement of trashracks, penstocks, etc. ; and

(4) experimental methods of stress analysis in hydraulic structures ; and

(5) investigation on compaction of different soils in wet conditions and standing water, with particular reference to construction of earthen dams.

An outlay of Rs. 120 lakhs has been provided in the Third Plan for the programmes of fundamental research in irrigation.

**Designs Organisations.** Large investments are being made on irrigation projects and it is, therefore, essential to ensure the maximum possible economies in the cost of construction by adopting improved techniques in design and construction and by proper choice of construction materials. It is recommended that every State should have a strong designs organisation, which, by working in conjunction with the research organisation, can produce the most suitable and economical designs. At the Centre, the Central Water and Power Commission has the organisation to render assistance to States in preparing designs of the more complicated structures.

**River Boards.** River basins, especially those of the larger rivers, naturally extend beyond the boundaries of individual States. In some cases, the most suitable site for harnessing the water resources of a river involving, for instance less submergence of land or smaller cost of construction, may lie in one State, while the area receiving irrigation or power benefits may lie in another State. For integrated and economic development of water resources, arrangements for inter-State cooperation are, therefore, essential. An important aspect which has to be considered in the long term planning of water resources is that, as industrialisation advances, the requirements of water supply for industries and for the growing urban populations will constitute major problems in development. The setting up of River Boards for important river basins, as envisaged in the River Boards Act, 1956, would enable a coordinated view to be taken of the needs of a river basin as a whole, including soil conservation in the catchment area. Steps to establish River Boards for the more important rivers are being taken in consultation with the States.

**Public Co-operation.** Flood controls drainage, anti-waterlogging and anti-sea-erosion schemes as also certain portion of irrigation works are especially suited for people's participation. These schemes involve mostly work which does not require any great skill on the part of most of the workers. They are also generally located at convenient distances from the villages benefited by these scheme. It is important that beneficiaries should be persuaded to contribute towards these schemes by offering voluntary labour and/or money in lieu thereof. These works should be carried out in close cooperation with the local organisations, especially the Panchayat Samitis and the Village Panchayats. To the greatest extent possible, labour cooperatives should be utilised. Voluntary organisations such as the Bharat Sevak Samaj can also help, for instance, in maintaining supplies of tools, obtaining contracts from the Departments concerned, and arranging for the execution of works and for the welfare of the workers. Community development organisations have an important role in these matters. They should foster a climate which will arouse the enthusiasm of the people, enlist their participation and give them a sense of partnership in the projects. They should also educate the people in their obligations as well as in the adoption of improved methods of agriculture thereby enabling them to derive the maximum benefits from irrigation.

Use of manual labour and machinery.The use of construction machinery on river valley projects should be viewed against the background of the large manpower resources available in the country and the urgent need for providing gainful employment. Extensive use of machinery imposes much strain on foreign exchange resources. Ordinarily, construction of projects should be carried out manually, unless resort to manual labour delays completion of the work abnormally, or adds to its cost prohibitively, Where necessary, judicious use of machinery and equipment to assist manual labour may be resorted to. Stress should be laid on the necessity of improving the techniques of manual labour to achieve greater efficiency and speed in construction. These aspects should be considered carefully and in detail in respect of the projects included in the Third Plan.

**Maintenance of Existing Works.** Before Independence, Irrigation Departments were primarily engaged in the maintenance and operation of existing irrigation works, as few new irrigation works were being taken up. Under the first two plans, however, large-scale programmes in irrigation have been initiated. With this change, resulting in more attention being given to construction works than to maintenance and operation, a degree of deterioration in the standards of maintenance of irrigation channels appears to have taken place. A contributory cause for this is that financial provisions for maintenance of existing channels have not been increased in many cases to the extent justified by increase in wages for labour and the costs of materials. The cumulative effect over a period of the resulting deterioration is likely to be serious. While it is important to increase irrigation facilities by constructing new projects, it is equally important that maximum benefits should be derived from existing facilities by efficient maintenance and operation.

**Technical Personnel.** Adequacy of properly trained technical personnel at ail levels is an essential requirement for the satisfactory implementation of irrigation and power programmes.

It is expected that, while the availability of degree-holders in the Third Plan would be adequate, there might be a slight shortage of diploma-holders, which would be met by suitable expansion of training facilities during the first two years of the Plan. In addition, for efficient operation and maintenance of costly earthmoving equipment, it is necessary to have properly trained operators and mechanics to handle them. Arrangements have been made for the training of operators and mechanics in two Technical Training Centres set up at the project sites at Kotah (Rajasthan) and Nagarjunasagar (Andhra Pradesh) by the Central Government.

**Control Boards.** Control Boards have already been set tip for some of the larger projects under execution, namely, Bhakra, Chambal, Rihand, Kosi, Hirakud, Nagarjunasagar, Tungabhadra, Rajasthan Canal and Koyna. The functions of these Control Boards are to ensure the efficient and economical planning and implementation of the projects, inclu- ding optimum and speedy utilisation of benefits accruing from them at different stages. Several large projects are being taken up in the Third Plan. For some of these, it would be helpful to set up Control Boards as soon as the projects are approved. This suggestion is being examined in collaboration with the States concerned. For other large projects, for which no Control Boards are set up, there should be arrangements for periodical review by the Ministry of Irrigation and Power with a view to removing bottlenecks and ensuring speedy implementation.

## POWER

### Sources of Energy

Electricity can be generated from any one of the primary sources of energy available in India : coal, lignite, water falls, uranium and thorium, oil, natural and refinery gases. Tidal power, wind power. geothermal power and solar radiations are other possible sources but their impact on electricity development in India has been insignificant so far.

A large proportion of the total workable reserves of coal estimated at 50,000 million tons for the entire country, is confined to Bihar and West Bengal with small outlying fields in Assam, Madhya Pradesh, Maharashtra, Orissa and Andhra Pradesh. Besides, lignite deposits estimated at about 2000 million tons are known to occur in parts of Madras, Rajasthan, Gujarat and Jammu & Kashmir, Reserves of good quality coal required for metallurgical and other industries are, however, limited thus necessitating the setting up of coal washeries. Poor quality coal with high ash content and middlings from coal washeries cannot be transported economically over long distances and is best burnt in stationary boilers of power stations.

Furnace oil could be utilised in boilers of steam power stations in lieu of coal. Oil refineries are being located at Gauhati in Assam, Barauni in Bihar and Cambay in Gujarat in addition to those existing at Digboi, Vishakhapatnam and Bombay. In order to minimise costs of carrige and to avoid strain on the transport system, it is desirable to locate steam power stations in the vicinity of collieries, washeries and refineries. In view of the high cost of power generation in diesel power stations and in view also of the, need for reducing import of diesel oil, expansion of this type of generation will be confined mainly to isolated locations and small nursery schemes or for peaking purposes. Refinery, blast furnace and coke-oven gases are used for power generation in a few cases. Reserves of natural gas have also been discovered in Nahorkatiya in Assam. It is proposed to utilise this gas, amongst other things, for generation of power during the Third Plan.

Installation of large thermal units employing higher steam temperatures and pressures would result not only in increased thermal efficiencies but also in reduction of capital costs per kW of installed capacity. The thermal efficiencies attainable with modern plants of 30, 60, 100 and 120 MW units are of the order of 26, 29, 32 and 34 percent respectively. The capital cost per kW of installed capacity of 120 MW units is about 20 percent cheaper than for 30 MW units. In India the overall efficiency of thermal power stations in 1959-60 was 19.5 percent because many of the units were small and old. With the general adoption and operation of larger units, the overall thermal efficiency is expected to improve considerably, thus enabling more kilowatt-hours to be produced from each ton of coal utilised.

Hydro-electric generation is of importance as, compared to coal, oil, natural gas and nuclear fuels which have to be consumed in order to produce energy, flowing water is an inexhaustible source of energy. In 1953, the Central Water and Power Commission undertook the task of systematically assessing the total power potential of rivers in the country. The possible hydroelectric sites were located on topographical maps and on the basis of available data on rainfall, run-off and river gauging, and allowing for other uses of the waters of these rivers, such as, irrigation, flood control, navigation, etc. a total hydroelectric potential of about 41 million kW has been assessed as technically and economically feasible.

It has been estimated that the thorium reserves in the country are among the largest in the world and are more extensive than those of uranium. In order to utilise thorium, the nuclear power programme in India has to be carried out in three stages, which is time-consuming. The first stage will utilise natural uranium as fuel, producing power and the fissile element plutonium. The second stage will employ reactors using plutonium as fuel and throium as fertile material, producing Dower and converting part of the thorium into U- 233. The third stage will use U-233 with thorium in breeder reactors, so that while electricity is generated, more U-233 is produced than is burnt up in the process. According to certain tentative estimates the cost of generation of electricity in this stage is expected to be lower than in the other two stages.

Having regard to the fact that one ton of uranium has potentialities of producing as much electricity as 10,000 to 11,000 tons of coal, the impact of nuclear power on transport facilities is obvious. Although at present. the capital cost of nuclear stations is nearly 1 1/2 to 2 times that of thermal power stations. threshold conditions exist for setting up of nuclear power stations in relation to coal-based power stations in areas remote from coalfields and having no other alternative economic sources of Dower gene-ration. Construction and operation of nuclear devices for production of electricity require a high degree of scientific and engineering skill. It is desirable that technical personnel in the country should obtain the necessary training and experience so as to undertake a large nuclear power programme at the appropriate time.

Tidal and geothermal power plants have been in use only to a very limited extent. Prospects of economic power generation from these sources in India are, for the present, negligible. Research on direct conversion of solar energy into electricity is being carried out in many parts of the world. Wind power plants have been in use in India for pumping water in isolated locations. Recently the Council of Scientific and Industrial

Research has set up a wind power division in the National Aeronautical Laboratory in Bangalore for the purpose of making wind surveys and conducting pilot studies on a few windmills and wind behaviour. The fluctuating wind power would necessitate installation of storage batteries for obtaining continuous power. The consequent high unit cost for building wind power stations is at present an obstacle to extensive introduction of such plants for power generation.

## PRESENT STAGE OF POWER DEVELOPMENT

The total installed generating capacity in the country at the beginning of the First Plan stood at 2.30 million kW-0.63 million kW in State-owned public utilities, 1.08 million kW in company-owned public utilities and 0.59 million kW in industrial establishments having their own power stations. During the First Plan, the aggregate installed generating capacity increased by about 49 per cent, the actual addition being 1.12 million kW, as against the target of 1.40 million kW. During the Second Plan, generating capacity increased by about 67 per cent from 3.42 million kW to 5.70 million kW (Annexure VI). As against the initial target of 3.48 million kW, the actual addition was 2.28 million kW. The shortfall occurred mainly because of foreign exchange difficulties that arose during the early years of the Second Plan and also because of delays in the execution of some of the projects such as Bhakra-Nangal, Koyna, Rihand and Hirakud.

To avoid conditions of severe power shortage in the early years of the Third Plan, steps were taken to provide foreign exchange for implementing the remaining power schemes of the Second Plan, which. had earlier been classified as "non-core" projects. Work was also taken up on a few additional power schemes which were not originally included in the Second Plan with a view to meeting increased demands that arose in certain regions during the Second Plan. Arrangements were also made to commence preliminary works on selected Third Plan schemes during the last year of the Second Plan. Important power stations commissioned in the First and Second Plans are listed in Annexure VII.

The total investment in electricity utilities at the beginning of the First Plan was about Rs. 150 crores, less than half of which was in the public sector. Investment in self-generating industrial establishments was estimated at Rs. 40 crores. During the First Plan, the total outlay on power development was Rs. 302 crores- Rs. 260 crores in State-owned utilities, Rs. 32 crores in company- owned utilities and Rs. 10 crores in self-generating industrial esta- blishments. The corresponding figures for the Second Plan are Rs. 525 crores, 460 crores, 37 crores and 28 crores respectively. The figure of Rs. 460 crores includes investment by the Damodar Valley Corporation and some State Electricity Boards from their own resources. Thus the total investment on power upto the end of the Second. Plan is reckoned at Rs. 1017 crores, of which State-owned public utilities would account for Rs. 790 crores.

## PERSPECTIVE OF POWER DEVELOPMENT

The additional generating capacity installed during the Second Plan averaged about 0.45 million kW per annum. While it is proposed to step up this programme by commissioning 1.4 million kW per year on an average during the Third Plan, the pace of development in the Fourth and subsequent Plans would be higher. Thus, by 1975-76, the aggregate installed generating capacity in the country may be of the order of 35 million kW. According to present estimates, roughly fifty per cent of this capacity could be provided from hydroelectric projects and the balance mainly from thermal stations. In order to achieve these targets, new hydroelectric sites will need to be investigated speedily and works commenced in time to avail of the benefits in the subsequent Plans. Having regard to the available energy resources, nuclear power is expected to play progressively increasing part in meeting energy demands in future years.

## PROGRAMME FOR THE THIRD PLAN

Basic considerations and criteria.-In deciding particular methods of power generation suited to different areas, the key factors are, the capital cost per kilowatt of installed capacity, the foreign exchange component, the cost per kilowatt-hour generated, the period required for construction, impact on other allied development activities such as coal mining, washeries, irrigation, exploitation of natural gas, stimulus to the development of new technology etc. The average production costs of electricity for hydro, coal-fired and diesel power stations are in the neighbourhood of 1.2 nP. 3 nP and 25 nP per kilowatt-hour respectively. The cost of atomic generation, tentatively estimated at 3.5 to 4 nP, may be comparable to that of coal-fired power stations in areas remote from the coalfields. The foreign exchange component of coal-based power stations is two to three times that of hydro-stations, while nuclear stations require still more foreign exchange. Because of the different characteristics of the various types of power generation, optimum economy can be achieved by proper balance in the different modes of generation and by interconnecting them as far as possible to meet the varying conditions of power demand such as base, peak and seasonal loads in a grid.

The expected load demand in the next few years has been the main criterion in determining the size of the power programme in the States during the Third Plan. Detailed load surveys conducted by the Central Water and Power Commission towards the end of the Second Plan indicated much higher demands than were assessed at the time of the preliminary load surveys in 1958.

The former alongwith the proposed industrial programme have formed the basis for inclusion of generation schemes in the Third Plan. Considerable increase in irrigation pumping is envisaged in the States of Madras, Maharashtra, Punjab and Uttar Pradesh.

In some areas, as in West Bengal-Bihar region industrial demands are expected to rise steeply. The electrification of the railway track between Calcutta and Kanpur and of certain other sections will increase traction demands considerably. In some States, where the additions to generating capacity during the Second Plan were not significant, the power programme would have to cater for a sizeable backlog of unsatisfied demands. Annexure VIII sets out the principal generation schemes included in the Third Plan. Annexure IX gives the State-wise abstract of costs of the power programme and the benefits envisaged in the Third Plan.

## PHYSICAL BENEFITS AND PHASING

By the end of the Third Plan, the aggregate capacity of the plants in commission and under erection and testing will be of the order of 13.40 million kW of which 12.69 million kW are expected to be in commercial, operation, representing an increase in installed generating capacity of 123 per cent over the Second Plan. With the completion of this programme, per capita generation of electricity would have risen from 18 kWh in 1951, 28 kWh in 1956, 45 kWh in 1961 to about 95 kWh in 1966.

A nuclear power station is planned for construction at Tarapur near Bombay. It will consist of two reactors, each producing 150 MW of power. One of these is expected to be in commission before the end of the Third Plan and the other in the first year of the Fourth Plan. Investigations regarding a suitable site for a nuclear power station in the Delhi-Punjab-Rajasthan-Uttar Pradesh region have recently been authorised.

The phasing of benefits from power schemes will depend largely on availability foreign exchange and the capacity of Electricity Boards who are generally in charge of the execution of power projects In the public sector to implement the programme approved for the Third Plan.

it is essential that detailed programmes should be worked out for the preparation of project reports, preparation of specifications and tender documents, analysis of tenders when received and placing of orders, deliveries of equipment, erection, testing and commissioning of plants, and obstacles likely to upset the scheduled programme should be anticipated and dealt with in advance. Power shortage in different regions cannot be mitigated unless a strict watch is kept on the progress of the schemes and every effort made to shorten the period of construction.

Although there are a number of uncertain elements at the present stage the following Table suggests the likely phasing of benefits during the Third Plan.

### *Table 7 : Phasing of benefits*

| | additions during year the by year (million kW) | aggregate installed generating capacity the end of the year (million kW) |
|---|---|---|
| 1961-62 | 0.60 | 6.30 |
| 1962-63 | 0.73 | 7.03 |
| 1963-64 | 1.05 | 8.08 |
| 1964-65 | 2.07 | 10.15 |
| 1965-66 | 2.54 | 12.69 |

It may be pointed out that despite the large programme of development envisaged above, owing to the rapid growth in demand, power shortages are likely to continue to exist in some regions, particularly in the early years of the Third Plan. Power development has to be a continuous process, and work has to be commenced on a series of projects which will yield benefits in subsequent Plan periods. With this in view projects such as, Beas, Punasa, Idikki and others, have been included in the Third Plan.

The transmission network will be further strengthened and extended during the Third Plan as shown in the Table below:

### *Table 8 : Transmission lines*

| | transmission lines 11 kV and above at the end of circuit miles | circuit kilometers |
|---|---|---|
| 1955 | 36500 | 58400 |
| 1960-61 | 84000 | 134400 |
| 1965-66 | 150000 | 240000 |

## FINANCIAL OUTLAYS

The estimated cost of the power program. me in the public sector in the Third Plan is Rs. 1039* crores. Investment in the private sector is expected to be of the order of Rs. 50 crores. The approximate break-up of the programme in the public sector is Rs. 661 crores for hydro and thermal generating schemes. Rs. 51 crores for atomic power and about Rs 327 crores for transmission and distribution schemes including Rs. 105 crores for rural electrification. This programme provides for power supply to the Bokaro steel plant and includes the outlay required for the 150 MW extension in the Neiveli power station. The provision of Rs. 24 crores for uranium mining, fabrication and plutonium extraction plant shown originally under "Power" in the Draft Outline, is now shown in the "Industry and Minerals" sector.

The total foreign exchange required for the power programme in the Third Plan is estimated at Rs. 320 crores. Experience in the Second Plan has underlined the fact that our dependence for electrical equipment on imports is a serious obstacle to rapid development of power. Even during the Third Plan, a large proportion of the machinery and equipment required wig, have to be imported. In addition to the completion of the first Heavy Electrical Manufacturing Plant at Bhopal and its further expansion, two other plants for manufacturing boilers, steam and hydraulic turbines and other heavy electrical equipment have been provided for in the Third Plan in the public sector. Units in the private sector will undertake further expansions in capacity for the manufacture of transformers, motors and switchgear. A substantial, portion of the requirements of equipment for power projects will thus be met from indigenous production.

## PATTERN OF CONSUMPTION

During the ten years 1951-61, except for traction and irrigation pumping, the other types of consumption do not show significant variations. As the growth of electric traction has not kept pace with the growth of power generation, consumption in this sector has shown a downward trend from 4.4 percent of generation in 1951 to 2.3 percent in 1960-61. The consumption in irrigation pumping has registered an increase from 2.7 to 4.2 percent. It is noteworthy that whereas the overall consumption has increased by about two and a half times, the use of electricity for irrigation pumping has increased more than four-fold since 1951 and progress is expected to continue to be rapid. Growth in electricity consumption in different sectors during the First and Second Plans is given in detail in Annexure XI. Indus- tries consume about 61-63 percent of the total amount of electricity generated or, to put it differently about 72 percent of power sold to consumers. This underlines the importance of coordinating power programmes with industrial programmes. With continued emphasis on heavy and basic industries in the Third Plan corresponding increase in power generation has been provided for.

## RURAL ELECTRIFICATION

An important objective of the Third Plan is to develop efficient small-scale industries in small towns and in rural areas so as to increase employment opportunities, raise incomes and living standards and bring about a more balanced and diversified rural economy. In achieving these aims a major limiting factor is the lack of power. Where electricity is available, it becomes possible to reorganise the traditional industries and to introduce small industries based on steadily improving techniques, which are capable of meeting the new needs of the expanding rural economy. In several States, electricity is being increasingly used for irrigation pumping, and the scope for this is likely to increase rapidly. Thus, in relation to the development of the rural economy, rural electrification has a growing importance, and indeed, its value cannot be assessed only in terms of the immediate economic benefits.

By the end of the Second Plan, the total number of towns and villages electrified in the country is reckoned at 23,000, as against 7,400 at the end of the First Plan. The Third Plan provides for an outlay of Rs. 105 crores for rural electrification. This does not include the outlay required for providing the necessary generating capacity for meeting rural loads which is included in the provision for generation. By the end of the Third Plan the number of towns and villages electrified is likely to increase by about 20,000 to about 43,000. In determining the scope of the rural electrification programme in each State, the need for balance between increase in generating capacity and extensions in transmission, distribution and rural electrification has been kept in view. Much larger outlays and more rapid development in rural electrification are envisaged for the Fourth and Fifth Plans.

It will be seen that by the end of the Third Plan all towns and villages with population exceeding 5,000 may be expected to be electrified. As regards villages with a population range of 2,000 to 5,000, it is envisaged that nearly 50 percent that is 10,000 villages will receive the benefits of electricity,

There are a number of isolated areas where small hydro plants of 10 to 100 kW each can be set up at modest cost. Small hydro units upto 100 kW capacity are now being manufactured in the country. In the long run , they will be more economical than diesel-alternator sets and relatively easy to maintain, and will not involve foreign exchange for their procurement or operation. A cell has been set up in the Central Water and Power Commission for initiating and assisting in field surveys and in the installation of such plants. This aspect of power development is of special importance in hill areas and suitable programmes should be formulated.

Rural extension of electricity become relatively uneconomic mainly because of distances separating individual villages, the low level of power consumption and the seasonal character of the requirements of power specially in agriculture. Consequently the load factor is low and the available generating capacity is not fully utilised. With a view to improving the load factor it is essential that different types of economic activities in each district requiring the use of power should be developed in a coordinated manner. This object can be secured through a carefully formulated development programme for each area covering activities in different fields of development such as minor irrigation credit and service facilities for equipment, improved seeds and village and small industries, so that rural electrification makes the maximum con- tribution possible to the increase of agricultural and industrial production. There should be forward planning for rural electrification over a period of two or more years ahead of taking up the work so that simulataneous action is initiated in other sectors also.

To facilitate the drawing up of definite schemes for the utilisation of power as part of the district development plan, State Electricity Boards should indicate in advance to the district agencies concerned, their estimates of the amount of power likely to be available for rural areas and small towns during the Third Plan, year by year. It has been recommended to States that, in every district where electric facilities exist or are likely to be available small committees should be set up to plan and advise on rural development programmes. These programmes should be worked out in sufficient detail and with the necessary phasing in terms of limited areas, such as a small town and its neighbourhood or a group of villages which have a common source of power and can, therefore, develop on the basis of a well-conceived economic programme. These district plans should be implemented as part of the State plan so that the development of rural electrification keeps in step with the programme for additional generating capacity.

Dispersal of industries in rural areas, which is discussed elsewhere in this Report, presupposes availability of power. There should be a close link between schemes for the development of village and small industries and the programme for generation and distribution of power. Similar coordination is called for in respect of minor irrigation schemes which require electricity for pumping.

Several aspects of rural electrification, such as those relating to the adequacy of power supply for rural loads, rates for supply and the role of Panchayat Samitis and village panchayats in distribution of electricity are being studied further.

## PROBLEMS OF COORDINATED DEVELOPMENT OF POWER

The Electricity (Supply) Act, 1948, laid down that a sound, adequate and uniform national power policy should be developed. coordinating the activities of planning agencies in relation to the control and utilisation of national power resources. This calls for exploitation of the natural resources in the most economical manner for the benefit of the entire region regardless of State boundaries. Thus, steam power stations should be sited near collieries, washeries and oil refineries. The cheapest hydro sites in any river basin should be harnessed in an appropriate order of priority. Nuclear power stations should be located in regions where other resources of energy are inadequate or expensive.

All power stations should be inter-connected to form State, zonal or super-grids, so that the energy is pooled and used to the best advantage of the region. Interconnected operation of power stations and power systems will improve the performance of electricity supply undertakings by raising the load factor reducing the requirements of stand-by machinery and enabling the efficient operation of the available plant.

There has been inter-State collaboration in the past in the execution of projects such as Bhakra-Nangal, Machkund, Tungabhadra, Chambal and others. Such co-operation needs to be further extended so that power generation may be undertaken on a regional or a zonal basis and not merely to meet demands within one State. This will also pave the way for eliminating the disparities in electricity tariffs in neighbouring States. Also, in the absence of the zonal approach there is a danger of large energy resources concentrated in some States remaining unutilised, either because of the inability of the State Governments to finance the project from their own resources or because of the power demand in the State not being sufficient to call for this development immediately. Problems relating to planning and construction of generating stations, which serve more than one State, are being examined.

Studies are being undertaken by the Central Water and Power Commission for the establishment of super-grid in the Southern region, linking up Andhra Pradesh, Mysore, Madras and Kerala power systems. Meanwhile, the construction of 220 kV inter-State link lines designed to provide immediate facilities for interchange of power to a limited extent between the States is being taken up. During the Third Plan, power systems in Maharashtra and Gujarat will get inter-connected as also the

Chambal grid of Rajasthan with the Satpura power system of Madhya Pradesh. Other inter-State links which should be considered are : the Rihand system in Uttar Pradesh with the Amarkantak-Korba system in Madhya Pradesh and the latter with the Hirakud system in Orissa, Ganga grid of Uttar Pradesh with the Delhi-Punjab system, and the Sharavathy system in Mysore with the Koyna system in Maharashtra. A special unit in the Central Water and Power Commission is being set up for undertaking studies and planning of regional super-grids in association with State Electricity Boards and other electricity supply undertakings.

## FINANCIAL ASPECTS

In accordance with the requirements of the Electricity (Supply) Act. 1948, autonomous Electricity Boards have been set up in all the States. These Boards are charged with the general duty of promoting the coordinated development of the generation, supply and distribution of electricity within the State in the most efficient and economical manner, with particular reference to such development in areas not for the time being served by any licensee.

It is essential that electricity undertakings in the public sector should earn reasonable surpluses and provide resources for financing future development. On account of the capital intensive nature of power development and the rapid growth in demand, large investments will be required in the public sector.

# 12

# Village and Small Industries

## ROLE IN PLANNED DEVELOPMENT

Village and small industries have, made a significant contribution in the First and Second Plans in realising the objectives of expanded employment, larger production and more equitable distribution. With the larger dimensions of the tasks to be accomplished in the Third Plan, their role will be even more important.

The objectives of the programmes for these industries as set out in the Industrial Policy Resolution, 1956, and in the Second Plan are to create immediate and permanent employment on a large scale at relatively small capital cost, meet a substantial part of the increased demand for consumer goods and simple producer's goods, facilitate mobilisation of resources of capital and skill which might otherwise remain inadequately utilised and bring about integration of the, development of these industries with the rural economy on the one hand and large- scale industry on the other. They also offer a method of ensuring more equitable distribution of the national income and avoiding some of the problems that unplanned urbanisation tends to create. With improvement in techniques and organisation, these industries offer possibilities of growing into an efficient and progressive decen- tralised sector of the economy providing opportunities of work and income all over the country. One of the principal aims of planning in this field, therefore, is to assist in the adoption of improved techniques and more efficient forms of organisation, so that full advantage is taken of the basic facilities and services available as a result of general economic development, and over a period the, entire sector becomes self-reliant and self-supporting. At the same time, the pace of technical change will have to be so regulated that large- scale technological unemployment with consequent hardship and misery to millions of people is avoided.

An important lesson of the past decade is that where individual small industries, including village industries, have failed to adopt improved techniques or to achieve economies of scale and organisation through cooperation, production costs have remained relatively high and problems of unsold stocks and of decline in production and employment have arisen. These problems have come up in some of the traditional industries. Constant adaptation to the conditions of rapid change in a dynamic economy and the adoption of new techniques, methods and forms of organisation are important factors in the stability and development of various village and small industries. In the last ten years, large programmes of assistance have been organised for these industries and considerable support has been given to them through provision of loans, subsidies, technical and marketing advice and, in some cases, through reservation of spheres of production. In the latter part of the Second Plan, marketing conditions for some of the small scale industries improved markedly following the intensification of import restrictions. The need for these restrictions may not continue indefinitely. Moreover, with the supply of electric power over large areas of the country, improvements in means of transport and communications, use of modem machines and techniques and the general advance of science and technology, the entire economy is being transformed. The problems of village and small industries, therefore, need to be constantly reviewed and necessary measures taken to realise the full potential of decentralised industry as an essential and continuing element in the national economy.

The progress during the First and Second Plans of different small industries, including handloom, khadi, village industries, small scale industries, handicrafts, sericulture and coir, was reviewed towards the middle of the Second Plan by a number of Working Groups and Committees. A special Study Team assessed the working of 25 industrial pilot projects which were taken up in community development blocks about six years ago. The Programme Evaluation Organisation also made a study of rural industries in selected community development blocks. Data collected in the course of these studies and the findings and conclusions reached have been of considerable value in formulating programmes for the Third Five Year Plan. A brief re- view of the progress of these industries in the first two Plans is given in the following paragraphs.

## REVIEW OF PROGRESS

In the First Plan, a major step taken for the development of village and small industries was the establishment of All-India Boards to advise and assist in the formulation of programmes of development for the Handloom Industry, Khadi and Village Industries, Small Scale Industries, Handicrafts, Sericulture and Coir. The Khadi and Village Industries Board not only prepared programmes for the industries with which it was concerned but also had them implemented through registered institutions and cooperative societies. In the case of other industries, responsibility for the implementation of programmes mostly rested with State Government, although for a few programmes the Boards functioned on behalf of the Central Government for purposes of implementation.

A notable development during the Second Plan was the establishment of a statutory Khadi and Village Industries Commission with more extensive executive powers than those enjoyed by the Khadi and Village Industries Board, which continued as an advisory body closely associated with the Commission. Further, in almost all States, statutory State Khadi and Village Industries Boards were created under legislation sponsored by State Governments. Steps were also taken to strengthen State Departments of Industries. Thus, a three-tier organisation was developed-the Ministry of Commerce and Industry at the Centre, All-India Boards, and State Departments of Industries and State Boards. In addition, industries officers were appointed at the district and block levels. At the end of the Second Plan, Extension Officers for

Industries had been provided in more than 1650 develop- ment blocks out of 3110 blocks. Steps were also taken for the co-ordination of programmes by setting up at the Centre a Co-ordination Committee for Small Industries consisting of the representatives of the Ministries concerned and the Chairmen of the All-India Boards and the Khadi and Village industries Commission. Coordination Committees were also constituted in most of the States.

An essential feature of development programmes in the First Plan was the provision of assistance in different forms such as credit, training facilities, technical advice, supply of improved tools and equipment on easy terms and establishment of sales depots. In the Second Plan, the scale of assistance for all these purposes was considerably enlarged, the total anticipated outlay being a little less than Rs. 180 crores as against about Rs. 43 crores in the First Plan. A number of new programmes were also organised. About sixty industrial estates were set up for providing factory accommodation and a number of common facilities for the promotion of small scale industries. A programme for the manufacturer and distribution of Ambar charkhas on a large scale was under taken by the Khadi and Village Industries Commission. A scheme was also introduced to assist handloom weavers' cooperatives to change over to powerlooms. Apart from these various programmes of assistance, steps were taken to provide a more assured market for the products of some of the industries. Production of certain varieties of cloth was reserved for the handloom industry and of certain types of agricultural implements for small scale industry. It was also decided that there should be no further expansion in certain large scale industries like vegetable oils, rice milling, leather footwear, match, etc. where the existing capacity was not being already fully utilised. Separate targets of production were laid down for the small-scale and the large-scale sectors of certain industries like bicycles and sewing machines.

In many of the industries, particularly small scale industries and handicrafts, assistance had to be given to individual artisans and entrepreneurs because a sufficient number of artisans' organisations had not developed at the field level. In handloom and coir however, assistance was channelled mostly through cooperative societies and in khadi and village industries mostly through registered institutions. In the First Plan considerable emphasis was laid on the organisation of industrial cooperatives as a means of promoting village and small industries. The number of industrial co- operative societies increased from 7105 in 1951 to about 15,300 in 1956. The handloom industry accounted or about 8000 cooperative societies; the next largest group was of palmgur societies, followed by tanners' and leather workers' societies, societies of small scale industries including light engineering goods, and sericulture. By 1959-60, the total number of industrial cooperatives increased to about 29,000, including about 11,200 handloom weavers' societies. On the whole, however, industrial cooperatives did not cover more than a small proportion of those engaged in village and small industries. In 1958, a special Working Group examined the difficulties impending rapid progress in the formation of industrial co operatives and recommended measures for ensuring their accelerated development. Action is being taken on the proposal of the Working Group.

The strengthening of administrative and organisational machinery and the expansion of assistance programmes combined with measures for giving an assured market for certain industries produced conditions favourable to the development of village and small industries. A detailed assessment of the progress made over the past ten years cannot be given for each industry in the absence of complete and reliable data, but in several industries a notable advance has been recorded.

According to information available at present, production of handloom cloth increased from about 742 million yards in 1950-51 to about 1900 million yards in 1960-61. Fuller employment was provided for nearly 3 million weavers and exports of handloom cloth on an annual average have been about 36 million yards during the last three years, valued at over Rs. 5 crores. The number of looms in the cooperative fold increased from less than 7 lakhs in 1953 to almost 13 lakhs by the middle of 1960. Production of traditional khadi (cotton, silk and woollen) increased from 7 million yards in 1950-51 to about 48 million yards in 1960-61. Employment, mostly part-time, was provided to nearly 11 lakh additional spinners besides whole-time employment to about 1.4 lakh weavers, carpenters, etc. Production of Ambar khadi (produced from the admixture of Ambar yarn, and ordinary charkha yarn) increased from 1.9 million yards in 1956-57 to about 26 million yards in 1960-61. Mostly part-time employment was provided by this programme to about 3 lakh spinners, besides fulltime employment to about 51,000 weavers and others.

As regards the progress of village industries information is available only about the activities of registered institutions, cooperative societies and centres assisted by the Khadi and Village Industries Commission. The total disbursements for the programmes during the Second Plan period were a little over Rs. 18 crores, of which the major portion was accounted for by assistance in the form of supply of improved equipment and training and marketing facilities for the processing of cereals and pulses, crushing of oilseeds, tanning and leather, palm gur, nonedible oils and soap, match, hand-made paper, gur and khandsari, bee-keeping, pottery, etc. A substantial part of the disbursed amount remained unutilised in the earlier years of the Second Plan period. The Evaluation Committee for Village Industries which about the middle of the Second Plan reviewed the working of certain production centres set up with the assistance of the Khadi and Village Industries Commission, concluded that the results obtained in respect of both production and employment were not commensurate with the expenditure incurred. Since then, however, there has been considerable improvement in the utilisation of funds and also in the working of these centres. Village industry programmes in the Second Plan have provided partial relief to about 5 lakhs of artisans and under-employed women workers in villages. They have also furnished experience which should be useful in working out future patterns of industrial development in rural areas.

The programme for sericulture has been directed mainly towards improvement in the methods of mulberry cultivation and of the quality of silkworm seeds, supply of improved spinning and reeling equipment and organisation of research. The Central Sericultural Research Institute at Berhampore and its sub-section at Kalimpong was expanded and a training institute at Mysore and a Silkworm Seed Station at Srinagar established. Production of raw silk rose from 2.5 million lb in 1951 to 3.6 million lb in, 1960. At the end of the Second Plan period, it was reckoned that the industry provided part- time employment to about 27 lakh persons, besides full-time employment to about 35,000 persons. The high cost of production continued to be the main problem of the industry largely due to the low yield of mulberry per acre, low yield of cocoons, etc.

Progress in the coir industry was generally slow owing to organisational deficiencies of coir cooperatives, inferior quality of coir yarn due to the inefficient equipment used for spinning, and competition from substitutes in foreign markets. Exports of coir yam and goods suffered serious setback in 1957-58 and, although they have since increased to some extent, they are still below the level reached at the end of the First Plan period. The industry is at present estimated to provide employment to about 8 lakh persons.

Handicrafts programmes were enlarged in the Second Plan and included the establishment of four Regional Design Centres, and a number of emporia and sales depots, besides training and production centres for specific crafts like ivory and conch shell products, bidri, decorative pottery, toys, bamboo articles, papier mache products, etc. There has been an increase in internal sales as well as exports of handicrafts. Over 100 emporia and sales depots have been set up and the annual sales through these increased from about Rs. 1 crore at the end of the First Plan period to about Rs. 2.5 crores in 1959-60. It is estimated that handicrafts including carpets worth over Rs. 6 crores per annum were exported during the last three years of the Second Plan period. Favourable conditions for stable and fuller employment were created for skilled craftsmen which in turn resulted in considerable improvement in their earnings. Progress was somewhat retarded by the shortage of technical personnel and certain basic raw materials and the difficulty in channelling credit to the artisans.

In the field of small scale industries progress during the past five years has been quite impressive. In spite of shortages of certain basic raw materials, many small industries, notably machine tools, sewing machines, electric fans and motors, bicycles, builders' hardware and hand tools have expanded considerably, the increase in production being as much as 25 to 50 per cent per annum.

Import restrictions have to some extent given an impetus to the growth of these industries. The number of registered companies, with authorised capital of less than Rs. 5 lakhs each and engaged in processing and manufacturing, increased during 1957-61 by about 1160. In the programme of industrial estates also, considerable progress has been made, and by 1960-61 about 60 industrial estates were completed, of which 52 with about 1035 factory sheds employing about 13,000 persons were actually functioning. The programme for small scale industries as a whole is estimated to have provided full-time employment to about 3 lakh persons.

## APPROACH IN THE THIRD PLAN

The main objectives to be kept in view in implementing programmes for village and small industries in the third Plan will be :

(i) to improve the productivity of the worker and reduce production costs by placing relatively greater emphasis on positive forms of assistance such as improvement of skill, supply of technical advice, better equipment and credit, etc.;

(ii) to reduce progressively the role of subsidies, sales rebates and sheltered markets;

(iii) to promote the growth of industries in rural areas and small towns;

(iv) to promote the development of small scale industries as ancillaries to large industries; and

(v) to organise artisans and craftsmen on cooperative lines.

The policies and measures proposed for achieving these objectives are out-lined below.

Improvement of skill and productivity. Training facilities for meeting the requirements of technical and managerial personnel in the. field of village and small industries will be considerably enlarged in the Third Plan. The arrangements to be made in this regard for the training of craftsmen and engineers are given in the Chapter on Technical Education. For rural artisans, a scheme has been drawn up to set up in selected areas 'cluster-type' institutions serving groups of villages for providing courses in certain allied trades such as blacksmithy, carpentry, etc. extending over a year or more with a view to training the artisans in the maintenance and repair of agricultural implements and parts of heavy agricultural machinery, etc. These institutions are intended to replace, where necessary, the production-cum-training centres set up earlier. In addition, training facilities will be available from peripatetic demonostration and training parties organised in rural areas by State Governments. Besides these general training programmes, special schemes for training in khadi, village industries and handicrafts will be taken up as a part of the development programmes for these industries. An All-India institute will also be set up to provide facilities for training in industrial extension techniques.

In all village and small industry programmes, emphasis is being laid on the introduction of improved tools and equipment. For small scale industries, a scheme for supply of machines on hire- purchase terms was introduced during the Second Plan period and it is proposed to expand it in the Third Plan so as to supply machines to a larger number of small industrialists and cooperatives. In the hand- loom sector, provision has been made for the introduction of 'take-up motion attachments' and semi automatic looms and also for continuing the limited programme introduced at the beginning of the Second Plan for conversion on a cooperative basis from handlooms to powerlooms. In the field of khadi and village industries, research and experiments for further improvements of the Ambar charkha and oil ghanis and of equipment used in hand-pounding of paddy and in- other village industries will be continued. In the coir industry., on the basis of a pilot scheme for the introduction of improved coir spinning equipment, it is proposed to undertake the manufacture and supply of such equipment on a large scale. In sericulture, an important item of the programme is to encourage the use of cottage basins, in place of charkhas for reeling. Similarly, in handicrafts the adoption of improved tools will be encouraged and assisted.

Efforts will be organised on a larger scale to provide technical advice to artisans and craftsmen engaged in various industries. In the field of small. scale industries, an industrial extension service has been built up through the Small Industries Service Institutes, the Extension Centres and the Extension Officers (Industries) at the block level. In the field of khadi and village industries, similar advice is made available through technical officers in the various registered institutions and centres and through extension officers in the blocks. Much, however, remains to be done to provide technical assistance and advice to every artisan and craftsman who needs it and efforts in this direction will have to be pursued more vigorously in the Third Plan.

Special attention will be paid to research for developing improved tools and equipment, processes of manufacture, designs, etc. The programmes for the expansion of existing facilities are outlined in the Chapter on Scientific and Technological Research.

Credit and finance.-Credit facilities which are an essential requirement of all village and small industries, have to be organised on a larger scale in the Third Plan to be made available on reasonable terms and with the minimum of procedural delays. In the allocation for small scale industries in the Third Plan, a substantial provision has been made for loans under State Aid to Industries Acts to meet the need for long and medium term capital as well as working capital. Similarly, in the allocation for khadi and village industries, substantial amounts have been provided for the grant of loans. However, the provision which can be made for loans in the Plan is necessarily limited in relation to the requirements, and the aim to be kept in view is that increasing measure the credit required for village and small industries should be available from normal banking and financial institutions. Under a pilot scheme operated by the State Bank of India for coordinated provision of credit to these industries, the credit limit sanctoined and in force by the end of March, 1961, was nearly Rs. 9 crores. Three other notable measures were taken during the Second Plan period for making credit available to village and small industries through institutional agencies. The Reserve Bank of India provides special facilities for advances to central cooperative agencies to meet the working capital requirements of the handloom. industry. A Pilot credit guarantee scheme under which Government shares with certain specified banks and other financial institutions risks on loans granted by them to small industries was introduced in July, 1960, and guarantees for loans amounting to Rs. 2 crores were issued by the end of 1960-61. A proposal was also formulated for providing a Government guarantee for loans given by banking and institutional agencies to Well-established organisations in the field of village and small industries such as the Khadi and Village Industries Commission, the National Small Industries Corporation, etc. In the Third Plan it is proposed to continue efforts along these lines.- To ensure that the credit needs of artisans in rural areas are not overlooked while providing loans under State Aid to Industries Acts, it has been agreed that a portion of the funds to be disbursed under these Acts should be earmarked for artisans in rural areas and an equal amount for the same purpose should be made available from the budget of community development blocks.

Role of subsidies, sales rebates, etc.The progressive enlargement of programmes of positive assistance is expected to make it possible to reduce the role of subsidies, sales rebates and sheltered markets in the Third Plan. In the field of khadi, it is hoped to bring about a gradual reduction of prices through technical improvements, pooling of production costs and economy in transport and other distribution charges. Rebates on sales of khadi, particularly of silk and woollen khadi, will be reviewed with the object of replacing them, as far as possible, by suitable management grants. As regards village industries also, it is proposed that the present subsidies and/or rebates on sales in respect of their products should be replaced by gradually tapering management grants. Similarly, in the handloom industry emphasis will be shifted from sales rebates to more positive forms of assistance.

Positive measures of organisation and assistance including arrangements for the supply of raw materials and coordination for research, training, etc. were mentioned in the First and the Second Plans as being among the element of a common production programme. The term 'common production programme' was adopted as a convenient way of describing the basic approach adopted for determining, while formu- lating programmes of development for different sections of an industry, the respective contributions which the large-scale and small scale and cottage sectors could make towards the total requirements of the community, in the context of the social and other objectives. The other elements of the programme which had the object of providing a degree of preference or assurance in marketing to the small-scale sector were reservation of spheres of production, limiting the expansion of the capacity of the large sector of the industry, imposition of cesses on large-scale units and giving a price advantage to the smaller units through differential taxation, subsidies, sales rebates, etc. It was recognised that the general principles underlying common production programme should be applied only after detailed study and investigation of the problems of particular industries. For instance, in the case of some of the traditional industries, measures for ensuring preferential treatment and assurance of market for their products may have to be continued for a somewhat longer period than in the case of small scale industries.

Industrial development in rural areas and small towns.- Although several industries such as village industries, khadi, sericulture, coir and to an appreciable extent, handloom, are already located in rural areas, the development of small scale industries has so far been, by and large, in or near the cities and the larger towns. Since one of the principal objects of programmes in this field is to provide opportunities of income and employment in a dispersed manner all over the country, emphasis in the implementation of the programmes in the

Third Plan will be on encouraging the further growth of industries in rural areas and in small towns as well as in less developed areas having a marked industrial potential. The first step in this direction should be to identify the areas in which various basic facilities such as electricity, larger supply of agricultural raw materials and improved means of transport will become available as a result of development envisaged in other sectors during the course of the Third Plan and to prepare programmes for assisting the growth of industries in such areas. The desirability of linking up the promotion of small industries with programmes of power development in the rural areas has also been stressed in the Chapter on Irrigation and Power. The other essential step will be to provide various kinds of assistance such as training facilities, credit, technical advice, tools and machines, etc. in an integrated manner to those who set up industries in the rural areas and small towns. This aspect should be borne in mind in implementing schemes for cluster-type training centres for groups of villages, provision of credit to rural artisans, setting up of common facility workshops and rural industrial estates. For the better utilisation of resources under the Plan, the attempt should be to provide assistance intensively at points where conditions are relatively more favourable and to build up in this manner a number of successful centres. which may serve as models and as nuclei for more widespread development. This would not only promote the growth of small industries under conditions favourable to their continuous growth, but will also help integrate industry with development in related fields.

With the increase in the production of cereals, pulses and a number of cash crops like suagrcane and oilseeds visualised in the Third Plan, there will be considerable scope for the expansion of processing industries in rural areas, With a view to providing fuller employment and strengthening and diversifying the rural economy, it will be desirable to develop these industries to the maximum extent in the decentralised and small scale sector and on a cooperative basis. The availability of basic facilities like power, trained labour and organised arrangements for the storage of raw materials and finished products will facilitate economic working of these industries.

In rural areas, where such basic facilities may not be available for some time to come, rural artisans should be assisted to organise on cooperative lines to purchase and stock raw materials, adopt improved techniques and to establish arrangements for the sales of their products.

Development of small industries as ancillaries.-Some efforts were made during the First and Second Plans to promote the development of small scale industries as ancillaries to large industries, and such industries also grew up spontaneously in some measure. Various me- thods of promoting such growth are being examined by a special Committee. In the Second Plan an important scheme was taken in hand for linking up the production of small units located in a new industrial estate at Bangalore with the production of a large project in the public sector, viz., Hindustan Machine Tools Limited.

It is proposed to encourage similar schemes for some of the other projects in both the public and private sectors. In each branch of industry, with a view to planned development it is essential to take a comprehensive view of the requirements of the community, the contribution which small industries can make in relation to large- scale industries and the extent to which processes and stages of production can be decentralised. During the First and Second Plans, spheres of production of small and large units were demarcated in the case of some industries, such as cotton textiles and agricultural implements. In a few other industries such as bicycles, sewing machi- nes and storage batteries, after estimating requirements, separate targets of production were laid down for the large-scale and the small-scale sectors. Various aspects of integration between large and small industries have to be considered in detail for each industry. Among industries which are at present being studied are agricultural implements and machinery, machine and hand tools, bicycles and bicycle parts, sewing machines and sewing machine parts, automobile and diesel engine parts, radio receivers and amplifiers, tanning and foot-wear, fruit and vegetable preservation, cotton textile machinery parts, electric motors (fractional) and fans, paints and varnishes, storage batteries. scientific and table glassware, surgical and mathematical instruments and plastic products.

Industrial cooperatives.-In those industries where considerable progress has been made in the formation of cooperatives such as handloom and coir, the emphasis in the Third plan will be on consolidation of the organisation and finances of the existing cooperatives and on bringing more of the workers within the co- operative fold. In other industries efforts will be directed towards the formation of industrial cooperative societies. The main steps proposed to be taken include provision of financial assistance to cover the expenditure on managerial and supervisory staff for a limited period, subsidisation of the rate of interest charged by the central cooperative financing agencies to the primary cooperative societies, expansion of facilities for the training of staff particularly at the middle level for industrial cooperatives and strengthening of the staff in the State Departments of Industries or Cooperation dealing with industrial cooperatives. A small nucleus organisation is also being set up at the Centre for ensuring coordinated implementation of the programmes for the promotion of industrial cooperatives. In some selected areas, separate industrial cooperative banks may be set up provided certain conditions such as a large concentration of industrial units organised on cooperative lines and the prospects of raising of part of the resources through deposits are satisfied. In the case of those small scale industries where industrial entrepreneurs or partnerships predominate, the formation of industrial associations will be encouraged for obtaining and distributing raw materials and for undertaking other functions such as dissemination of technical and other information, maintenance of accounts, etc.

Arrangements for coordination.-While at the Centre and at the State levels overlapping and duplication of effort in the formulation and implementation of, programmes for village and small industries are avoided, as far as possible, in practice some overlapping and duplication do come about in such matters as establishment of emporia and sales depots, exhibitions, training, etc. Further means will need to be devised to secure coordination among the various Boards and agencies concerned with the implementation of the programmes. However, it is more at the field level that the need for greater coordination is being felt. This applies particularly to/the programmes for khadi and village industries where the activities of State Governments, State Khadi Boards, registered institutions and the block level staff have to be more closely integrated. Moreover, with developments envisaged-in the field of agriculture, power, transport, etc. it is necessary to take a unified view of the entire problem of rural industrialisation. The existing Boards may not always be able to take such a view because each of them operates in its own specified field. The rural industries programme of the Khadi and Village Industries Commission is at present limited to only 12 traditional industries. A comprehensive programme of rural industrialisation will have to take into account the various aspects of development in each area and it will be necessary to ensure that close cooperation of the, various institutions and agencies working at the regional or block level is obtained for preparing local plans and implementing them. it is proposed to examine the various aspects of this question further in consultation with State Governments and the Boards.

## OUTLAY AND ALLOCATIONS

In the Third Plan, a total outlay of Rs. 264 crores has been proposed for programmes of village and small industries, as compared with an estimated expenditure of a little less than Rs. 180 crores in the Second Plan This is made up of about Rs. 141 crores for schemes of the States and Union Territories and about Rs. 123 crores for the Central and Centrally-sponsored programmes and schemes.

In addition to the outlay indicated above, there is a provision of about Rs. 20 crores made for the development of these industries in the programmes of community development and some provisions for the purpose have also been made in the programmes for the rehabilitation of displaced persons, social welfare and the wel- fare of backward classes. Further, about Rs. 275 crores are expected to be invested from private sources including banking institutions.

## HANDLOOM, KHADI AND VILLAGE INDUSTRIES

The development programmes for the Third Plan have been formulated in the light of the experience already gathered and the findings and suggestions of the Evaluation Working Groups referred to earlier. In the case of khadi and village industries, there have been some modifications in the general conception of the programme, Under each programme, it is essential that expenditure on buildings and overheads is kept to the minimum.

Handloom and powerloom industries.The principal aim of the handloom programme during the Third Plan period will be to bring about further expansion of handloom production through fuller employment of the handloom weavers and the introduction of improved techniques. Emphasis will be shifted gradually from rebate on sales-which has already been reduced from 6 nP. to 5 nP.-and other schemes involving, subsidy to more positive forms of assistance. Loan assistance on a more liberal scale will be provided to weavers, so that on the basis of the larger share capital in the cooperatives, it becomes possible for them to borrow larger funds from institutional agencies. Further, a higher priority will be accorded to the supply of improved appliances including semiautomatic looms, provision of facilities for processing and training, introduction of improved designs and purchase of yarn requirements increasingly from cooperative spinning mills. It is proposed to revitalise a number of weak cooperative societies and also to set up some worksheds for common weaving centres on a pilot basis mainly to meet export requirements. Steps will also be taken to stimulate the exports of handloom cloth. The bulk of the handloom programme will be implemented by the State Governments and the Administrations of Union Territories. The programme which the Hand- loom Board will itself implement includes the expansion of the weaver's service centres already set up at Bombay, Madras, Varanasi, Calcutta and Kancheepuram, reorganisation of the two Institutes of Handloom Technology and publicity and propaganda.

With a view to improving the economic condition of handloom weavers, a programme for conversion. of handlooms into, powerlooms .on a. cooperative basis was undertaken early in the Second Plan period. This envisaged the installation of 35,000 powerlooms during the two years 1956-58. Progress was, however, very slow and only 3500-4000 powerlooms were installed out of about 13,000 sanctioned upto the end of the Second Plan period. The remaining 9000-9500 will be installed during the next few years. Effective steps have already been taken to check installation of powerlooms except by the handloom weavers' cooperatives.

Of the total production target of 9300 million yards of cloth set for the last year of the Third Plan period, the share of the decentralised sector, namely, the handloom, powerloom and khadi industries, has been fixed at 3500 million yards, as compared with its output of about 2350 million yards in 1960-61. The major portion of the additional production is expected to come from the handloom industry but no precise allocation of it between these different sections has yet been made. The position will be reviewed from time to time in the light of progress made in each sector.

Khadi-traditional and Ambar.-With the introduction during the Second Plan period of the Ambar charkha with its superior efficiency and output, it was thought that traditional khadi might, relatively speaking, become less important and the Ambar charkha might play a larger part in the future development of khadi.

These expectations were not entirely fulfilled. Work on the Ambar charkha was new to the spinners and altogether different from that on the traditional charkha; the Ambar charkhas manufactured in the earlier stages were not all upto the mark and arrangements for servicing could not be organised to the extent required. Because of these initial difficulties, the Ambar charkhas were worked on an average for about two hours in a day for about 200 days in a year and the average production was only 1.8 hanks per day. The results fell considerably short of the earlier assumptions that the Ambar charkha could be plied for 8 hours in a day for 300 working days in a year and produce 8 hanks per day (the Ambar Charkha Enquiry Committee estimate was 6 hanks per day).

The assumptions themselves might not have been realistic as hand-spinning is done largely by women and only as a part-time occupation. Even so, the earnings of spinners who took to the Ambar charkha show a fair improvement over those of traditional spinners, the average annual earnings being about Rs. 52 for Ambar as against about Rs. 35 for the traditional charkha. In some regions this average for spinners on the Ambar charkha has risen to about Rs. 80 to Rs. 100, and is similar to the average earnings of a large proportion of agricultural labourers. The Ambar spinners have been able to earn this amount in spite of the fact that the rate of spinning wage for the Ambar charkha has been fixed at 2 annas per hank, as against 2 3/4 annas for the traditional charkha. It is also deserving of note that the prices of khadi have not been allowed to rise in spite of the substantial rise which has taken place in the prices of cotton, and which has led to a rise in the prices of mill cloth. On the other hand, the increased production of khadi, both traditional and Ambar, resulted in the accumulation of large stocks in the last two years of the Second Plan period. Special steps have been taken for further development of sales including absorption of pro- duction locally.

Further development of khadi in the Third Plan will, be mainly along the lines of the reoriented programme drawn tip by the Khadi and Village Industries Commission in which the emphasis will primarily be on intensive efforts to secure integrated rural development of selected compact areas or gram ekais, It is proposed to organise 3000 gram ekais, each covering a village or group of villages having a population of 5000 each. The areas to be selected will be those in which some work has already been carried out under the Commission's intensive area scheme or the community development programme, or by some of the voluntary organisations, registered institutions and cooperatives.

Another distinguishing feature of the future programme will be the preparation of local plans for the maximum exploitation of available resources for local use with a view to achieving Local self-sufficiency to the extent possible, These plans are to be executed by registered institutions as well as service cooperatives and gram panchayats. Thus, the responsibility of the Commission will be largely limited to provision of financial and technical assistance and training facilities and the preparation and execution of the programmes will be left to the State Boards, the institutions and the local agencies at the village level. Some steps have already been taken to ensure coordination with the other agencies engaged in rural development programmes but arrangements for bringing about coordination with the programmes for public participation like the Lok Karya Kshetra Programme, etc. have not yet been completed.

The programme for khadi for the Third Plan will aim at gradual reduction of dependence on urban markets and correspondingly greater production for local use and improving the techniques of spinning and weaving so as to raise the output and earnings. Special attention will be given to improvement in the quality of khadi. By the end of the Third Plan period, about 40-50 per cent of the khadi production is expected to be marketed locally and the prices to be reduced by 15-20 per cent. Certain improvements in the Ambar charkha have already been introduced which are expected to raise the productivity from 1 hank per hour to 1.5 hanks per hours. These improvements are at present undergoing field trials. A Committee has also been set up to suggest measures for increasing the sales of hand- spun yarn and khadi.

The traditional charkha will continue to play a definite role, but greater efforts will be made to popularise the Ambar charkha. It is also proposed to bring into effective use 2.5 lakh Amber charkhas out of 3.5 lakh charkhas already distributed and to introduce another 3 lakh charkhas in the gram ekais. Efforts will continue to be made to increase the productivity of the Ambar charkha from the present average of about 2 hanks to an average of 4 hanks and also gradually to increase their working period in the gram ekai centres, so that during the Third Plan period they will be worked on an average for considerably more than 2 hours in 200 days in a year, which was the average during the Second Plan period. As stated earlier, no precise allocation of production targets of cloth has been fixed for the different sections of the decentralised sector but a target of about 160 million yards of khadi is envisaged at present.

**Village industries.** Rural artisans are usually dispersed in a large number of scattered villages and this, combined with their low standard of literacy and poor economic condition, is a considerable impediment to rapid implementation of development programmes. Among the other factors responsible for the slow progress of village industries programmes have been the general lack of previous experience in regard to the development of these industries, lack of trained and qualified staff, location of production centres in unsuitable places, lack of adequate funds and organisation for procurement of raw materials in bulk and failure to introduce more efficient techniques of production. Even such technical improvements as were introduced did not go far enough to secure a material increase in productivity. They did not, therefore, gain general acceptance.

An intensive area scheme was undertaken during the Second Plan period which aimed at intensive development of khadi and village industries as part of a larger effort for developing an integrated rural economy. The basic unit for working out the scheme was a selected area comprising 30-40 villages with a population of about 20,000. The approach in this work has been to prepare village plans for utilising all available manpower and other idle resources and, therefore, the scope of the scheme includes measures for improvement of agricultural production through construction of wells and distribution of seeds and manure as well as construction of houses, roads, dispensaries, etc. At the end of September, 1960, the scheme was in operation in 65 intensive areas and 18 pre-intensive areas. Experience of the working of the scheme has suggested three man conclusions. Firstly, there is great scope for introducing improved techniques and mechanical power in villages without creating any difficulties in regard to the full employment of manpower. This is because there is considerable development potential in the village economy. Secondly, through proper local planning and organisation, it is possible to convert idle manpower into a productive resource. Thirdly, the development of village industries, if it is to be enduring, has to be closely linked up with the development of the rural economy as a whole.

In conformity with the reoriented approach and the aims referred to above, programmes for village industries for the Third Plan period have been prepared for implementation in compact areas and mainly to meet local requirements. Schemes for aid and assistance will be continued but, as mentioned earlier, present subsidies and/or rebates on sales in respect of the products of certain village industries will be replaced by suitable management grants on a progressively decreasing scale. The existing character of many of these industries is expected to change through the use of improved techniques and also the use of power. wherever available and considered desirable.

Some of the more important details of the programmes for different industries are given below :

(i) Hand-pounding of paddy.-It is proposed to introduce improved processes of parboiling, to, train persons in improved methods of production, to continue research for production of improved equipment and to construct godowns.

Under the Rice Milling Industry (Regulation) Act, 1958, powers were delegated to the State Governments for licensing the installation of new rice mills or resumption of operation of defunct mills keeping in view not only the likely effects on the existing hand-pounding industry but also the scope for its further development, further it was also laid down that in permitting new rice milling capacity, preference should be given to rice mills to be run by cooperative societies. The actual working of the Act shows that new milling capacity has been licensed in some of the States and some of the main intensions of the Act have not been fulfilled. It is proposed to consider further the problems which have arisen with a view to ensuring that the policies visualised in the legislation are carried out effectively.

(ii) Oilseeds crushing.-The programme consists of storage of oilseeds and arrangements for their distribution, effecting improvements in the existing Wardha ghani and developing cheaper models with higher productivity. The improved ghanis are proposed to be manufactured in the centres for blacksmithy and carpentary.

(iii) Tanning and leather.-A study group is already examining the working of the flaying and carcass recovery centres with a view to suggesting a practical scheme for better flaying, curing and grading hides and skins and for improving the tanning of hides and skins. In the meanwhile, a special drive has been initiated to, intensify the development of flaying, carcass recovery and tanning and it is proposed to set up 200 centres for intensive development.

(iv) Match.-There has been a change in the pattern of techniques and tools with the object of producing matches with a better marketability. In pursuance of the recommendations of the Cottage Match Special Enquiry Committee, it is proposed to set up 200 new 'D' class production units.

(v) Gur and khandsari.-Production units of varying sizes, equipped with hand-driven or pedal-driven centrifugals will be set up with a view to facilitating the use of power. Introduction of power- driven sugarcane crushers is also being encouraged and assisted.

(vi) Bee-keeping.-The main emphasis during the Third Plan period will be on a gradual expansion of the industry wherever possible on more intensive lines and developing the industry with a view mainly to the secondary results such as improvement of, crops and fruits, etc. rather than the primary results. The programme envisages organisation of 44 area offices, 975 sub-stations and distribution of 94,500 bee- boxes.

(vii) Other village industries.-The programmes, for other village industries like palm gur, hand-made paper, soap, fibre etc. include schemes for setting up production units, distribution of improved equipment, etc. It is also proposed to set up a few centres for the production of methane gas and to draw up a programme for the development of the lime industry.

## SERICULTURE AND COIR

**Sericulture.** The emphasis in the development programme for the sericulture industry will, be on reducing the cost of production, creating a suitable marketing organisation and exploring possibilities of increasing exports. The main factors affecting the cost of production of raw silk are of a continuing nature and a determined effort will have to be made in the Third Plan to bring about an appreciable improvement in the existing position. The cost of mulberry constitutes 60 per cent of the cost of raw silk and it is necessary that the yield per acre of mulberry which is at present comparatively low should be increased. At present only a small proportion of the area under mulberry is irrigated and mulberry culti- vation has to face competition from more remunerative cash crops. The first step to be taken is, therefore, to make mulberry cultivation a paying occupation by increasing the yield per acre through irrigation and application of fertilisers.

The other important factors affecting the cost of production of raw silk are the supply of disease-free seed and of more efficient reeling equipment. Greater attention will be given to these aspects in the Third Plan. It is proposed to develop an adequate seed organisation so that the supply of disease-free seed could be increased. In regard to reeling equipment, experience of the programme in the second Plan is that where cottage, basins have been introduced in place of traditional charkhas, the quality of silk has improved. In the Third Plan, it is intended to encourage this process of substitution further, especially as it would be easier to shift over to cottage ,basins from traditional charkhas without changing the decentralised character of reeling industry. Regarding marketing facilities, organised efforts will have to be made during the Third Plan period to provide facilities for cooperative marketing for both cocoons and raw silk. This would ensure an economic price to rearers and prevent an undue rise in prices of raw silk. The possibilities of increasing exports will have to be explored, in view of keen foreign competition, by producing fabrics of oriental design, colour and pattern. The efforts of the Central Silk Board and the State Gov- ernments will be directed towards the achievement of these objectives in the Third Plan. It is envisaged that production of mulberry and non-mulberry silk will increase to 5 million lb in 1955-66, as against 3.6 million lb in 1960.

**Coir Industry.** Over 55 per cent of the production of the coir industry is exported and the main emphasis in its development programme in the Third Plan will have to be on stepping up exports. The internal organisation of the industry which has grown up around the four process of collecting husk, retting the husk, spinning coir yam and making coir goods such as mats, mattresses, etc. has not been sufficiently strong and stable and has not helped in the growth of the industry on sound lines. Success of the development programme depends largely on organising properly the primary producer of coir yarn who is often a person with meagre resources "hemmed in between the husk dealer at the bottom and the exporter of fibre and yarn at the top who are in a position to dictate terms".

A number of primary cooperative societies for these small producers have been formed, but quite a num- ber have run into losses and it is essential that stricter control and greater supervision over their operations is introduced to ensure healthy development. Apart from placing the coir co., operatives on a more stable footing an important task in the Third Plan will be to supply to the coir spinners treadle spinning machines with a view to improving the quality of yarn and also to make suitable arrangements for dyeing. A special export promotion scheme has been drawn up to assist registered manufacturers-cum-exporters of coir yam and other products, who will be given facilities for import of baling hoops, sisal yam and dyes. Other important items in the programme will be (i) promotion of new lines of production like bristle and mattress fibre, rope-making, utilisation of coconut pith and coir waste and blending of coir with other fibres and materials like rubber, and (ii) setting up of defibring plants for the manufacture of matress and bristle fibre.

## HANDICRAFTS

The All-India Handicrafts Board is concerned with the development of about 40 different crafts. Specific measures of development are being adopted for 12 of these crafts namely, carpets, art metalware, hand-printing, ivory, zari, wood work, papier mache, lacquerware, cane and bamboo and allied crafts, dolls and toys, pottery and jewellery. For these crafts the Board is assisted by special craft committees composed of representatives of craftsmen, manufacturers, dealers, exporters and State Governments. As a result of work undertaken in recant years, the key problems of various crafts have been identified and special steps will be taken to deal with them more fully during the Third Plan. Progress in some crafts depends largely on arrangements for the import and distribution of imported raw materials, as in art metal-ware and ivory; and in some, on improvements in processing and design and the solution of urgent technical problems, as in wood-work, lacquerware, pottery and papier mache; and in some on quality control and observance of specifications and standards, as in zari and brassware. In all crafts more effective organisation of the artisans is a prerequisite for assuring sustained employment, bringing about technological improvements and providing larger facilities.

The number of handicratf cooperatives has increased from about 1000 in 1957-58 to nearly 1600 at the end of the Second Plan. Handicrafts emporia, of which there are now 115, can do much to facilitate the development of cooperatives by providing orders, technical advice and raw materials and credit and other facilities. In the Third Plan work along these lines should be expanded. While cooperatives will constitute the main lint of development in the field of handicrafts, there is scope also for the organisation of small entrepreneurs engaged in handicrafts into associations with a view to ensuring the adoption of improved business standards, control over quality and better conditions for artisans.

With a view to carrying to artisans throughout the country the results obtained. at the four regional design development centres which were established during the Second Plan at

Delhi, Bombay, Bangalore and Calcutta, it is proposed to set up design extension centres at selected places in which there are concentrations of craftsmen. Other activities to be undertaken include market research, promotion of inter-State marketing, laying down standards and specifications and extension of training facilities in the management of emporia, sales manship and display. A Central Handicrafs Development Centre has been recently established with the object of studying the tools and techniques. employed in different handicrafts and evolving suitable improvements. Common facility centres have been set up for certain crafts and will need to be extended during the Third Plan.

For undertaking surveys and providing for training and experimentation, it is proposed to develop craft institutes for carpets, handprinting, bamboo and cane work, metalware, embroidery and various carving crafts. There is considerable scope for the expansion of exports in handicrafts, specially through ensuring quality control, pre-shipment inspection, provision of raw materials, credit and other services to exporters of handicrafts, securing orders from abroad and greater publicity with a view to the development of new markets. These programmes should be accelerated. In the past handicrafts catered mainly to the needs of foreign markets and the higher income groups. In addition to exports, the production of handicrafts has to be oriented towards meeting the needs of custom- ers in different income groups within the country itself and the promotion and development of rural crafts.

## SMALL SCALE INDUSTRIES

The growth of small scale industries constitutes one of the most significant features of development during the Second Plan. This is illustrated by such statistical data as are available for individual small industries. For instance, between 1956-60, the number of small scale units engaged in the production of bicycles increased from 44 to 150, of sewing machines from 35 to 75, of machine tools from 344 to well over 500, of electric motors from 6 to 74 and of electric fans from 22 to 47. The production of bicycles in the small-scale sector increased from about 25,500 in 1956 to 228,000 in 1960 and of sewing machines from 23,600 to 52,000. The value of ungraded machine tools produced by small units rose from Rs 1.3 crores in 1956 to Rs. 4.0 crores in 1960. Large numbers of new units have also come into existence for the manufacture of dyestuffs and plastic products. There is little doubt that the growth of the economy anticipated during the Third Plan will provide large opportunities for both existing and new small scale industries. Development programmes in this sector have to be oriented and strengthened so as to enable small units to take the fullest advantages of these opportunities.

In the course of the Second Plan, a series of measures have been initiated with a view to making technical advice and information, credit and other facilities available for small scale industries. These will need to be developed further in line with the larger tasks set by the Third Plan. In addition to increase and diversification of production, programmes in the Third Plan must aim at securing closer integration between small-scale and large-scale units over a wide range of industries and the development of small industries as ancillaries. Small scale industries which now tend to concentrate in the larger cities and towns, should be promoted increasingly in small towns and at rural centres. Special efforts will also be made to develop cooperatives for production to the extent possible and also for purchase and distribution of raw materials, provision of common facilities, assembling of parts and components, marketing of products and securing orders in bulk. Along with cooperatives, trade associations comprising all small-scale units in each industry can also play a useful part. An essential aspect of development in the Third Plan will be to secure the fuller utilisation of available capacities through the adoption of two shifts and the provision of the requisite raw materials.

In the course of the Second Plan, the organisation for the development of small scale industries has been strengthened both at the Centre and in the States. It now includes 16 Small Industries Service Institutes with 4 Branch Institutes and 53 Extension Centres. Together, these have a corps of technical and specialised. personnel which now comprises over 300 officers and 1500 other staff. In the States also, Departments of Industries are now much better equipped.

More than one-half of the development blocks served by the community development programme already have Extension Officers for Industries. Small Industries Service Institutes have undertaken surveys of about 60 small industries and 102 different areas. In several districts, special studies of the possibilities of developing small scale industries have been carried out. Surveys of individual small scale industries undertaken at regular intervals ran materially assist the planned development. 'Prospect Sheets' are being prepared for a series of industries. A large number of model schemes have also been drawn up. Guidance along these lines for starting new industries should be made available to new enterpreneurs and to cooperatives of artisans as well as educated youth. The programme for the expansion of training facilities during the Second Plan included training in business management and in engineering and non-engineering trades as well as training for district industries officers and block level extension officers. Mobile workshop vans provided a measure of training for artisans in the operation of machines. In each area, in cooperation with State Industries Departments and other agencies, the existing facilities will be further extended during the Third Plan.

Besides building up the necessary organisation for the development of small industries, progress was made in the Second Plan in establishing facilities for the provision of credit, supply of machines and development of marketing and stores purchase. In each of these directions considerable expansion is envisaged for the Third Plan, the main aim being to provide larger facilities for cooperatives, small entrepreneurs and new entrants. Although a beginning has been made in the grant of credit facilities through the scheme operated by the State Bank of India and guarantees for bank loans provided by the Reserve Bank of India, there is vast scope for the extension of credit to small industries by commercial banks gene- rally. Similarly, State Financial Corporations could also provide a larger measure of assistance to small scale industries. The National Small

Industries Corporation has supplied machines on hire-purchase terms of the total value of about Rs. 4.2 crores, including over Rs. 1 crore during 1960-61. It should be possible to extend this scheme and to enable much larger numbers of cooperatives and small entrepreneurs to avail of hire-purchase facilities. Extension of hire-purchase facilities on the part of State Governments and their various agencies would facilitate the development of small scale industries. Stores purchase policies can make a valuable contribution both towards increase in the production of small units and towards the development of new lines of production. Thus, the value of purchases made by the Central Government from cottage and small scale industries rose from Rs. 74 lakhs in 1953-54 to nearly Rs. 6 crores in 1960-61. The bene- fits of stores purchase can be considerably enhanced if purchases are planned for sufficiently in advance and this is accompanied by carefully worked out development programmes. Stores purchase policies and related programmes need to be developed more extensively in the States and also at the Centre.

Among other developments in the field of small scale industries envisaged in the Third Plan, reference may be made to the proposed establishment of depots for stocking raw materials in short supply to be made available to small units with a view to assisting in the fuller utilisation of existing capacity, Facilities for training in the manufacture of small machines will be enlarged through the establishment of additional prototype production and training centres. It is also proposed to set up an industrial design institute and to encourage inventions through prizes and other means. Schemes for quality marking of certain products, such as were initiated during the Second Plan in some States, will be further developed. Three States have recently set up Small Industries Corporations for constructing industrial estates and running raw material depots and common service facility centres. Similar Corporations are being considered in some other States.

Industrial estates.-The programmes for industrial estates was very popular in the Second Plan and about 60 estates were set up. While many of these estates have been successful in their main aim of providing suitable factory accommodation and other conditions favourable to working efficiency, expenditure on some of them has been on the high side and the new employment created is not yet commensurate with the expenditure incurred. Moreover, since most of the industrial estates have been located close to fairly large towns, the objective of establishing new centres of industries has been achieved only to a limited extent.

Besides the 60 industrial estates mentioned above, there are another about 60 industrial estates, started or sanctioned during the Second Plan period, which have still to be completed. It is proposed to set up during the Third Plan period about 300 more new industrial estates of varying sizes and types. They will be located as far as possible near small and medium-sized towns. It is also intended to start a number of industrial estates in selected rural areas where power, water supply and other essential facilities are available or can be readily provided. A rural industrial estate will consist mainly of worksheds for use by artisans along with certain common service facilities and will have only a limited number of regular factory sites and premises. Care will have to be taken to locate such estates in areas where there is a sufficient concentration of artisans and craftsmen who will be in a position to make use of improved techniques, better tools and relatively modern facilities.

At appropriate places, particularly near large cities and towns, it is envisaged that only developed sites should be provided on which small entrepreneurs could erect their own factory buildings, instead of establishing an industrial estate complete with factory With a view to promoting small ancillary industries. it is proposed to start some 'functional estates' for the specific purpose of accommodating small units which will be working as ancillaries to related large-scale industries. A few industrial estates are also proposed to be set up on a pilot basis in selected universities to enable students to earn while they are pursuing their studies and also to provide them with training, so that later they can start their own businesses. Certain suggestions have already been made by a team set up by the Committee on Plan Projects for securing economies in the general lay-out of industrial estates and the construction of factory buildings, etc. These will have to be followed closely in setting up new industrial estates during the Third Plan.

## EMPLOYMENT

On the basis of the total investment under the Third Plan, including outlay in the public sector and investment from private sources. it is estimated that the development programmes for village and small industries outlined in this Chapter will provide part-time employment or fuller employment for about 8 million persons and whole- time employment for about 9 lakh persons. Programmes for the production of khadi are expected to provide mostly part-time employment and those for the handloom industry, powerlooms in the handloom sector, village industries, sericulture and coir industries to provide mainly fuller employment to those already engaged in them. The programmes for small scale industries, including industrial estates and handicrafts and, to a limited extent, some of the other industries, are expected to create mostly whole-time employment.

## EXPORTS

Exports of coir yarn and manufactures, handloom fabrics and handicrafts are valued at an annual average of about Rs. 21 crores. In several directions products of small scale industries have also begun to contribute towards exports. For instance, 600,000 pairs of leather shoes supplied by small units were exported during the Second Plan. Items of production like cotton hosiery, sports goods, build- ers' hardware, leather goods, canned fruits and vegetables and other products have been recently selected for export promotion. It should be possible to secure stable and expanding markets for a growing range of products of small industries. It will, however, be essential to give constant attention to improvement and standardisation of quality, reduction of cost, introduction of new designs and to the proper organisation of production. Schemes of quality marking should be extended widely as they are an important means for bringing about improvements in production and for creating confidence among foreign buyers.

## STATISTICS

Although surveys of a number of industries and specific areas have been carried out by different agencies and organisations in the past, basic statistical data for small industries for the country as a whole, which are essential for making a quantitative assessment of the impact of the programme and for drawing up new plans, are still lacking. A complete list of industrial units is, however, expected to be available through the Census of 1961 and, using this as the 'frame', it is proposed to conduct bi-annual surveys to cover initially all units which employ 10 or more workers (whether using power or not) and having a capital investment not exceeding Rs. 5 lakhs each.

# 13

# Industries and Their Development

## REVIEW OF PROGRESS UNDER THE TWO PLANS

The past decade has witnessed the beginning of an industrial revolution in India. During this period the growth and diversification of industry have been quite remarkable and parti- cularly rapid in the five years of the Second Plan. In this short space of time three new steel works, each of one million tons capacity, have been completed in the public sector and two existing steel works in the private sector have been doubled so as to bring their ingot capacity to two and one million tons respectively.

The foundations have been laid of heavy electrical and heavy machine tools industries, heavy machine buliding and other branches of heavy engineering, and the production of machinery for the cement and paper industries has been started for the first time. In the field of chemical industries there has been an advance on a wide front, leading not only to larger units and greatly increased output of basic chemicals, eg., nitrogenous fertilisers, caustic soda, soda ash and sulphuric acid, but also to the manufacture of a number of new products e.g., urea, ammonium phosphate, penicillin, synthetic fibres, industrial explosives, polythylene. newsprint, and dyestuffs.

The output of many other- industries has increased substantially, e.g. bicycles, sewing machines, telephones, electrical goods. textile and sugar machinery. New skills have been learnt by the workers and, at the other end of the Scale, a large and growing class of industrial managers has come into being. In overall terms organised industrial. production has practically doubled in the last ten years, the index of industrial production having risen from 100 in 1950-51 to 194 in 1960- 61.

This bare recital of facts hardly does justice to the progress that has been achieved. To the eye-of the beholder much more impressive testimony of the upsurge of industrial activity is conveyed by the great new steel works, the huge new open cast mines, the new industrial townships and the various factories springing up in the environs of the main cities of the country. Viewing the industrial 2scene as a whole, independent expert opinion has borne testimony to the great progress achieved in quite a short space of time and has characterised the broadening of the industrial base and the buoyancy of manufacturing enterprises as the most striking change in the Indian economy since the beginning of the Second Plan.

There can be no doubt that in the industrial field far-reaching gains have been secured. It must, however, be recognised that this success, considerable though it is, has so far been insufficient to make any great impact on the general condition of the mass of the population or radically to alter the structure of the eco- nomy. Moreover, compared with the industrial targets which the country set itself, there have been some large shortfalls. Thus, while the setting up of the three new steel plants under the Second Five Year Plan was by itself a most impressive achievement, their combined output of steel was only 0.6 million tons in 1960-61 as against the target of 2 million tons. Similarly in the case of the Tata Iron & Steel Works (TISCO) production has fallen short of the target set for the Second Plan period, the actual output of saleable steel for the five-year period being only 4.5 million tons as against 5.2 million tons reckoned upon in the 1955 forecasts of the Tariff Commission. In the field of fertilisers, the expansion of the Government Sindri Fertilizer Factory and, in the private sector the ammonium chloride project at Varanasi were not completed till 12 to 18 months after the scheduled date and have since been facing serious teething troubles in reaching capacity output. The three new fertiliser plants in the public sector at Nangal,

Neiveli and Rourkela, have all been delayed by one or two years; whereas they were all planned to be more or less in full production in 1960-61, the Nangal plant came into partial production only in January, 1961, while the other two are still under, construction.

The delay in their case, as also in that of the Heavy Electrical Project at Bhopal is mainly due to foreign exchange difficulties. The same cannot be said of the Heavy Machinery, the Mining Machinery and the Foundry/Forge Projects. All these three projects which should by now have been quite far advanced in their construction are still in their initial stages and instead of making a valuable contribution to the Third Plan will only begin to yield output at the end of it. In the case of the project for the manufacture of organic intermediates, which is of cardinal im- portance for the dyestuffs, plastics and drugs industries, the delay in implementation has been due, apart from the time involved in defining the exact scope and content of the project and other preliminaries, to difficulties in concluding negotiations with overseas collaborators. The experience of the Second Plan has shown that the gestation period of a project; especially in the case of heavy engineering industries, is generally longer than expected. This highlights the importance of advance planning.

The main industrial targets which have not been achieved are those set for iron and steel. fertilisers, certain items of industrial machinery, e.g. paper and cement plant machinery, heavy castings and forgings, aluminium, newsprint, raw films, chemical pulp, soda ash, caustic soda, dyestuffs and cement. The shortfalls have unfortunately occurred in some of the very industries which are of crucial importance and have deprived the economy of benefits reckoned on for the start of the Third Plan.

Broadly speaking, it can be said that the industrial advance has been in keeping with the avowed objective of enabling the economy to reach as soon as possible the stage of self-sustaining growth, for, despite the shortfalls, notable progress has been achieved in the development of iron and steel, heavy engineering and other capital goods industries.

The actual cost of many of the projects has. been more than what was envisaged when the Second Plan was drawn up. For instance, on the basis of preliminary project reports, a provision of Rs. 425 crores was made in the Second Plan for the three public sector steel plants, their townships, ore mines and quarries.

The first detailed estimates available by the end of 1956 indicated the revised investment requirements as Rs. 559 crores exclusive of escalation. The latest estimate of the actual outlay on the steel plants and ancillaries referred to above amounts to Rs. 620 crores. The further rise in cost as compared to the 1956 estimates has been explained as due primarily to increases in the quantities of work and to escalation. Similar divergences between actual outlay and the project cost estimates have occurred in the case of TISCO in the private sector. The capital expenditure on their expansion programmes has increased by about Rs. 30 crores over the initial estimates. While differences of this kind may have been inescapable in the past in view of the lack of experience in project engineering, the importance of achieving more accurate estimates requires to be emphasised. In other countries consultant organisations specialising have played an important part in this field and in the last few years similar agencies have begun to spring up in this country also, and they should be able to assist entrepreneurs in project evaluation and in esti- mating capital costs in a more thorough and scientific manner.

In the last ten years, some success has been achieved in the dispersal of industry. The selection of the locations for the three new steel plants (Bhilai, Rourkela and Durgapur), the Heavy Machinery Plant (Ranchi) and the Heavy Electrical Project (Bhopal) and the decision to exploit the lignite deposits at Neiveli in Madras, justified as these all were on purely economic grounds, have also had the effect of creating new centres of industry in areas of the country hitherto untouched by it. Preference in fact has always been given to the location of public sector projects in relatively backward areas whenever this could be done without significant prejudice to technical and economic considerations; and this will be the guiding principle for the future also. Similarly in the licensing of private sector projects the claims of under-developed regions have generally been kept in view to the extent possible.

## FINANCING OF THE INDUSTRIAL PROGRAMMES

The overall fixed investment on public sector projects in 1956-61 has been about Rs. 770 crores as against the original estimate of Rs. 560 crores. For the private sector, the corresponding investment figures are Rs. 850 crores and Rs. 685 crores respectively. Except in the case of the expansion of the Sindri Fertiliser Factory, where internal resources played some significant part in financing new investment, public sector projects were carried out by means of advances from Government in the form of equity capital and loans. The foreign exchange cost of Government steel works, machine-building, mining equipment and heavy foundry/forge projects was met mainly from credits advanced by friendly countries. The equity participation that was originally proposed by Krupp-Demag in the Rourkela Steel Works was the only sizeable private investment envisaged in a public sector project. This was given up in 1956 in the course of negotiations regarding contracts for the purchase of machinery. The steel expansion programmes in the private sector were assisted to the extent of Rs. 70 crores by the International Bank for Reconstruction and Development (I.B.R.D.) and by credits from other international sources and by Rs. 20 crores of interest-free advances from the Government of India. The high levels of investment recorded by private enterprise in other fields were facilitated by deferred payment arrangements resorted to on a considerable scale.

The quantum of funds drawn by private enterprise from each of the recognised sources as compared with the Plan expectations is currently estimated.

The current assessment of the break-up of the overall investment in organised industries as compared with the estimates as forecast in the Introduction to the volume on the Programmes of Industrial Development : 1956-61.

In spite of the large investment (about 30 per cent above the Plan estimate) the physical targets set under the Second

Plan are broadly estimated to have been achieved to the extent of only about 85 to 90 per cent. The wide gap between the rather high target originally set for the cement industry and the capacity actually achieved accounts for a high proportion of the overall shortfall in the physical performance.

## THIRD FIVE YEAR PLAN : OBJECTIVES AND OVERALL APPROACH

The industrial plan for the period 1961-66 has to be governed by the over-riding need to lay the foundation for further rapid industrialisation. over the next 15 years, if long-term objectives in regard to national income and employment are to be achieved. From this point of view it is essential to stress forward with the establishment of basic capital and producer goods industries- with special emphasis on machine building programmes-and also with the acquisition of the related skills, technical know-how and designing capacity, so that in the following Plan periods the growth of the economy in the fields of power, transport, industry and mineral production will become self-sustaining and increasingly independent of outside aid.

There are, however, other factors which have also to be kept in mind. Thus, while longterm objectives require concentration on capital goods industries and increased production of processed industrial raw materials, the industrial programme for the Third Plan has also to provide, to the extent possible, for meeting the demand likely to be generated over the next 5 years for a wide range of other manufactured goods. Owing to the need to devote a large portion of available resources to laying the foundation for future development, it may be difficult to meet this demand in all cases. The aim is to provide fully for essential needs, but restraint on consumption will be unavoidable, especially in the case of goods of luxury or semi-luxury character the production of which it will be difficult to increase pari passu with the growth of demand.

The operation of industries depends not only on markets but also on the supply of raw materials, power, fuel and facilities for transport. Industrial programmes have, therefore, necessarily to take into account, and will in fact be limited by, the rate at which the supply of raw materials, power, etc. can be increased. In particular, power and fuels are likely to be inhibiting factors in the first half of the Third Plan period. This may entail forgoing in some instances the adoption of industrial processes which make a heavy demand on electric power, notwithstanding their attractiveness.

**Industrial Policy.** The expansion of industry will continue to be governed by the Industrial Policy Resolution of April, 1956. As in the Second Plan the roles of the public and private sectors are conceived of as supplementary and complementary to one another. For example, in the case of nitrogenous fertilisers where the public sector has already assumed a dominant role, it is envisaged that during the Third Plan the private sector will enter this field in a bigger way than in the past and supplement the efforts of the public sector. In the case of pig iron, the policy has been relaxed to allow the establishment of plants in the private sector with a maximum capacity of 100,000 tons per year as compared to units of 15,000 tons permitted so far. Programmes for the manufacture of dyestuffs, plastics and drugs in the private sector will be largely complementary to the programme for the manufacture of primary aromatic compounds as by-products at the steel works and of organic intermediates to be undertaken in the public sector. Similarly, whereas the manufacture of bulk drugs will be organised in a big way in the public sector, the further processing of bulk drugs will also be undertaken in the private sector.

Against the background of the goal of a socialist pattern of society, it is necessary in encouraging and approving programmes in the private sector to guard against industrial development being concentrated in the hands of a few entrepreneurs and leading to complete or partial monopolies.

**Industrial Priorities.** Plans for industrial expansion have to hold a balance between different and competing claims of nearly equal importance. There are, however, certain general considerations which require to be mentioned. In the first place, where there are wide gaps between capacity and production or where, by multi-purpose shift operation or the addition of balancing equipment, it is possible to secure greater output at diminishing cost, fuller utilisation of existing installed capacity must take precedence over expansions or the setting up of new units. Secondly, expansion of existing plants will have to be given preference over establishment of new units since the creation of additional capacity in this manner will not only be quicker but will also assist in bringing down the investment costs per unit output. For example, the expansion of the Bhilai, Rourkela, and Durgapur Steel Plants will lower the investment from about Rs. 2000 to Rs. 1500 per ton of finished steel and have a beneficial effect on the level of retention prices.

As regards new developments the accent will have to be on projects which, by contributing to exports, will earn or, by replacing imports, will save foreign exchange. It will not be possible to allow significant expansion of industries, which are heavily dependent on the import of raw materials and whose expansion, therefore, until these materials are available within the country, swells the demand or foreign exchange or maintenance account. On the other hand, having regard both to the short-term and, the long-term needs of the economy, special attention will have to be given to the development of industries for whose products there are reasonable prospects of finding export markets.

Subject to these general considerations the emphasis to be given to programmes and projects over the next few years will have to be broadly in accordance with the following priorities :

(1) Completion of projects envisaged under the Second Five Year Plan which are under implementation or were deferred during 1957-58 owing to foreign exchange difficulties.

(2) Expansion and diversification of capacity of the heavy engineering and machine building industries, castings and forgings, alloy tool and special steels, iron and steel and ferro-alloys and step-up of output of fertilisers and petroleum products.

(3) Increased production of major basic raw materials and producer goods like aluminium, mineral oils, dissolving

pulp, basic organic and inorganic chemicals and intermediates inclusive of products of petrochemical origin.

(4) Increased production from domestic industries of commodities required to meet essential needs like essential drugs, paper, cloth, sugar, vegitable oils and housing materials.

## INDUSTRIAL DEVELOPMENT PROGRAMMES

The development programmes for industries and minerals envisaged under the Third Plan will entail in all about Rs. 2993 crores of investment in order to reach the physical targets set for achievement. Their foreign exchange component is placed at about Rs. 1338 crores.

The estimate of investment on replacement shown in the above Table falls short of the minimum requirements of the cotton textile, jute textile and woollen textile industries in regard to which special studies have been made recently. The backlog of replacements in these three industries alone has been estimated at about Rs. 169 crores. The estimate that investment on replacement account in the Third Plan will be of the order of Rs. 150 crores is more or less a projection of the actual performance during the Second Plan. Even so, it is on the optimistic side in view of (a) the pressure on the available resources of private enterprise and institutional agencies for new investment and (b) the fact that mills with large backlogs of replacement are in no position to provide resources for renovation commensurate with needs and (c) the small allocation made in the Plan to enable the N.I.D.C. to assist these programmes financially.

It is necessary to emphasise that in the case of several projects the estimates of cost, on the basis of which the overall figures have been calculated, lack at this stage the required degree of precision, since these projects are in very preliminary stages of formulation in respect of scope, processes, location and other relevant particulars. Further, some of them fall under industries about which no experience is available in the country which might facilitate more accurate estimates. The esimates of foreign exchange requirements have been made on the assumption that payments wilt be made in cash and that, broadly, machinery and equipment will be obtained from the cheapest sources of supply. These estimates will be vitiated if changes have to be made in these underlying assumptions. For instance, the estimates will go up considerably if, in order to utilise the credits that have been made available by different countries, a large part of the equipment has to be obtained from sources which are not the cheapest.

As compared to these estimates of requirements, the resources available both for the public and the private sector programmes are expected, on present reckoning, to be deficient. The current allocations for industries and minerals in the public sector and the estimates of resources likely to be available for private sector programmes amount only to Rs. 2570 crores-Rs. 1470* crores for the public sector and Rs. 1100 crores for the private sector. In addition, it is hoped that about Rs. 150 crores will be forthcoming for meeting the continuing arrears of replacement and modernisation in certain pre-war industries.

These estimates point to the probability that in both sectors there will be a sizeable spill-over into the Fourth Plan and that the physical targets will not all be achieved by the end of the Third Plan period. Some spill-over would be probable in any case considering the very preliminary stage which some of the projects have so far reached, the uncertainties about foreign exchange and the relatively long gestation periods in the case of heavy industries. It is difficult at this stage to forecast with any great degree of accuracy which projects will get delayed and spillover into the Fourth Plan and which of the physical targets will not be achieved. The mat- ter is, however, discussed further in connection with the public and private sector programmes.

## PUBLIC SECTOR PROGRAMMES

General observations.-The industrial and mineral programmes of the public sector, exclusive of defence industries and projects of the Ministries of Railways and of Transport and Communications designed to meet their own operational requirements, e.g. electric and diesel locomotives, telephones and teleprinters are shown in Annexures I and II. Their overall cost is about Rs. 1882** crores, whereas the provision that it has been possible to make for them is only Rs. 1520 crores (Rs. 1450 crores at the Centre and Rs. 70 crores in the States). It is probable, therefore, that, as already stated, their full implementation will take rather more than five years. It is not possible at present to say what stage each one of the public sector projects will have reached by 1965-66 but some general indications can be given. It will be seen that in Annexure I projects of the Central Government have been grouped in three categories, viz.

(1) projects under execution and carried over from the Second Plan; (2) new projects for which external credits are already assured wholly or partly; and (3) new projects for which external credits have yet to be arranged.

It may reasonably be assumed that all the projects falling in category (1) will be completed during the Third Plan. This should also apply to most of these in category (2); at any rate considerable progress should be made with all these projects. But some of them e.g. the precision instruments project and the two heavy electrical projects are still only at the preliminary stage of formulation and their scope and content are yet to be defined. It is possible, therefore, that some of these projects may spillover to some extent into the Fourth Plan. Obviously, the largest element of uncertainty attaches at present to those projects falling in category (3). Some of these, however, e.g. the alloy steel plant, are of very high priority and every thing possible will have to be done to expedite them.

The industrial programme for the Third Plan takes into account the contribution towards meeting civilian needs that can be expected from expansions envisaged by the defence establishments in the field of alloy steels, tractors, trucks, electric equipment, nitrocellulose and chemical products. The possibilities in this regard are expected to be exploited by making full use of the capacity in the ordnance factories with a view to maximising and diversifying production and achieving consequent investment economies.

The major industrial projects in the public sector included in the Third Plan are in the field of iron and steel, industrial machinery, heavy electrical equipment, machine tools, fertilisers, basic chemicals and intermediates, essential drugs and petroleum refining, These are briefly reviewed later in this Chapter under individual industries alongwith developments in the private sector in allied groups of industries.

Financing of Central Government projects.-Although, as in the Second Plan, the bulk of the funds required for industrial projects in the public sector will be found by Government, quite considerable contributions are likely to be made by some undertakings from their own internal resources. Thus, based on the forecasts of production from public undertakings, it is estimated that about Rs. 360 crores will be available from their internal resources for financing industrial investments. The bulk of this amount will be contributed by the steel plants and fertiliser factories established in the public sector. it is also proposed that the Hindustan Machine Tools should set up one or two new machine tool works under its aegis, financed mainly from its own internal resources in respect of rupee expenditure.

Assistance to institutional agencies and other miscellaneous requirements.-The Central Government's plan for industries has also to take into account the resources required to be made available to the Industrial Finance Corporation and the National Industrial Development Corporation to enable them to operate at somewhat higher levels than in the Second Plan. Provisions have also to be made for plantation industries, the National Productivity Council, the Indian Standards Institution and the extension of the metric system. The financial requirements of all these miscellaneous activities reckoned on an austere basis are shown in Annexure I.

Industrial projects of State Governments.-The major projects proposed for development as public sector undertakings by State Governments are shown in Annexure II. Many of these are spill-over projects from the Second Plan, e.g. the expansion of the Mysore Iron & Steel Works and of the Andhra Paper Mills, the doubling of the Durgapur coke ovens and the piping of gas from Durgapur to Calcutta. The major new projects of State Governments are the third stage expansion of FACT for additional production of ammonium phosphate, am- monium sulphate and ammonium chloride alongwith coordinated developments at Travancore-Cochin Chemicals, and the organic chemicals project of the Durgapur Industries Board for the manufacture of caustic soda, phenol, phthalic anhydride and some other organic chemicals.

Within the allocation for industries in the plans of State Governments, funds have to be found not only for the above projects but also for the State Financial Corporations and for the financing of industrial development area schemes. The latter are intended to contribute to the growth of industries in regions which are at present relatively backward industrially. The idea is to acquire in industrially backward regions suitable tracts of land at focal points where good communications exist or can be easily developed, to develop factory sites thereon, provide the basic facilities like power, water, sewage, etc. and then offer them for sale or on long lease to prospective entrepreneurs. The outlay proposed in the State plans for industrial development area schemes amounts to Rs. 5.4 crores.

## PRIVATE SECTOR PROGRAMMES

General observations.-Under the Industrial Policy Resolution of April, 1956, a very extensive field of activity is open to private enterprise outside the Schedule A Industries which are reserved for the State. Private enterprise has not been slow to take advantage of these opportunities; reference has been made earlier in this Chapter to the buoyancy of manufacturing enterprise. It must not, however, be forgotten that to this lively development of the private sector the large programme of public investment undertaken in the last ten years has very materially contributed both directly, by the provision of the necessary overheads, and indirectly, by stimulating demand and so, creating an atmosphere favourable to industrial growth. The further large-scale public investment planned for the next five years is likely to maintain the same favourable conditions for the operations have to fit themselves into the overall framework of industrial development and conform to the priorities outlined in paragraph 19 above. Moreover, shortages of foreign exchange and of power are likely to impose throughout the period of the Third Plan limitations on the free growth of the private sector such as have only begun to be seriously felt during the closing years of the Second Plan. Whereas during the Second Plan several of the original industrial targets were raised, in the Third Plan any revision of the industrial targets would have to be considered from the point of view of a totality of circumstances, including foreign exchange, domestic resources, transport, power supply and trained personnel as well as the priorities laid down in the Plan.

With a view to formulating capacity and production targets for the Third Plan, the Planning Commission had discussions with representatives of various industries prior to as well as following the publication of the Draft Outline in June, 1960. The Commission has also had before it the recommendations made by Development Councils and by other agencies who had been requested to consider the targets for specific industries. On wider issues, such as the finan- cial resources likely to be available to the private sector for investment during the Third Plan. discussions have also been held with premier industrial and commercial organisations of the country.

The statement at the end of the Chapter (Annexure III) shows the targets proposed for various industries under the Third Plan. These are overall targets for both the public and private sctors. For the engineering industries they are based on utilisation of installed capacity on double shift operation.

## FINANCING OF PRIVATE SECTOR PROGRAMMES

Sources of supply of investible funds for financing gross fixed assets formation in the. private sector during the Third Plan period and the quantum available from each source are estimated.

According to these estimates the funds likely to be available fall short of the requirements of the private sector programmes which are estimated to amount to Rs. 1350 crores. Apart from the overall shortage of financial resources, there is the still more difficult problem of finding the foreign exchange required for achieving all the targets. This is estimated to amount to not less than Rs. 530 crores. Foreign aid or credit to meet these requirements in full is not at present in sight. It cannot be said at this stage in which specific industries the actual performance will fall short of the targets. Much will, depend on the success attained in securing foreign collaboration and investment in industries where these are felt to be desirable. An endeavour will, however, be made to ensure the full achievement of targets in the case of industries of high priority. To this end, it is intended that the industrial programmes should be regularly reviewed and allotments of foreign exchange/credit made every six months for individual industries in the light of the progress achieved and the priorities which may suggest themselves from time to time. In this way it is hoped to achieve balanced progress.

In determining priorities, an important consideration will be the contribution an industry can make towards mitigating the pressure on foreign exchange either through a reduction in the level of imports or through additional exports. Thus industries which will directly save or earn foreign exchange will be given priority over industries which would only contribute to an increase in the supply of manufactured goods for the home market. In estimating import savings more stringent criteria will have to be applied than hitherto.

## MAIN FEATURES OF THE INDUSTRIAL PROGRAMME

The salient features of the development programmes of major industries in the Third Plan are discussed in the following paragraphs:

## METALLURGICAL INDUSTRIES

Iron and steel.-The overall targets proposed under this industry are 10.2 million tons of steel ingot capacity and 1.5 million tons of pig iron for sale. The estimates of requirements of pig iron and of finished steel by 1965-66, which have provided the background for the planning of this industry, are indicated below alongwith the figures of the installed capacity available at the start of the Third Plan. A basic assumption made in connection with the demand forecast is that the current selling price of steel will hold good for the Third Plan period.

The share of the private sector in the steel target is 3.2 million tons of ingots. The existing installed capacity of TISCO and IISCO is 3.0 million tons. The expansion of capacity for steel in the private sector is expected to come from the installation of scrap- based electric furnaces which will augment the supplies of billets to re-rollers. The supply of billets to re-rolling mills from the main producers of steel is visualised at one million tons by the end of the Third Plan. As regards saleable pig iron, the output from the private sector is provisionally placed at about 0.3 million tons to be achieved through expansions of iron making capacity based on low shaft blast furnaces and/or electric smelting of iron ores.

As regards the public sector, rapid achievement of capacity output from the new steel plants whose construction was completed by 1960-61 will be the most important task in the initial years of the Third Plan. New developments included in the Plan comprise the expan- sion of the Bhilai, Durgapur and Rourkela steel plants and of the Mysore Iron and Steel works and the establishment of a new steel plant at Bokaro. In addition there is included in the Plan a project for a pig iron plant based on low shaft blast furnace techniques and the use of coke from the Neiveli lignite. The Neiveli pig iron project on which considerable prelimi- nary investigations have still to be conducted in regard to the proc- ess as well as the raw materials intended to be used, represents an intermediate stage towards the establishment of a steel plant of about 0.5 million tons in the Southern region. The financial provision included for this scheme in the Third Plan covers mainly the require- ments of a high temperature carbonisation plant for the production of lignite coke.

The expansion programme of the Mysore Iron and Steel Works comprises mainly the spillover expenditure on the ferro-silicon plant and provision for steel making by the L.D. process and for a light structural mill.

The layout of the new steel plant at Bokaro is being planned for a capacity of two million tons of steel ingots, but in the first phase of development it is proposed to instal facilities for the production of one million tons. This plant is expected to specialise in the production of different types of flat products. The exact types to be produced in the first phase and the nature of the finish- ing facilities to be provided therefor are currently under examina- tion.

On the completion of these development programmes, the capacity for mild steel of the public sector steel works will be raised from three million tons to seven million tons, making along with the capac- ity of the private sector a total of 10.2 million tons of ingots.

The overall investment required for the public sector steel development programmes included in the Third Plan is estimated at Rs. 525 crores. This is inclusive of the investments required for in- creasing the production of limestone at Nandini and iron ore at Dalli Rajara and Barsua in the case of the expansion programmes. It also includes the investments required for the additional production of coal and iron ore for the Bokaro steel plant and the expenditure on townships at all the four steel works,

The total production of finished steel in the country during the Third Plan period is tentatively estimated to be of the order of 24.1 million tons inclusive of an output of 0.3 million tons from the Bokaro steel plant in 1965-66.

On the basis of the above forecast of production and of the tonnages of different end-products likely to be available, shortages are expected to be significant, particularly in the initial years of the Plan period, in the case of flat products, e.g. tin plate, sheets, skelp and plate. This will call for the formulation of a scheme of priorities for determining the quantum of imports and allocation of flat products to different classes of consumers. Prima facie, it should be possible to narrow down the margin between the demand and the indigenous supply of steel products in short supply by free inter- change of steel ingots between the public sector plants so as to achieve the most intensive use of the rolling mill facilities for flat products. This possibility should receive attention in production planning in the light of the situation that may obtain from year to year. The output of the main producers of steel will include electrical steel sheets produced by TISCO and at Rourkela. Similarly finished steels turned out by the producers operating on electrical furnace billets and by the ordnance factories will include spring steels and free- cutting steels, The level of production of these special varieties of mild steel will be related to the demand estimated for 1965-66 placed at 75,000 tons for spring and free-cutting steels and 70,000 tons for electrical steel sheets.

Tool, alloy and stainless steels.-The Second Five Year Plan envisaged the establishment of an alloy, tool and special steel plant in the public sector. Preliminary project reports for a plant of 25,000 tons annual output in terms of different finished products were received in 1958 from some of the leading producers abroad. Action on the implementation of this scheme was delayed as a result of the decision taken to get a more detailed project report the scope of which was modified in the course of its preparation, to facilitate the establishment of a more viable unit in line with the higher levels of demand for alloy steels visualised under the Third Plan. After the receipt of the report from the consultants in July, 1960, it was decided in November, 1960, to establish at Durgapur an alloy and tool steels plant of 48,000 tons annual output with built-in capacity in certain primary units so that it could be rapidly expanded to 100,200 tons.

The current heavy demand for imports of these high priced but essential raw materials of the engineering industries is a serious problem on maintenance account. The manufacture of tool, alloy and stainless steels has, therefore, to be assigned very high priority in the Third Plan from the point of view both of the requirements over the five-year period and of the probable long-term growth of demand for these products. The demand estimates for 1965 and 1970, which have been kept in view as a guide for planning in this field, are indicated below along with the end-product pattern of the public sector project to be established at Durgapur.

The projected Durgapur alloy steel plant will incorporate some of the latest equipment and processes for the manufacture of these products developed recently in advanced countries. Thus, it is proposed to instal electric soaking pits in preference to gas-fired Pits. The desirability of using sponge iron instead of scrap as the starting raw material and of introducing continuous casting facilities is expected to be kept in view in connection with, the further expan- sion of this plant. In the current phase of development, it is planned that the plant should draw supplies of pedigree scrap from the adjoining Durgapur steel works. The outlay on the project is estimat- ed at Rs. 50 crores in all of which Rs. 20 crores would be the foreign exchange element.

The ordnance factories of the Ministry of Defence are expected to function as a second source of supply of alloy steels in the public sector. The combined output of the Ishapur and Kanpur ordnance factories, mainly in the category of constructional steels but includ- ing some output of spring steels as well, is estimated at 50,000 tons.

The rest of the development in this industry is envisaged in the private sector where additional production facilities will be planned having regard to the deficits in different categories of these products still outstanding.

Aluminium.-In the field of non-ferrous metals, aluminium is expected to continue to retain its dominant position. The target of 87,500 tons set for 1965-66 is expected to be achieved as a result of the following projects in the private sector which have already been cleared for implementation:

(1) Expansion of the Indian Aluminium Company's plant at Hirakud by 10,000 tons per annum and the Alwaye plant by 5000 tons per annum;

(2) Establishment of a smelter at Rihand of 20,000 tons annual capacity;

(3) Establishment of a smelter at Koyna of 20,000 tons annual capacity;

(4) Establishment of a smelter near Salem of 10,000 tons annual capacity; and

(5) Expansion of the plant of the Aluminium Corpora- tion of India by 5000 tons per annum.

In the context of the rising demand for electrolytic copper and the relatively meagre possibilities of substantially increasing its domestic production during the Third Plan, further expansion of capacity for aluminium production appears prima facie desirable. The amount of such expansion would mainly have to be determined by the pace at which it is considered feasible from the technological angle to substitute aluminium for copper over the next five years, though the possibility of exporting aluminium would also be a relevant con- sideration. The additional foreign exchange needed for developing further capacity would be quite considerable if, as seems almost certain, arrangements have also to be made for the connected power facilities, The attractiveness of new proposals for further expansion of aluminium production would depend largely upon the extent to which they can provide for these additional foreign exchange requirements.

**Copper.** The production of electrolytic copper will commence in the early years of the Third Plan with the commissioning of the unit at Ghatsila by the Indian Copper Corporation. The smelter and the electrolytic refinery associated with the Khetri and Daribo copper mines for an annual production of 11,500 tons of electrolytic copper are likely to be established by the middle of 1964.

**Zinc.** The production of zinc for the first time in India is expected to be achieved by the middle of the Third Plan period with the commissioning of the zinc smelter based on zinc Concentrates from the Zawar Mines in Rajasthan. The annual capacity of the plant will be 15,000 tons. It is also being equipped to operate a by-product sulphuric acid plant based on the smelter gases which will be used for the manufacture of phosphatic fertilisers.

## ENGINEERING INDUSTRIES-HEAVY AND LIGHT

Large-scale developments are proposed in this sector in view of the prospects of increased supplies of pig iron and steel, the emphasis on machinery manufacture and the scope in many instances for wide employment opportunities in relation to investment. The public sector will mainly concentrate on projects for the production of heavy machinery and heavy machine building.

Apart from this, targets have been proposed within this field, to be achieved mainly by private enterprise, in respect of an extensive range of manufactured items, i.e. agricultural machinery and constructional equipment like trac- tors, diesel engines, road rollers dumpers and shovels; power distri- bution and measuring equipment like transformers (below 33 KV), elec- tric cables and wires, and house service meters; rail and road transport items like locomotives, wagons, passenger coaches, commercial vehicles (buses and trucks); complete plants for the setting up of new units for the sugar, paper, cement and textile industries and certain chemical industries, steam-raising equipment (boilers) and machine tools, consumable stores like welding electrodes and durable consumer goods like passenger cars, sewing machines, bycycles and electric fans. These targets do not. however, cover all lines of expansion.

The production of new items in this field, of which various types of machinery are the most important, is expected to be developed both in independent plants specially established for the purpose like the A.V.B. (Associated Cement-Vickers-Babcock Wilcox.) plant at Durga- pur for the manufacture of equipment for the cement industry and high pressure boilers, and also by the deversification of the output of engineering workshops already in operation or currently under estab- lishment. In the latter case, the investment required for developing the production of new items of machinery will be substantially lower than would otherwise be the case.

This is the explanation for the apparently low estimates of investments vis a vis estimates of output in certain industries. In some of the manufacturing programmes, there is also the practice of entrusting the production of certain compo- nents to ancillaries or even major establishment with surplus capaci- ties. In the circumstances, the normal relationship between output and investment cannot be applied.

In the following paragraphs the programmes in the principal sectors of the engineering industries are briefly outlined.

## FOUNDRY AND FORGE SHOPS FOR CASTINGS AND FORGINGS

Foudry/forge capacity is of crucial importance for the machinery manufacturing programmes. Within the overall targets set for this field in the Third Plan-1.2 million tons of grey iron castings, 200,000 tons each of steel castings and forgings-the accent in the public sector programmes is largely on production in the higher ton- nage ranges for heavy machinery manufacture. The facilities which are being planned in the public sector projects are as follows:

Capacity for 45,000 tons of steel castings, 38,000 tons of grey iron castings and about 70,000 tons of steel forgings will be created in the foundry/forge which is being set up at Ranchi. Further capacity will become available from foundries attached to the steel plants at Durgapur, Bhilai and Rourkela, to the Heavy Electrical Project, Bhopal, to the Mining Machinery Project, Durgapur, and to the Hindu- stan Machine Tools. A steel foundry is under construction at the Chittaranjan Locomotive Works.

Castings and forgings will also be required by several other machinery projects in the public sector included in the Third Plan, but a clear picture of these requirements and the best arrangements for meeting them, i.e. whether through captive foundry/forges or through independent units, or a combination of, both will only emerge when the project reports are received.

A substantial part of the new capacity in the private sector is expected to come up as the result of demand stemming from the expansion of the automobiles industry and the manufacture of machinery for textiles, cement, sugar, paper and similar capital goods industries.

## INDUSTRIAL MACHINERY

The principal projects of the public sector in this field are the Heavy Machinery Plant near Ranchi; the Mining Machinery Project, Durgapur; the Heavy Electrical Equipment Plant, Bhopal and two other heavy electrical projects for which locations are currently under study by an expert committee.

The heavy machinery plant, which is being set up near Ranchi, on its expansion to 80,000 tons output per year will be able to supply the bulk of the equipment required for adding to steel making capacity at the rate of about one million tons annually. The expanded mining machinery project at Durgapur is being designed for an annual output of 45,000 tons of equipment. The three heavy electrical equipment projects are designed to ensure from indigenous sources a wide range of electrical equipment sufficient to enable power genera- tion to be increased at an annual rate of two million kW per year from 1971 onwards. They will also produce heavy motors, rectifiers and control equipment. Manufacture of high pressure boilers for thermal power plants with an annual capacity of about 28,000 tons (2500 tons of steam per hour) is another heavy engineering project tied with assistance from Czechoslovakia. Though it was originally visualised as a part of a composite heavy electrical equipment project, it is now proposed to develop it as an independent plant specialising in manufacture of high pressure boilers.

The targets set for the production in the private sector of complete plants to meet the demands of cement, paper, sugar and cotton textile mills and the levels of indigenous content envisaged.

It is highly desirable that the targets set for 1965-66 in re- spect of machinery items should be achieved and on the basis of the indigenous content specified in each case. The consortium approach for the manufacture and supply of complete plants for factories by groups of firms in association-which has been adopted for the manufac- ture of sugar mill machinery-may facilitate a speedy advance in other fields also.

## MACHINE TOOLS

Exclusive of the contribution from the small-scale sector reckoned at about Rs. 5.0 crores, the target for machine tools is envisaged at Rs. 30 crores, worth of output by 1965-66 as against an estimated production of Rs. 7 crores on the same basis in the last year of the Second Plan. Though there would thus be nearly a three- fold increase of output, this target of production falls substantially below the Rs. 50 crore level of yearly demand forecast for machine tools by the end of the Third Plan. There are physical limitations to a bigger step-up of production in this field arising from the large demand for skilled labour and the wide diversity in the categories of machine tools required. This is, however, a field of high priority where further developments should be undertaken, if feasible.

In the public sector, it should be possible within the foreign exchange arrangements so far made to proceed at once with the expansion of Hindustan Machine Tools, Jalahalli (HMT) and Praga Tools, Hyderabad, and with the establishment of a new heavy machine tools plant near Ranchi and one more machine tool works of the same size and type as HMT to be located in Punjab. It is estimated that the com- bined output of these machine tool works in the public sector inclusive of the contribution expected from the prototype factory, Ambernath, of the Defence Ministry, will rise to about Rs. 15.0 crores.

The expansion programmes in the private sector will broadly have to be complementary and supplementary to the public sector plans and formulated against the background of the demand forecast for the different groups and families of machine tools.

## RAILWAY ROLLING STOCK

In this field the most important development in the public sector will be the diversification of the Chittaranjan Locomotive Works so as to include the production of electric locomotives. The traction motors for these electric locomotives are proposed to be manufactured at the Heavy Electricals Ltd., Bhopal. The project for the manufacture of diesel electric and diesel hydraulic locomotives 2included in the Railway Plan will make a major contribution towards the achievement of self-sufficiency in respect of railway equipment. The Rs. 12 crore diesel loco project will have an annual capacity of 140 units with a turnover value of Rs. 10.0 crores. The diesel hy- draulic engines would also make use of the Suri transmission, an improved design developed recently by an engineer of the Indian Rail- ways which has been licensed for exploitation in West Germany. The private sector will continue to manufacture electric multiple coaches, wagons and meter gauge steam locomotives.

## SHIPBUILDING

The programmes under this head include the expansion of Hindustan Shipyard Ltd. and the construction of a drydock at Vishakha- patnam. With the completion of these developments, the Visakhapatnam shipyard will be capable of producing ships of a total tonnage of 50,000-60,000 D.W.T. per year.

A second shipyard at Cochin and a scheme for the manufacture of marine diesel engines form part of the public sector programme. The former is estimated to cost Rs. 20 crores and the latter Rs. 5 crores.

Manufacture of smaller vessels for coastal and river traffic, tugs and boats and propelling machinery therefor will continue in the private sector. Construction activity will be mainly on a jobbing basis and no specific targets have, therefore, been fixed for these 'custom-built' items.

## STRUCTURAL FABRICATION

As against the current structural fabrication capacity estimated at 500,000 tons, inclusive of the capacity of wagon build- ers, the target for the last year of the Third Plan is visualised at 1.1 million tons. The accent is expected to be much more on develop- ing fabrication facilities for heavy structurals than has been the case in the past. Allied to these structural shops, facilities for the manufacture of items like pressure vessels, heat exchangers and other types of chemical plant and equipment are envisaged to the developed through the establishment of heavy plate and vessels works. The manufacture of cranes is another important line of allied activity.

In the public sector plan, detailed proposals have been worked out for a heavy structural works and a plate and vessel works to be established at a single location in the Nagpur-Wardha area. The former would have a capacity of 10,000 tons and the latter 18,000- 20,000 tons per year on single shift basis. Together, these plants are estimated to cost Rs. 10.1 crores.

## INDUSTRIAL AND POWER BOILERS

In addition to the capacity to be developed in the public sector under the Czechaided heavy electrical project, facilities for the production of boilers for power plants as well as for meeting the steam raising demand of different industries are planned for develop- ment in the private sector. The value of the output of boilers in 1965-66 is envisaged at Rs. 25.0 crores.

## AUTOMOBILES AND ANCILLARY INDUSTRIES

The levels of development proposed for these industries are broadly in keeping with the recommendations made by the ad hoc Commit- tee on the Automobile Industry in its Report of March, 1960 and by the Development Council for Automobiles and Ancillary Industries. The capacity targets in respect of all the items conform to the minimum targets recommended by the Development Council with the exception of passenger cars, for which a lower figure as proposed by the ad-hoc Committee has been accepted. The targets tentatively proposed for passenger cars, commercial vehicles, jeeps, motor cycles and scooters are :

| | number |
|---|---|
| passenger cars | 30000 |
| commercial vehicles | 60000 |
| jeeps and station wagons | 10000 |
| motor cycles, scooters and three wheelers | 60000 |

The target for commercial vehicles includes 4000 units expected to be produced at the ordnance establishments.

To reach the targets of production of automobiles without excessive and continued strain on foreign exchange resources, it will be necessary to achieve at least 85 per cent indigenous content by 1965-66 as compared with less than 60 per cent at the start of the Third Plan. Investment designed to increase the indigenous content has to take precedence over investment for establishing new units or expanding existing capacity. Priority has also to be given to the production of commercial vehicles. Exclusive of the investment on facilities for producing castings and forgings to meet the full requirements of the automobile industry, the direct investment in this field vis-a-vis the targets is placed at about Rs. 85 crores with a foreign exchange element of Rs. 40 crores. Even more important than the direct investment is the demand for foreign exchange on maintenance account which for the Third Plan period, as a whole, has been estimated at Rs. 175 crores.

## OTHER ENGINEERING INDUSTRIES

With the exception of the following projects in the public sector, the expansion of capacity under other engineering industries vis-a-vis the targets in Annexure III to this Chapter is expected to be secured through the efforts of private enterprise : (a) Precision Instruments project. (b) Expansion of Precision Instruments Factory, Lucknow (c) Expansion of Hindustan Cables, Rupnarainpur. (d) Expansion of the Government Electric Factory, Bangalore. (e) Heavy Compressors and Pumps project. (f) Ball and Roller Bearings project. (g) Surgical Instruments, project, Guindy. The precision instruments project is of fundamental importance in relation to future growth and covers new ground in a highly specia- lised field. Manufacture of control instruments and equipment with an ultimate annual turn-over of about Rs. 20 crores is envisaged under this project. The surgical instruments plant near Guindy has been planned for the manufacture of 25 groups of instruments valued at about Rs. 2.7 crores per year. The expansion of Hindustan Cables is, like the Diesel Loco Project, linked with the growing demands of Government in the field of communications.

Where no targets have been fixed for specific items in this as well as in other fields, developments are expected to be regulated by ad hoc reviews.

## CHEMICAL AND ALLIED INDUSTRIES

The largest and most important investment under this head during the Third Plan will be in the field of fertilisers. Large- scale development of nitrogenous fertilisers has become necessary as a result of the steep rise in the demand for them in connection with the agricultural programme and has been facilitate by the availability of waste gases from the petroleum refineries and coke-oven plants, the associated gas liberated in the mining of crud petroleum and. most important of all, petroleum naphtha, Naphtha has also given a fillip to organic chemical industries which have so far had to depend mainly on alcohol from molasses and acetylene from carbide. A favourable climate for the production of organic intermediates has been created by the recovery of organic hydrocarbons, e.g., benezene, toluene, naphtha-lene, anthracene and xylene which is expected to be further stepped up in the public sector pari passu with the increased coking of coal at the steel plants. The extraction of some of these hydro- carbons is considered feasible at some of the petroleum refineries by marginal modification and additions. The programmes of some of the major industries falling under this head are briefly described below.

## INORGANIC CHEMICALS

Fertilisers.-The demand for nitrogenous and phosphatic fertilisers is expected to expand to about one million tons in terms of nitrogen and 400,000 tons in terms of P2O2 by 1965-66. In the case of phosphatic fertilisers the end-product will have to be at least 50 per cent water soluble in order to meet the requirements of the users. In the case of nitrogen, the following end-product pattern forms the basis for production planning.

***Table 9 : End-product pattern for nitrogenous fertilisers (000 tons of N)***

| | 1965-66 |
|---|---|
| ammonium sulphate | 230 |
| ammonium sulphate-nitrate | 30 |
| nitrochalk and nitrolimestone | 160 |
| nitrophophate complex fertiisers | 45 |
| urea | 305 |
| ammonium phosphate | 200 |
| ammonium chloride | 30 |
| total | 1000 |

It will be seen from the above that a significant portion of the additional output of nitrogen is being planned in the form of compound and/or complex fertilisers so that a part of the phosphate ($P_2O_5$) requirements will also be met simultaneously. The pattern of produc- tion is expected to keep within reasonable limits dependence on sul- phur and gypsum.

In addition to the completion of fertiliser projects carried over from the Second Plan, it is proposed that further capacity for nitrogenous fertilisers should be established in the public sector by both the Central and some of the State Governments.

At the time of the publication of the Draft Outline it was provisionally thought that the public sector capacity for nitrogenous fertilisers would be ex- panded to 800,000 tons and that the balance of 200,000 tons required to reach the target of one million would be provided by the private sector.

It now seems probable that the private sector will undertake rather more than previously contemplated and that the capacity in the public sector by 1965-66 will be somewhat less than 800,000 tons.

Applications from private enterprise have so far been approved, apart from the doubling of the Varanasi factory of Sahu Chemicals to 20,000 tons, for a plant at Ennore near Madras (8,250 tons of N) ; in Madhya Pradesh (50,000 tons of N) ; at Vishakhapatnam (80,000 tons of N) and Kothagudiam (80,000 tons of N) in Andhra Pradesh ; and in Rajasthan (80,000 tons of N).

In addition, private enterprise in partnership with the West Bengal Government is expected to put up a fertiliser factory at Durgapur (58,000 tons- of N).

It has also been proposed that fertiliser factories should be set up in Gujarat and Mysore, but their details are still being examined.

The capacity in the public sector by the end of the Third Plan is at present expected to be about 730,000 tons as shown below :

*Table 10 : Capacity for nitrogenous fertilisers in the public sector*

| | (tons of) |
|---|---|
| existing capacity (Sindri, Nangal, FACT) | 217000 |
| Rourkela | 120000 |
| Neiveli | 70000 |
| Trombay | 90000 |
| Nahorkatiya | 32500 |
| further ėxpansion of FACT | 40000 |
| Gorakhpur | 80000 |
| one more fertliser plant in the public sector | 80000 |
| total | 729500 |

As a general rule, the size of the new plants will be fixed at 70,000 to 80,000 tons of nitrogen in order to provide guidance and facili- tate the planning of the manufacture of fertiliser plant equipment.

Under straight phosphatic fertilisers, a capacity of 200,000 tons in terms of P205 has already been planned. No further expansion of capacity is envisaged in terms of superphosphate.

The production of nitrogenous and phosphatic fertilisers is expected to be somewhat as follows during 1961-66 :

*Table 11 : Estimates of production of Nitrogen and $P_2O_5$*

(000 tons)

| | N | P205 |
|---|---|---|
| 1961-62 | 140 | 100 |
| 1962-63 | 200 | 150 |
| 1963-64 | 300 | 225 |
| 1964-65 | 500 | 300 |
| 1965-66 | 800 | 400 |

The overall investment and the foreign exchange cost of the fertilisers programme on capital account are estimated at Rs. 225 crores and Rs. 100 crores respectively.

Sulphuric acid.-As a major barometer of industrial activity, the target of 1.75 million tons set for sulphuric acid provides an indication of the tempo of all-round expansion planned. The growth of sulphuric acid production in the public sector is visualised in con- junction with fertiliser production, by-products recovery and pickling operations at the steel plants, petroleum refining and manufacture of organic intermediates and drugs, and uranium extraction from the ores. The overall demand for the acid in the public sector by 1965-66 is ex- pected to be about 550,000 tons as against a capacity of about 150,000 tons in existence in the public sector at the end of the Second Plan.

The break-up of the estimated consumption of this acid in 1960-61 and the requirements in 1965-66 are assessed as follows:

(000 tons of suphuric acid)

| | estimated consumption 1960-61 | estimated inrepuirement in 1965-66 |
|---|---|---|
| fertilisers | 210 | 1090 |
| steel works | 26 | 30 |
| rayon and staple fibre | 59 | 135 |
| Sulphates and other inorganic | 24 | 40 |
| salts petroleum refining | 8 | 20 |
| miscellaneous | 33 | 185 |
| total | 360 | 1500 |

Whereas the production of sulphuric acid has so far been based on sulphur, a part of the capacity proposed to be set up in the Third Plan period will be linked with by-product smelter gases (zinc and copper smelters) and with pyrites from the Amjor deposits in Bihar. The pyrites-sulphuric acid plants, it established in conjunc- tion with large-scale fertiliser plants near the steel works at Durga- pur and Bokaro, could find a profitable outlet for the 'spent oxide' for use in the sintering of iron ore.

**Sulphur.** It has been estimated that the consumption of sulphur will increase from about 175,000 tons in 1960-61 to about 600,000 tons inclusive of the sulphur equivalent of pyrites and by- product smelter gases in the last year of the Third Plan. With the development of new sources of sulphur supply in other countries, no serious rise in the import price of this basic industrial raw material is anticipated. Even so, it still remains important to establish some indigenous source of sulphur. A major effort at tackling this problem will be made-during the Third Plan. A public sector project has been included in the Plan for the recovery of sulphur from pyrites.

Caustic Soda and Soda Ash.-The targets for these chemicals are based on meeting the estimated requirements for 1965-66 in full from indigenous sources. With the exception of the expansion pro- gramme of Travancore-Cochin Chemicals and the organic chemicals scheme of West Bengal, the development in these two industries rests entirely with private enterprise. The additional production required in order to reach the target for caustic soda is expected to be based on both the electrolytic and the chemical processes.

The relative shares of the capacity for caustic soda, processwise, in the last years of the Second and Third Plans are:

(tons)

| | **1960-61** | **1965-66** |
|---|---|---|
| chemical caustic | 27000 | 50000 |
| electrolytic caustic | 97435 | 350000 |
| total | 124435 | 400000 |

The expansion of soda ash production is also expected to cover the production of heavy soda ash. An indication of the growth of capacity for heavy and light soda ash is given below:

(tons)

| | **1960-61** | **1965-66** |
|---|---|---|
| soda ash (light) | 220000 | 370000 |
| soda ash (heavy) | nil | 160000 |
| total | 220000 | 530000 |

**Miscellaneous.** Apart from the major heavy chemicals whose programmes have been outlined above, the Third Plan envisages specific levels of development for other products like titanium dioxide, calci- um carbide, sodium hydrosulphite, sodium sulphate, potassium hydroxide and barium chemicals against the background of the expansion of de- mand.

## ORGANIC CHEMICALS

Large-scale developments are envisaged in the field of organic chemicals almost for the first time. These may be said to have followed the build-up in the demand for marry items as a result of the development of allied chemical industries over the last decade e.g. plastics, dyestuffs, drugs. New industries visualised in the Third Plan like nylon and terylene and further expansion in the exist- ing lines over the next five year have been taken into account in fixing the levels of development appropriate in this field. The undermentioned targets for the three major items have to be regarded as provisional since it is not yet clear at what pace the industries which would be important customers for the products and are to be established in the country for the first time, are likely to develop.

(tons)

| | capacity target for 1965-66 |
|---|---|
| phathalic anhydride | 15000 |
| phenol | 15000 |
| methanol | 40000 |

Manufacture of plastic monomers, vinyl chloride and styrene, butadiene, carbon black and rubber chemicals, butyl alcohol and its esters, citric acid and oxalic acid, which are proposed to be undertaken for the first time in the private sector, deserves mention in this connection.

Major developments are also envisaged in the public sector through the Basic Chemicals and Intermediates (BCI) plant near Panvel in the Maharashtra State. The B.C.I. project as the supplier of intermediate chemicals, is firmly linked with the synthetic drugs project proposed for establishment at

Sanatnagar near Hyderabad. As a result of these two projects, valuable technical know-how in a virgin field is expected to become available during the Third Plan period. The programme under the BCI project covers the manufacture of 40 organic intermediates with an aggregate output of 25,160 tons. Provision is also being made for further expansion in due course by about 15,000 tons. Several basic inorganic chemicals are consumed in the manufacturing operations which include inter alia chlorination, sul- phonation, alkaline fusion, nitration, reduction and oxidation. The manufacture of some of these inorganic chemicals is also envisaged in captive plants within the project.

## PETROLEUM REFINING

A project report is to be obtained with a view to establishing in the public sector a plant for the manufacture of high viscosity index lubricating oil products. Government is also considering a proposal for establishing a plant for this purpose in association with private enterprise. Apart from this, developments in the field of refined, petroleum products are visualised entirely in the public sector. The programme includes, the completion of the refineries under construction at Nunmati (Gauhati) and Barauni and the establish- ment of a third public sector refinery with an annual capacity of about two million tons of crude throughput in Gujarat. External credit and technical assistance have been assured for this third refi- nery and the site for it is being selected. The product pattern of this refinery will have to be designed, as in the case of the Nunmati and Barauni refineries, to cover as far as possible the deficits in kerosene and diesel oil. Every effort is being made for the construc- tion of the refinery by the middle of 1964, and on present indications it is likely to be in a position to undertake a throughput of approximately 3.5 million tons of crude oil during the Third Plan period.

The requirements of furnace oil might prove to be higher if fiscal incentives are given to encourage industries in areas far removed from the coal fields to change over from coal to fuel oil. This matter is under examination.

In common with several other countries, India will face the problem of imbalance between the output of motor spirit (gasoline) and the demand for it. While exports have so far provided an outlet for surplus motor spirit, the disposal of it, in this manner, is expected to become more and more difficult with the all-round expansion of refining capacity in neighbouring countries. The solution to the im- balance problem will have to be found by the adoption of the following methods :

(1) Technological measures to increase the production of middle distillates. There is, however, only a limited scope for varying the production pattern. The question of increasing the production of kerosene and H.S.D. by changing the specifications in the flash point of these two products is being examined.

(2) Appropriate fiscal measures which will retard the growth of consumption of high speed diesel oil. This has been done to some extent in 1960-61.

(3) Promoting the use of mixed fuels which will reduce the demand for H.S.D. and at the same time increase the off-take of gasoline. Existing diesel vehicles could use mixed fuels containing upto 10 per cent gasoline without any changes being effected in them.

(4) The surplus of motor spirit can also be reduced or avoided by diverting the light distillate (naphtha) from which motor spirit is made to other productive uses such as production of nitrogenous fertilisers and petrochemicals. Naphtha has already been decided upon as the feed stock for the fertiliser plants to be constructed at Trombay, Visakhapatnam, Gorakhpur and Ennore (near Madras) and for the third stage expansion of Fertilisers and Chemicals. Travancore.

The public sector programmes in this field also visualise a project for the fractionation of the Nahorkatiya natural gas to isolate the ethylene, butane and other aliphatic hydrocarbons and make them available to petrochemical industries. The residual gases are proposed to be fed to the Nahorkatiya fertiliser project and the power plant planned for establishment close to the petrochemical plants.

## PHARMACEUTICALS AND DRUGS

A beginning has been made in the later. years of the Second Plan in the diversification of the production of essential drugs in both the public and private sectors. This is illustrated by the arrangements for streptomycin manufacture by Hindustan Antibiotics Ltd., and the synthesis of vitamin A from lemongrass oil by two leading pharmaceutical establishments in Bombay. New developments in this field are projected by Government as well as private enterprise which are expected to ensure the availability of essential drugs at reasonable prices and based on indigenous raw materials. The public sector projects in this field which are estimated to involve a combined outlay of Rs. 27.3 crores are :

(1) Synthetic Drugs Project at Sanatnagar, Andhra Pradesh, covering the manufacture of sulpha drugs, vitamins, phenacetin, other synthetic drugs (INH, lumi- nal, chloroquin, etc.) and intermediates (including ASC at 1500 tons per year)annual value of output, Rs. 6.4 crores.

(2) Antibiotics Pliant near Rishikesh, Uttar Pradesh, covering the manufacture of penicillin, streptomycin, chloro and other tetracyclins, new antibiotics. Annual value of output, Rs. 26 crores.

(3) Phyto-chemical Plant in Kerala, covering the manufacture of caffeine, ephedrine, digitalis glycosides, lanatazides, ergot alkaloids, atropine, scopolemine, reserpine, papin, vitamin P-yearly output, Rs 0.77 crores.

In connection with the manufacture of phytochemicals the establishment of modern drug farms has assumed crucial importance. Provision has been made in the Five Year Plan of some of the States for these related developments.

## PLASTICS

Within the overall target of 85,000 tons set for plastic materials as a whole, pride of place has been assigned to polyolefines (polyethylene, etc.) their proposed share being 27,000 tons. Next in importance from the point of view of the rate of growth envisaged are polystyrene and polyvinyl chloride for each of which appropriate targets are being fixed. Polyethylene has a high priority as a lining material for bagging fertilisers on account of its high resistance to moisture. Ethylene of petrochemical origin is expected to come into use as the raw material for its production on account of its price advantage as compared to alcohol. This is a field in which revision of the target might merit favourable consideration from the export angle as well as the potential of some of the plastics to provide substitutes for scarce Materials like rubber and leather.

## SOFT COKE

The manufacture of soft coke from lignite at Neiveli at the rate of 380,000 tons per year is a major spillover scheme from the Second Plan. Development of further capacity is prima facie desirable in the context of the heavy denudation of forests that has been taking place from charcoal production. The public sector programme includes a proposal for the establishment of low temperature carbonisation plants for the production of soft coke. The approach to developments in this field is, however, flexible.

## CEMENT

The capacity target for cement fixed at 15 million tons by 1965-66 represents about 50 per cent increase over the level expected to be reached by the end of the Second Plan. Recent trends in the demand for cement indicate that the estimated requirements for 1960-61 which were taken as the basis for the projections of growth, may have been somewhat on the low side. This matter is expected to be reviewed in another year. The possibility of having to revise the cement target upwards, if restraint on construction activities is not con- sidered necessary or desirable, cannot be ruled out.

In view of difficulties in expanding the output of limestone in step with the full requirements of the cement industry, greater attention should be devoted to the use of granulated slag from the steel works. Not much progress was made on the use of blast furnace slag in cement manufacture during the Second Plan.

## GLASS AND GLASSWARE

Important developments in this industry will be the manufacture of optical and ophthalmic glass The former is of basic importance to the instruments industry and its manufacture is to be started during the Third Plan on the basis of the know-how and experience built up by the Central Glass and Ceramic Research Institute of the Council of Scientific and Industrial Research. Manufacture of ophthalmic glass is to be undertaken at Durgapur with aid from U.S.S.R

## RAW FILMS

The plant for the manufacture of raw films, X-ray films and sensitised papers proposed to be set up near Ootacamund in Madras State with the technical collaboration of M/s. Bauchet et Cie of France is a major public sector project falling in this field. The capital investment on the scheme and its turnover are estimated at Rs. 8 crores and Rs. 5 crores respectively. On reaching full production tinder its current phase of development, availability of these products is estimated at 4.8 million sq meters of films and 1.5 million sq. meters of photographic paper.

## CONSUMER GOODS INDUSTRIES

Programmes for the manutacture of conSumer goods in the public sector occupy a relatively minor position in terms of direct investment in organised industries, the only exception being the manufacture of essential drugs discussed in Para 90 above. Watches and cameras. are two items of durable consumer goods projected for manufacture in the public sector with technical collaboration from Japan. The pro- duction of the latter will be developed by the National Instruments Factory, Calcutta. The interest of the public sector in the field of consumer goods will also be manifested through assistance afforded for the establishment and expansion of cooperative enterprises. Sugar and cotton spinning mills will continue to be the main beneficiaries of such assistance. The programmes and targets proposed for the major consumer goods industries under the Third Plan are briefly outlined below.

**Cotton Textiles.** The requirements of cotton textiles at the end of the Third Plan have been calculated on the assumption that 8450 million yards of cloth will be needed for domestic consumption and 850 million yards for export. The figure for domestic consumption pro- vides for an increase of about 20 per cent over the estimated level of demand in 1960-61 ; in other words it allows for an annual increase of 2 per cent in population and 2 per cent in per capita consumption. For the purpose of this calculation, the demand in 1960-61 has been assumed to be about 7000 million yards. The actual availability of cotton cloth for domestic consumption that year was of the order of 6750 million yards, but this relatively low figure is believed to have been mainly due to a shortage of raw cotton consequent on a poor cotton crop in 1959-60 and cannot be taken to reflect the actual level of demand in 1960-61. This view is also supported by the high prices ruling for cotton cloth which have had a restrictive effect on the offtake. The figure taken for exports is not much higher than the average level prevailing during recent years, as for some time past exports have been stagnant and have not shown any decidedly upward trend.

Out of the total target for cotton cloth of 9300 million yards, 3500 million yards have been allocated as the share of the decentralised sector (handloom, powerloom and khadi). The production target allocated to the mill sector is 5800 million yards as against the current level of output and estimated effective capacity of about 5000 million yards. To achieve the additional production of 800 million yards in the mill sector, it is envisaged that about 25,000 automatic looms will have to be installed during the Third Plan.

On the basis of a cloth production target of 9300 million yards, and taking into account also the yam required for purposes other than cloth weaving, e.g. hosiery and newar, the yam production target has been fixed at 2250 million lb. To reach this target of 2250 million lb of yam it will be necessary to increase the active spindleage of the mills to about 16.5 millions as compared to 12.7 millions at the end of the Second Plan. The addition that may be secured through the activisation of idle spindles as a result of modernisation programmes will ultimately determine the number of spindles required to be installed through new units and expansions.

The implications of the general observations made in Para 21 regarding investment on replacements have to be further examined and the contributions towards additional effective spindleage which may be obtained through modernisation programmes and through the establishment of new mills assessed or, realistic basis.

The estimated gross investment will, however, remain substantially the same whether the bulk of the additions to spindleage comes from modernisation or from new units. Out of the additional capacity for spindles and looms envisaged for installation during the Third Plan, it is proposed that a substantial proportion of the additional loomage shall be export—oriented.

**Rayon and Staple Fibre.** The programme for the rayon and staple fibre industry in the Third Plan period envisages expansion of capacity from about 100 million lb (52.3 million lb of rayon filament and 48 million lb of staple fibre) at the end of the Second Plan to 215 million lb (140 million lb of rayon filament and 75 million lb of staple fibre).

This expansion programme provides inter alia for an increase in the per capita consumption of rayon fabrics from 1.3 yards in 1960-61 to 1.8 yards in 1965-66. The overall target for rayon filament comprises 20 million lb of tyre cord yarn required for the automobile tyre industry, 76 million lb of viscose filament, 24 million lb of acetate yam, 10 million lb of cuprammonium and 10 million lb of synthetics. Considerable importance has, been attached to the phasing of investments in this industry so as to reduce the burden on foreign exchange on current account.

Thus it is proposed that expansion of capacity for the manufacture of rayon grade pulp should be given preference over further expansion of output of rayon filament and staple fibre The position will have to be periodically reviewed so as to ensure that additional capacity in this field is created in step with the progress in the manufacture of the raw materials. The future planning of this industry, particularly staple fibre, will also be influenced by the extent to which it proves possible to increase the production of long staple cotton, since staple, fibre can be regarded as a substitute for it.

**Paper and Newsprint.** The expansion programme of the paper and paperboard industry broadly conforms to the aim of achieving self- sufficiency in respect of this essential item. To meet the estimated demand of 700,000 tons by 1965-66, it is proposed to increase the capacity of the industry from the present level of 410,000 tons to 820,000 tons by the end of the Third Plan period.

A sizeable proportion of the additional capacity to be established during the Third Plan period will take the form of small paper plants using local raw materials.

The Security Paper Mill to be established at Hoshangabad with an annual capacity of 1500 tons envisages the production of specialised paper on the import of which a considerable amount of foreign exchange is at present expended.

In the case of newsprint, a five-fold expansion from 30,000 tons to 150,000 tons has been proposed in step with the anticipated growth of demand during the Third Plan period Additional capacity is expected to be achieved through the doubling of the Nepa mills and through the establishment of new newsprint factories based on baggasse and on the soft woods available in the Himalayan region.

For the achievement of these targets, the paper and newsprint industries will have to depend upon new raw materials in place of bamboo which has so far been their mainstay. New industrial uses of bamboo, e.g. for rayon grade pulp will also accentuate the shortage of bamboo for the paper industry. While new plantation and replantation programmes can, to some extent, provide a long term solution, in the Third Plan the paper and newsprint expansion will have to depend heavily on the use of bagasse which is currently being used as fuel by the sugar mills. The diversion of bagasse to the the paper industry will have to be based on providing the sugar mills with an alternative fuel.

**Sugar.** In the case of the Sugar industry, the stage of self-sustained growth has been reached by the beginning of the Third Plan as a result of the progress made in the manufacture of mill machinery in the country. A second major factor which would influence the pace of growth of this industry is the expected availability of sugarcane.

The Third Plan has envisaged expansion of sugarcane output to 100 million tons mainly through improvements in yield per acre. After allowing for diversion of sugarcane for jaggery manufacture and other miscellaneous uses, about 35 million tons of sugarcane are expected to be available for sugar production.

To cope with the crushing of these supplies in this seasonal industry, expansion of capacity to 3.5 million tons per year (in terms of gur) has been projected under the Third Plan. Cooperative industry during the Third Plan and it is estimated that their share of the enterprises are expected to make further progress under this overall mill capacity will rise to about 25 per cent.

A provision of about Rs. 6 crores has been envisaged in the Plan for contribution by State Governments to the share capital of cooperative sugar factories, Throughout the Third Plan period, the production of sugar in the country is expected to meet the demand in full and the surplus will be exported.

**Vegetable Oils.** In the case of vegetable-oils, further expansion of production is largely dependent on the programmes for cultivation of the five major oilseeds, viz., groundnut, sesamum, rape and mustard, linseed and castor

The production of these oilseeds is planned to be raised from an estimated 7.1 million tons in 1960-61 to 9.8 million tons by 1965-66. From the trends of consumption and the rate of population growth, it is felt that the availabilities of edible oil will not be adequate to provide for sizeable exports after meeting the internal needs in full.

In order to augment the supply of vegetable oils, various proposals form a part of the overall programme,one of which is the expansion of the production of cotton seed oil to one lakh tons per year. The realisation of this target will depend on the success achieved in promoting the use of cotton seed cake as an animal feed instead of the whole seed and in ensuring the offtake of the cotton linters as an industrial raw material. The additional production of cotton seed oil is largely to be used in the manufacture of vanaspati thereby relieving the pressure of demand on groundnut oil.

Another important programme calculated to augment the vegetable oil resources which has been envisaged in the Plan, is to increase solvent extraction of oil cakes to 160,000 tons of oil per year from its current level of about 40,000 tons. Oil thus produced would be used chiefly for industrial purposes.

Other subsidiary sources of supply of oil, though relatively of minor importance from the point of view of tonnage output, have also been borne in mind, e.g. rice bran oil. The overall production of vegetable oils inclusive of coconut oil is expected to amount to about 2,9 million tons by 1965-66.

## PROBLEMS OF DEVELOPMENT AND GENERAL RECOMMENDATIONS

The nature and levels of industrial development proposed under the Third Plan present a major challenge to both the public and private sectors in view of the manifold problems to be attended to in a limited period of time. Resources and foreign exchange, though important, are not the only problems which have to be tackled.

Those involved in maintaining rising levels of production and at the same time carrying out the expansion of steel plants have been found by the two private sector companies to be quite complex and the fullest use must be made of their experience in overcoming the difficulties that may arise in expanding the public sector plants while at the same time bringing them to full production.

For machine building activities, which figure prominently in the public sector programmes, as well as for machinery manufacture in the private sector, designs development and project engineering are of paramount importance. In regard to the latter, which has been briefly referred to in paragraph 6, the N.I.D.C. is arranging to assume responsibilities with reference to its own public sector projects as well as those of the Commerce and Industry Ministry, and a Technological Consultancy Bureau was established by it in 1960-61.

The functions of the Bureau will include preparation of preliminary studies, investigation and selection of sites, preparation of detailed project reports and the designing of structures. As regards designs development, though to begin with the fabrication of plant and equipment will necessarily be based predominantly on 'bought out' designs, the object should be to manufacture in the not distant future industrial machinery on the basis of indigenous designs.

In the public sector, it is intended that the nucleus organisations functioning under Hindustan Steel Ltd. and Sindri Fertilisers and Chemicals should be rapidly expanded and similar agencies brought into being in an appropriate manner under other machinery projects.

A central designs institute for machine tools is projected at Bangalore. Similar programmes should be accorded high priority in the private sector also and appropriate steps taken to push forward these programmes vigorously. Since performance guarantees are customary in this field, establishment of the necessary testing facilities will also become essential. A high voltage laboratory is being set up for the testing and design development of switchgear at Bhopal. This problem will have to be attended to by the private sector also wherever necessary.

Since the, industrial sector has also to play its part in the export drive, thought and attention must be given not only to securing expansion of output but also to all factors that contribute to enhanced productivity and reduction of costs.

As regards production costs, the high levels are partly attributable to factors capable of remedy, if the sizes of plants proposed for establishment are of optimum size and economic outlets for by-products and/or co- products as in the case of electrolytic caustic soda plants, are also developed. A high level of utilisation of capacity will be conducive to economies on overheads. These are aspects that should be continuously studied by Development Councils at the expert level.

Many of the heavy industries envisaged for development, e.g. steel plants, petroleum refineries, fertiliser factories require very large quantities of water for process use. Machine building projects, which give rise to concentration of industrial labour at the selected location, similarly demand largescale water supply facilities for potable and other township requirements, though the direct consumption in the processes is not considerable.

In the studies undertaken by special committees entrusted with the task of recommending suitable sites for some of the major industrial projects included in the Third Plan, the availability of water has figured as a very material factor influencing the ultimate choice.

It has been noted that several areas which are otherwise well suited for the location of heavy industries have had to be ruled out owing to lack of water on the scale demanded. Without long-term planning of water, supplies, the opportunities for industrialisation in such areas will be thwarted.

No less important is the, problem of effluent disposal, particularly in the case of chemical and allied industries. Without proper arrangements for treatment and disposal of effluents, the pollution of the rivers in proximity to chemical factories-many chemical plants are getting established in the upper reaches of the Ganges and other rivers-will present a serious public health problem. These twin problems should receive attention commensurate with their growing importance in detailed studies relating to factors ancillary. to industrial expansion.

## OUTLOOK FOR THE INDUSTRIAL SECTOR IN 1965-66

The gains from the industrial development, as formulated for the Third Plan, will be many sided. The rapid growth of public sector investment and output will considerably further the objective of a socialist pattern of society. The dependence of some of the vital sectors of the economy like agriculture, electric power, railways, motor transport on imports of equipment and material from abroad will be substantially reduced. Within the industrial sector itself, the development of heavy engineering and machine-building will enable a large amount of capital equipment required for industries, which is at present imported, to be manufactured here.

The imports required for the maintenance of a number of important industries will also be reduced through the production of the basic raw materials within the country itself, e.g. rayon grade pulp, organic chemicals, synthetic rubber, intermediates for dyestuffs and the drug industries. Thus, with the completion of the industrial programme drawn up for the Third Plan, the essential foundations for self-sustaining growth will have been laid. In 1965-66 the general index of industrial production, which is one of the conventional indicators, of progress, is expected to reach the level of 329 (1950-51 = 100) as against 194 provisionally estimated for 1960-61 and 139 for the last year of the First Plan.

# Bibliography


**Angel, Bradley:** *Toxic Threat to Indian Lands: A Greenpeace Report*, San Francisco, Greenpeace, 1991.

**Barnett, P.G.:** *Survey of Research on the Impacts of Pesticides on Agricultural Workers and the Rural Environment*, Davis, CA: California Institute of Rural Studies, 1989.

**Bryant, Bunyan:** *Environmental Justice: Issues, Policies, and Solutions*, Washington, DC, Island Press, 1995.

**Campbell, R. R., and Wade, J. L.:** *Society and Environment: The Coming Collision*, Boston, Allyn and Bacon, 1972.

**Daubenmire, R. F.:** *Plants and Environment*, New York, Wiley, 1947.

**David Sadava:** *Plants, Genes and Crop Biotechnology*, Sudbury MA, Jones and Barlett Publishers, 2003.

**Gelobter, Michael:** *The Distribution of Air Pollution by Income and Race*, Berkeley, University of California, 1989.

**Hill, David:** *The Quality of Life in America; Pollution, Poverty, Power, and Fear*, New York, Holt, Rinehart and Winston, 1973.

**Johnson, Hazel:** *Financial Institutions and Markets: A Global Perspective*, NY, McGraw Hill, 1993.

**Merchant, Carolyn:** *Radical Ecology: The Search for a Livable World*, New York, Routledge, 1992.

**Petty, Keown, Scott, and Martin:** *Basic Financial Management*, Prentice Hall, 1993.

**Schall and Haley:** *Introduction to Financial Management*, McGraw-hill, 1988.

**Sontheimer, Sally:** *Women and the Environment: Crisis and Development in the Third World*, New York, Monthly Review Press, 1991.

# Index

## F



## G



## H



## I



## L



## M

♦♦♦